Flexibility in Labour Markets

Edited by

ROGER TARLING

Faculty of Applied Economics
University of Cambridge
England, UK

1987

ACADEMIC PRESS

Harcourt Brace Jovanovich, Publishers
London   Orlando   San Diego   New York
Austin   Boston   Sydney   Tokyo   Toronto

ACADEMIC PRESS INC. (LONDON) LTD
24–28 Oval Road,
London NW1

United States Edition published by
ACADEMIC PRESS INC.
Orlando, Florida 32887

British Library Cataloguing in Publication Data

Flexibility in labour markets.
1. Labour supply
I. Tarling, Roger
331.12   HD5706

ISBN 0-12-683740-6

Printed in Great Britain by St Edmundsbury Press Ltd
Bury St Edmunds, Suffolk

Contributors

J. P. DE GAUDEMAR, DATAR, 1 Avenue Charles-Floquet, 75007 Paris, France

RAINER DOMBOIS, Universität Bremen, ZWE "Arbitat & Betrieb", Universitätsallee, 2800 BREMEN, FRG

ELIZABETH GARNSEY, Management Group, Department of Engineering, University of Cambridge, Trumpington Street, Cambridge, England, UK

ANNIE GAUVIN, Séminaire d'Economie du Travail, Université de Paris 1, 90 rue de Tolbiac, 75013 Paris, France

GABOR KERTESI, Center for Value Sociology and Applied Social Research, Institute for Sociology of the Hungarian Academy of Sciences, Budapest 1, Uri utca 49, Hungary

FRANÇOIS MICHON, Séminaire d'Economie du Travail, Université de Paris 1, 90 rue de Tolbiac, 75013 Paris, France

JILL RUBERY, Department of Applied Economics, University of Cambridge, Sidgwick Avenue, Cambridge, England, UK

WERNER SENGENBERGER, International Institute for Labour Studies, CP6 1211 Geneva 22, Switzerland

JEAN-JACQUES SILVESTRE, CNRS, Laboratoire d'Economie et de Sociologie du Travail, 35 Avenue Jules Ferry, 13626 Aix en Provence, France

GIOVANNI SOLINAS, Dipartmento di Economia Politica, Via Giardini 454, 411000 Modena, Italy

GYORGY SZIRACZKI, Department of Labour Economics, University of Economics, 1093 Budapest, Dimitrov ter 8, Hungary

ROGER TARLING, Department of Applied Economics, University of Cambridge, Sidgwick Avenue, Cambridge, England, UK

PAOLA VILLA, Istituto di Scienze Economiche, Universita Cattolica, Largo Gemelli 1, 20123 Milan, Italy

JILL WALKER, The Research School of Social Sciences, The Australian National University, PO Box 4, Canberra, ACT 2601, Australia

FRANK WILKINSON, Department of Applied Economics, University of Cambridge, Sidgwick Avenue, Cambridge, England, UK

Contents

Acknowledgements

This book is the second to be produced by the International Working Party on Labour Market Segmentation, based on papers presented at their conferences held in Modena, North Italy and Oslo, Sweden. The Working Party is indebted to Sebastiano Brusco and his colleagues at the University of Modena and to Ted Hanisch and his colleagues at the Institute for Social Research in Oslo for organizing the conferences, and to the Regional Government of Emilia-Romagna and the Norwegian University of Labour for sponsoring the conferences.

The editing of the book was carried out with the help of Jill Rubery and Frank Wilkinson in the Department of Applied Economics of the University of Cambridge. Andrew Wilson translated the papers by Michon, Gaudemar, and Nohara and Silvestre.

Preface

This volume is based on papers presented to meetings of the
International Working Party on Labour Market Segmentation and
considers the question of flexibility in the working of the
labour market and in the utilization of labour. The ideas
discussed were given foundation and perspective by the
previous book published by the group (Wilkinson, 1981), which
called for attention to be concentrated on "the practical
importance of this research and consequently to draw out the
policy implications of its findings for both economic and
social problems" (p. xii).

One of the difficulties in developing an international
comparative approach and establishing collaborative research
on labour market organization was the absence of a coherent
framework for the analysis to establish its position relative
to economic orthodoxy. This was not a matter of detail, but
an issue of fundamental differences in interpreting how the
economy worked. The proposition that the framework was a
dynamic non-equilibrium one was developed in the previous
volume by emphasizing the interrelatedness of social,
political and economic factors and the evolutionary nature of
processes which conditioned economic structures. A more
complete framework was published by Wilkinson (1983) where
attention was drawn to system dynamics that could encompass
the variety of processes underlying change.

   That framework was an attempt to identify how economic,
social and political factors came together and interacted.
The aim was to provide an integrated overview of a changing
system extending far beyond the traditional sphere of
economists; a broad frame into which more detailed analysis
of the firm or the workplace could be located.

   The first section of this volume contains articles by
Tarling and Wilkinson and by Michon which attempt to provide
the bridge between the general framework and the detailed
analysis. Tarling and Wilkinson argue that the costs of
production are fixed by: the techniques of production and the
nature of the product which determine the resource
composition of the commodity; the organization of production
which determines how effectively assembled productive factors
are utilized; and the prices of production factors which are
determined by power relations within the firm and between the
firm and its suppliers. The flexibility of costs is then
determined by the extent to which firms can adjust techniques
of production, products, organization and power
relationships.

   Michon analyses "non-standard job forms" in France and
challenges accepted notions of discontinuities and
segmentation in the labour market. He shows that the changing
boundary of the firm within the universe of its factor supply
and product markets is of crucial importance in determining
the "division of labour", "segmentation" and the
"specification of wage relationships". This puts flesh on the
bones of the Tarling and Wilkinson paper and again
concentrates attention on the importance of understanding the
link between "the concentration of individual capital of
unequal size and power on the one hand, and the multidimensional fragmentation of the productive organization on
the other" (Michon, Chapter 2).

   These two papers argue for a view of the firm which is
made coherent not by the impersonal workings of a market, but
by the power and social relations which govern the
organization and control of production. The firm is no longer
a well-defined entity and the implications of this
flexibility of form for the labour market processes are
complex and difficult to describe in detail.

   The next section of the volume contains four papers
which discuss specific labour market processes within the
broad analytical framework provided by the first section.
Rubery takes as her topic the institutional form of labour
market regulation. Union and non-union firms of different
sizes are compared and it is shown that firm-specific factors
are very important in explaining the institutional forms
taken by labour organization. But these firm-specific factors

cannot be explained by a dichotomizing classification based
on firm size, product market conditions and the specificity
of skills as in the dual labour market approach. Nor can the
degree of flexibility achieved by non-union firms, and
particularly those of small size, be regarded as evidence of
the working of the competitive market of orthodox theory. A
more embracing explanation is couched in terms of social and
economic advantage and disadvantage as secured by
organization (or lack of it) which can be found on both sides
of the labour market. Thus the greater degree of flexibility
and lower wages in small non-union firms is evidence not of
the free working of the labour market, nor of the quality of
labour employed, but of the different configurations of
disadvantage found in the labour market segment in which such
firms operate.

How the needs of a firm and of an individual are
"reconciled" in the labour market depends on the links that
exist between the labour market, its operation and the social
groups from which the firms' workforce is drawn. De Gaudemar
describes "mobilization networks" as a means of understanding
these links. The networks are formed by sets of social
relations which can be activated by firms and individuals, or
by their mutual interaction. These relations can then be used
to understand how power is exercised.

Social and economic advantage is a major feature of
these networks and Garnsey looks at the impact of working
time arrangements in this context. She draws out the links
between the traditional full-time working pattern and female
labour supply, conditioned as it is by culture and
traditional family divisions of labour. Dutoya and Gauvin
examine female employment in France with a much greater
emphasis on arrangements in the workplace. They show that
working conditions and sex segregation (dependent on
unrecognized skills and qualifications) reflect company
strategies which combine aspects of the organization of work
and personnel management practices. The particular combinations are determined in the context of firm-specific factors
and the external labour market so that discriminatory
practices arise to exploit disadvantage.

The final section of the volume draws on particular case
studies which examine in greater detail how changes in the
structure of employment take place. Nohare and Silvestre
compare employment structures in France and Japan and point
to the differences in recruitment and mobility patterns. In
France mobility more generally takes the form of job changes
between enterprises, so that recruitment from new entrants to
the labour market or the unemployed form a smaller percentage
of the total than in Japan. However, the consensus under-

pinning the evolution of the Nenko system has institutionalized mobility within Japanese enterprises, so that there is
considerably more inter- and intra- plant mobility within the
same organization in Japan. These systems of recruitment,
mobility and reward are then shown to have had major
implications for the changes in the structure of employment
in the 1970s.

The paper by Kertesi and Sziraczki explains how
liberalization in Hungary has led to the emergence of new
employment structures. Labour shortages created pressures for
change, and growth of consumer demand encouraged the growth
of a second, non-socialist economy. This permitted workers to
choose between the security of the socialist sector and the
income growth available in the second economy whilst in
socialist enterprises elite groups developed as a solution to
labour shortage. The closure of the elite group, who have
security and income, strengthens the hierarchy in the
socialist sector and forces others to seek new ways of
achieving higher incomes. Thus the structure of employment
within enterprises evolved in response to economic and
institutional change. The evolution of the regulatory system
in Hungary introduces a degree of flexibility into the system
and provides ways of overcoming shortages in the state
sector; developments in which both the state and the workers
have an interest.

In the UK there is no obvious community of interest in
the Government's drive to privatize services provided by the
"local state"; an intention of which is to cut wages and
worsen conditions of work. There is confusion in the academic
debate between issues of finance and of production which,
when translated into policy discussion, obscure the argument
about who benefits and who loses. The Walker and Moore paper
clarifies this debate, separates the issues, and shows that,
for direct employees, the lowering of real incomes and
intensification of work is the crux of the production crisis.

Flexibility in labour input is also achieved in the
private sector by forms of employment which allow work
intensification when required and which are often associated
with lower rates of pay. Dombois and Osterland provide
evidence from a number of industries, particularly retailing
and shipbuilding in West Germany, to show how part-time and
contract working provides employers with these benefits.
These forms of employment are not new but are usually
associated with disadvantaged groups. However, Dombois and
Osterland emphasize the growing institutionalization of some
of these "buffer" groups, with employers attracted by lower
costs of a more flexible workforce and employees attracted by
potentially higher, if more uncertain, earnings.

By comparing behaviour in the automobile industry in two countries – the US and Germany – Sengenberger and Kohler are able to investigate the role of institutional factors in determining methods of workforce reduction. Rather than evolving institutionalized "buffer" groups, the automobile industry copes with product demand variation in Germany by an assortment of instruments affecting hours of work and recruitment, and in the US by more direct action on the numbers employed.

The final two papers extend the analysis by locating industry studies of the flexible use of labour firmly in their social context. Solinas provides an extensive discussion of the Italian knitwear industry. He argues that a full understanding of the emergence of "good " jobs for a large proportion of the workforce needs to draw on the characteristics of the industrial "district", its social as well as its economic organization, the subordination of sub-contractors and homeworkers outside the "district", and the sector's success in international markets.

Villa relates events in the Italian steel industry in the 1970s and shows how strategies evolve with growing trade union power. This made the rigid hierarchical system of labour organization highly costly and inefficient. The symbol of union dominance was the "Inquadramento Unio" and it became the focus for the struggle to control production. However, this allowed management, freed from some of the rigid rest-rictions of the detailed hierarchical system, to experiment with new terms of organization. The outcome was the "opera-tive unit" whereby work organization was handed over to employees, but control was retrieved by management who set the production targets for the units.

The common theme of the papers in this book is that the level, structure and flexibility of costs depend on social organizations and power relations as well as what are conventionally defined as technological and economic factors. This does not mean that this volume belongs in the "institutionalist" tradition if by that it is meant that its contribution rests on the premise that institutions dominate economic forces. The proposition is more radical than that: the authors believe that there are no ways of separating the economic and the technical from social organizations and power relations. In fact, technology and economic relations are examples of social organization and power relations given a specific point of reference.

This notion is not incompatible with conventional economic theorizing which rests on particular assumptions about social organization and power relations. Thus, for neo-classical theory, it is assumed that technology is

completely malleable so that changes in relative prices can
be immediately counteracted by changing the factor
composition of the productive unit; individuals are motivated
by self-interest which, along with the appropriate financial
rewards secure the planned factor input; each actor is
sufficiently endowed with out-of-market resources to allow
freedom of choice in market activity; and the presence of
many buyers and sellers and no restriction on the choice of
pairing between buyer and seller ensure the exercise of power
by any individual is just counter-balanced by the power of
others to avoid market situations where that power would be
exercised. Within this framework the working of "economic"
laws can be isolated and it can be demonstrated that "costs"
are equally matched by "benefits" to optimize economic
welfare and that the system ensures the necessary flexibility
to maintain that desired state.

    This collection of essays rests on the belief that the
"true" social and political organization and the resulting
structure of power relationships cannot be taken as given –
or as an article of faith – to be safely incorporated as
axioms in the process of model building; it requires
empirical investigation. Only then can an understanding of
the real complexity of the "economic" process and its
adjustment mechanisms be developed, the costs and benefits of
innovation across the broad range of social relations be
identified and a sound basis for policy be constructed.

REFERENCES

Wilkinson, F. (ed.) (1981). "The Dynamics of Labour
    Market Segmentation". Academic Press, London and
    Orlando.
Wilkinson, F. (1983). Productive systems. Cambridge
    Journal of Economics, 7 (3 and 4), 413–429.

Part I

General and Theoretical

The Level, Structure and Flexibility of Costs

R. TARLING and F. WILKINSON

I. THE COST OF PRODUCTION

There are four distinct elements in the formation of the
costs of production; the nature of the product, the technique
of production, the organization of production and the prices
of the productive factors. Whilst these elements can be
discussed separately, they necessarily interrelate. The
nature of the product has an important influence on the
techniques of production and the feasibility of production
influences the design of products. Furthermore, the technical
and organizational aspects of production cannot be easily
separated in the fixing of the method of production (and
therefore in determining the demand for the different factors
of production) and this has an important influence on price.
Nevertheless, a study of the level and flexibility of costs
requires an analysis of the separate influences on their
formation as a basis for understanding how these influences
interrelates. This section considers in turn the tech-

*The authors are grateful to the ESRC for supporting the
research which underpins this paper.
*Numbers in square brackets refer to numbered notes at the
end of each chapter.

nical, organizational and price aspects of the costs of
production.

A. The Resource Costs of Production

This first section is a purely abstract discussion of the
utilization of the factors of production assembled as a given
set of techniques of production designed to produce a given
set of products. Why they were so assembled is a question of
history, and is of no concern here. Our interest is in their
effective use, and for the purposes of this section it is
assumed that the factors of production are passive – that
their productive power is available for use without coercion.
     The resource costs are the productive resources used up
in production and there are two separate elements in their
determination. The first relates to the composition of the
product – the physical quantity of each productive factor
embodied in it – and the second to the technical efficiency
of production – the completeness by which the productive
factors assembled for production are fully converted into
products.

1. The factor composition of the product

The technical requirements of production consist of the
inputs of labour, and the means of production – machines, raw
materials and intermediary goods – which the process of
production transforms into new products in which they lose
their separate identity. They are physical quantities which
are separately measurable but for which there is no common
measure (for example, no standard exists for a direct
comparison of a unit of human effort with a ton of steel).
Moreover, the different inputs are complementary in the
production process and so whilst in input terms the different
factors of production are separable, there is no way to
measure their independent contribution to the product of
their joint effort.
     The essence of production is therefore a complemen-
tarity between the labour and the means of production and the
way these are combined is called the technique of production.
The same product can be produced by different techniques of
production: a hand operated machine can produce the same item
as a machine driven by an electric motor. Equally, with a
slight modification of the input of materials, it is possible
for a given machine to produce different products: for
example, man-made fibres can replace cotton in the weaving of

different types of cloth. However, once the techniques of
production and the product are given, the input of the
productive factors to each unit of product is given and is
invariable with respect to the scale of output: each unit of
output has the same factor composition as each previous and
each successive unit.

2. The technical efficiency of production

Once the product and the method of production have been
fixed, how effectively the productive resources are used
depends on the scale of output (the most efficient level of
which is defined by the technical specifications of the
method of production); the organization of production (which
ensures that the assembled resources are put to the most
effective use possible whatever the level of output); and how
well production is managed in terms of, for example, the
adequate provision of supplies and the proper maintenance of
machines. Assuming that the productive system is well managed
in this latter sense, the technical efficiency of production
depends on the scale of production and the organization of
production.
    An important determinant of the most efficient scale of
output is the extent of the divisability of productive
resources into unit inputs. If all inputs were completely
divisible, the minimum efficient scale of production would be
one unit, and the productive unit could expand and contract
directly in line with the level of output. However, although
the idea of the complete divisibility of all factors of
production underlies much of economic theory, it is
practically impossible in any technical sense. Raw materials
and intermediary products are generally technically
divisible into unit input quantities, but labour and machines
are not. Even with the simplest technique the unit inputs of
labour and machine power are indivisibly embodied in the
worker and the machine. When a single labourer works the land
with a digging stick, the full productive power of the
labourer and the stick are present however fully they are
used. It is this technical indivisibility which determines
the input of each productive factor into the production
process and this means that all productive factors are only
fully utilized if output changes by discrete amounts
determined by the lowest common denominator of the
indivisibilities of the various types of factor inputs.
    The indivisibility of unit inputs is not the only reason
why the average requirement of productive factors per unit of
output may fall as output rises. In the initial stages of

Production productive resources additional to those embodied
in the product may be required for what can be called start-
up costs. These will include, for example, extra energy
required to raise the speed of the machine to its most
efficient operating level, the number of operations performed
before the operator reaches full dexterity and, in the longer
term, learning-by-doing by which the full productive
potential is realised.

   At that scale of output which makes the most efficient
use of resources given the indivisibility of unit inputs and
the existence of start-up costs, the maximum exploitation of
productive resources embodied in techniques of production
will be determined by the level of output relative to the
rate of depreciation of labour and the means of production.
Characteristically, labour and machines are able to repeat
the productive tasks established by the method of production, and it is in this constant repetition that the embodied
productive power is transferred to the product. Consequently,
the capacity of labour and machines has two dimensions: the
quantity of products which can be produced in each cycle of
production and the number of cycles of production in the life
of labour and machines. Labour and machines lose their
effective productive power by wear and tear through usage in
production and by virtue of the passage of time whereby
labour and machines become less effective whether or not they
are used. This latter loss results from an ageing process
whereby workers and machines physically deteriorate and
embodied skills and techniques are rendered obsolete by new
technical developments [1].

   The time-related costs, ageing and obsolescence, set an
ultimate limit to the possible number of productive cycles,
whilst on the other hand, the wear and tear caused by usage
is liable to rise more than proportionately as the speed of
production (i.e. the number of production cycles per second)
is increased. Thus the speeding up of the machine will
shorten its life by increasing wear and tear, but if life is
shortened less will be lost from the process of ageing and
growing obsolescence. The number of productive cycles will be
maximized when those lost by more intensive exploitation are
just offset by those saved by shortening the ageing process.

3. Organization of production

The discussion so far has taken the organization of
production as given. At one level this may be reasonable
because the machine and labour functions are both determined
by the technique of production and therefore given. However,

although the machine functions are built into specific items
of equipment these can be organized in different ways so as
to improve the effectiveness of their use, and for a similar
purpose, different stages of the process of production can be
integrated to a greater or lesser extent. In addition,
considerable discretion can be exercised in the incorporation
of the labour functions into the design of particular jobs.
The design of the job would fix its technical function (in
much the same way as the design of a machine embodies within
it its technical role) but labour is more malleable than
machines, and the opportunities are greater for the redesign
of occupation without changing the technique of production.
For example, the operation of a lathe includes the setting up
of the machine, its operation and its maintenance. Each of
these tasks can be taken as technically determined and
invariable, but they can be combined into job contents in
different ways as shown in Table I.

Table I. Lathe operation and job contents

Tasks	Job content		
	Setting up	Operation	Maintenance
Setter/ operator/ maintenance	x	x	x
Setter	x		
Operator		x	
Maintenance			x
Setter/ operator	x	x	
Operator/ maintenance		x	x
Setter/ maintenance	x		x

Thus the three tasks involved in lathe operation can be
differently arranged to give seven occupations with the
number of tasks embodied in each occupation varying from one
to three.

There may be advantages and disadvantages from a greater
or lesser degree of the division of labour. Greater
specialization may allow each task to be performed more
effectively and, moreover, the concentration of the skills
associated with tasks in single occupations will allow their
more continuous use. For example, suppose a lathe is being
set up for 10%, operated for 80% and maintained for 10% of
its theoretically feasible operating time, and further
suppose that maintenance, setting up and operating are ranked
in descending order of skill. If occupations are not
specialized , i.e. each worker performs all the lathing
functions, each worker will need to be sufficiently skilled
to maintain the machine, but the total amount of maintenance
skill available will only be used for 10% of the time. In
contrast, complete specialization will allow the skill to be
used for 100% of the time and might have the additional
advantage of allowing the development of a higher degree of
skill. However, such a rigid separation could introduce
rigidities of its own which would prevent the most effective
use of labour. If operators had no maintenance skills, when
the lathe breaks down they would have to wait for the
maintenance worker. Unless the machines broke down in strict
rotation (so that 90% of the machines were always working and
10% were being maintained) then the average operating time
would fall below 80% and the operators would be less than
fully employed. The resulting "down-time" could be reduced if
the division of labour could be adjusted to allow operators
to perform simple maintenance and running repairs.

4. The resource costs of production per unit of output

The average resource costs of production per unit of output
depend on the factor composition of the product and, in
addition, how effectively the resources assembled for
production are utilized. The factor composition of the
product is fixed and invariable with respect to output once
the nature of the product and the technique of production is
given. The level of average unit resource costs above this
minimum is determined by the variability of the utilization
of factors of production with respect to output – the degree
of utilization of indivisible factors, start-up costs and
depreciation – and those which are independent of the scale
of output, determined by the effectiveness of the

organization of the labour process.

The resource costs of production can also be classified as those which are converted into the product, those which are not converted but are used up, and those which are not converted and which are not used up. The productive resources which are not converted but which are used up include start-up costs [2] and depreciation. The indivisibility of productive factors means that all the resources needed for production have to be assembled but may not be used. There is only one level of output and operating efficiency at which the productive powers embodied in the factor of production are fully utilized. At other levels they are being stored — available but not used — and in this case the resource costs of production are those associated with storage [3]. In some cases the storage costs may be close to zero but in others they may be substantial. For example, the human capacity to work needs substantial maintenance independently of the effort put into work, and if the temperature of a blast furnace falls below a certain level the linings collapse and require extensive renewal. In each of these cases inputs are required to maintain the productive factor at operating efficiency which are independent of the level of output — these can be called the costs of storage.

Unit resource costs of the factor composition will be constant, and the failure to organize the production process effectively might add a constant margin to this. But the other factors outlined above will have a variable influence on unit resource costs associated with the level of output. The addition to average unit resource costs resulting from the indivisibility of factors of production, start-up costs and the time-related element in depreciation will decline as the level of output rises whilst the cost of wear and tear will rise. The profile of the unit resource cost curve therefore depends on the relative importance of these factors.

B. The Money Costs of Production

Cost schedules cannot be constructed unless a common measure can be found for the different factors of production — it is not possible to sum tons of iron and units of human effort. The common denominator is money price and once this is known the contribution to average costs of the different productive resources and how they are used can be evaluated. However, relative prices cannot be taken, as in orthodox theory, to reflect the relative contribution of factors of production to output because factors are complementary in

Production and therefore their relative contribution to the
product cannot be known. Therefore, the investigation of the
determination of price is quite independent of that of the
technical costs of production.

1. Price

The discussion so far has concentrated on the technical and
organizational aspect of production and no attention has been
paid to the terms on which the services of productive factors
are secured: their price. Factors of production command a
price both because they are useful in production and because
they are separately owned so that their services can only be
obtained on terms agreeable to their owners. A price is paid
to obtain the service of the productive factor because it is
useful in the production of a product which in itself is
useful and therefore commands a price. In turn, owners of the
productive factors trade because in doing so the services
they own can provide them with command over products which
they find useful.

Usefulness and ownership explain the existence of price
but not its level. The formation of price has two dimensions: mutual interest and relative power. The productive
power embodied in labour and the means of production can only
be realized jointly and this interdependence brings the
parties together and forms the basis for price determination. But this mutual dependence also bestows the parties to
the trade with bargaining power, because the benefits of
production can be denied to others by the refusal to participate in production.

A consideration of the power relations raises important
differences between the determinants of the price of labour
and the inanimate means of production. The potential productive power of the means of production and labour is acquired
in the market whilst the extraction of that power – and hence
its effective price – is determined in the production
process. Whilst in this latter respect the means of production can be regarded as passive and the discussion of their
effective use is a technical matter and follows that of the
previous section, the introduction of power relations means
that the previous assumption that labour is passive must be
abandoned.

The agreement of a market price does not completely
transfer control over labour power to the employer.
Ultimately, the decision how and whether their skills and
effort are to be utilized rests with workers, whose attitudes are formed by education, socialization, traditions,

worker organization and other social forces. Consequently,
the negotiation over the use of labour power — what might be
called the effort bargain — continues into the production
process which adopts a coercive role reflected in systems of
supervision, methods of work organization, occupational
specification and the design of machines. In these respects
it is difficult to separate the aspects of the organization
which are technically based — designed to make the most
effective use of labour even if workers are entirely passive
— and those designed to control the <u>pace</u> of work. Production
line techniques, for example, allow for a finer division of
labour but also for machine pacing which eases supervision.
The redesign of occupations and methods of production to
concentrate skills and the conceptual aspects of the labour
function in managerial hands may also have a dual function in
improving the efficient use of labour, directly — by allowing
a more continuous use of skills for operating the productive
unit, and indirectly — by enhancing managerial control over
labour. Thus, "Taylorist" scientific management techniques ,
by making a more careful analysis of tasks, provide the basis
for a redesign of machines, methods of working and the
regrouping of tasks in new occupational structures which
allow a more effective use of labour at a given pace of work
and also, by giving management additional control over the
pace of work, facilitates hard driving [4].

2. The determination of price

The balance of power in the determination of price depends on
the degree and immediacy of the dependence each party has on
the sale, the number of alternative buyers and sellers in the
market and the legal, social and political context for
trading — an important determinant of the type and degree of
coercion which can be brought to bear.
    Dependence on the market will be determined by the
degree of separation of the ownership of the different
productive factors and the immediacy of that dependence will
rest on the extent of access to non-market resources —
domestic and other non-market forms of production, accumulated wealth and public and private transfers. In these
respects the bargaining power of individual workers relative
to capital is inherently weak. Their access to the means of
production is very limited and they are therefore dependent
on the labour and product markets for subsistence. Few
workers have sufficient resources to sustain a long period
without work, labour power is highly perishable so that if
unused is immediately wasted, and workers are numerous and

consequently difficult to organize. By contrast, capitalist
employers control the means of production which only slowly
lose their productive power if not used, and, to a varying
extent dependent on their size, have massed resources to
sustain prolonged periods without production, and are relatively few in number and so can more easily collude.

But whilst in general a power balance exists between
labour and capital, the extent of this imbalance varies both
between and within economies. In Britain the effects of
enclosures and the 1833 Poor Law legislation effectively
separated the working class from subsistence agriculture and
destroyed pre-capitalist forms of social welfare so that the
working class became almost totally dependent on the labour
market for maintenance. However, this degree of separation
from alternative forms of subsistence was much less complete
in other countries. In France, for example, widespread
peasant proprietorship had an important influence on the
development of an industrial proletariat and the form labour
organization has taken. On the other hand, responsibilities
for non-market economic activities may have an important
influence on the terms on which labour is supplied. Their
role in domestic production is an important determining
factor in the secondary labour market status of women and the
same argument would apply where workers retain significant
responsibility for subsistence agriculture.

Thus, non-market production and related responsibilities have an important influence on the bargaining power
of labour. The overall effect will depend on the extent to
which the standard of living requirement can be met without
recourse to the market. Easy access to land as an alternative
means of subsistence has provided an explanation for the
scarcity of labour and high wages in the US during the early
stages of settlement. In contrast, the need to top-up the
income of the primary wage earner to provide an acceptable
minimum standard for the family is a reason given for why
women accept low wages. In the latter case women's role as a
secondary income provider reinforces the responsibility for
domestic production in undermining their labour market power.

The extent to which workers can redress the imbalance of
power with capital other than by recourse to out-of-market
resources will also vary between different groups. Labour is
differentiated by, amongst other things, skill, organization
and by the conditions of its supply. The scarcity of skill in
itself enhances the bargaining power of skilled workers and
provides the organizational basis to maintain or even
increase skill scarcity. The process of exclusion operates
within the education and training system, at the level of the
market and in the labour process. Techniques of production

and occupational design will specify the skill content of jobs. The educational and training system will provide the skills, but can also act as a screening device by which entry to skilled trade is restricted. Within the labour process control of job areas and occupational design will allow skilled groups to extend their jurisdictional control over a wider area of tasks and to "capture" new occupations whatever their skill content. By these means "skill" becomes at least partly a question of organizational control and hence a social rather than purely technical category.

However, despite such differences, in general the power imbalance between labour and capital can only be offset by the collective provision of alternative forms of subsistence and by united actions in the labour market. Historically these have been secured by the strengthening of the family, community action, the building of trade unions and by organized pressure on the state. The ability to sustain such initiatives depends on the social and political systems such as the legal impediments under which workers' organizations operate and the extent of state and other provisions of social welfare. These vary widely between social classes, between economies and through time, and consequently the bargaining power, and hence the market prices of factions of labour, will vary widely.

Arguments similar to those outlined above can be adduced to show that capital is similarly fragmented. Difference in access to funds, levels of technology and size affect relative bargaining power and the terms on which firms trade with their suppliers (including labour), with sub-contractors and in the market for their products. Thus a structure of price of inputs of productive factors exists which is the outcome of social and political as well as technical and economic forces. The question then arises of the constraints on these prices.

3. The limit to price

Where production is entirely by factors acquired in the market the monetary costs of production form the lower limit to price. Unless these are met from the price of their output the producers will go out of business, except possibly in the short period when the deficit may be covered by running down reserves or by borrowing. This is quite clear in the case of production of machines and materials, but in the case of labour the question becomes rather more complicated. At some physiological minimum labour is much the same as non-human factors of production: unless wages meet the cost of

Production labour power will cease to exist. However, there
is no doubt that wages in advanced industrial countries are
significantly higher than the physiological minimum, but that
does not mean that wages can fall to the physiological
minimum. Each economic system has its acceptable standards of
living which are historically determined and which are
underpinned by social and political forces and below which it
is difficult to reduce wages. At any point of time this
customary standard of living can be taken as the cost of
producing labour.

Labour also differs from other factors of production in
the extent to which non-marketed resources contribute to its
production. The state provides health care, education and
social security, and domestic labour and other private non-
market activities play an important part in producing labour
power. The market price can therefore fall below that
necessary to maintain the customary standard of living to the
extent that this is "made-up" by resources from the state and
the private non-market sector [5].

At each stage of production there are two sets of
prices; those of inputs and those of outputs. Accepting the
customary standard of living as the cost of producing labour,
and making allowance for the possible contribution of non-
market resources to production, both the input and output
prices must be at least high enough to cover their costs of
production to ensure production. Within these constraints
price levels are determined by relative power, and the extent
to which the price is higher than the cost of production is a
measure of the successful exercise of power in securing a
proportion of the surplus produced by the system.

4. Pricing contracts

Before the technical cost of production can be translated
into monetary costs by the simple process of multiplying the
factor inputs by their price, one further question needs
resolving; that of the terms on which the use of productive
factors are secured. Three basic methods can be identified;
permanent transfer of ownership by sale, the temporary
transfer of ownership by forms of leasing, and the sale of
productive power with no transfer of ownership.

Clearly, the more permanent the transfer of ownership
the greater will be the extent to which the cost of storing
the productive factor when not in use and of depreciation
will be transferred to its user. Usually the means of
production are owned by the productive units, although
machines are frequently leased. On the other hand, employment

contracts secure for the capitalist the services of labour
for a limited period of time (contracts which are, in effect,
forms of leasing). However, payment by results and other
systems of incentive payments mean that the employer is
directly purchasing labour power even if the employment
contract fixes the normal hours of work. "Putting out" and
sub-contracting provide ways by which employers secure labour
power, and often the services of the means of production,
without any direct responsibility for their storage,
maintenance or depreciation costs.

If market powers are equally balanced there would be no
material difference between the forms taken by market
transactions. A productive unit may be faced, under normal
operation, with the prospect of all factors of production
being temporarily unemployed, or being under-employed where
technical indivisibilities required the total productive
power to be assembled whatever the level of output. But, in
either case, if the market power was balanced, the costs of
storage and depreciation would be fully taken account of in
the agreement on price [6]. However, if market power is
unequally distributed both the price and the form of the
contract might reflect the power imbalance. Typically, in
sectors of the labour market where the workers are poorly
organized, wage levels are low and employment is insecure and
in product markets where relative bargaining power expresses
itself in the security guaranteed by the contract as well as
the level of price.

5. Money costs of production per unit of output

Once the products, the techniques of production, the
organization, the price of productive factors and the forms
of contract are determined, then the unit costs of production and their variation with respect of output are fixed.
Costs of production can be changed by adjusting any of these
variables, and can be made flexible if this adjustment can be
made at will. But as cost formation includes technical and
power elements changes in costs can be secured by adjustments
in technical or power relationships, or in both.

C. The Firm and the Structure of Costs

At any point in time, then, the structure of industrial costs
is the outcome of an historical process involving economic,
technical and power relations and is fixed. At the centre of
this decision-making process is the firm: the unit

controlling production. the firm can be represented as in
Fig. 1, which emphasizes the central importance of the
organization of production, but which illustrates the
constraints within which the firm operates.

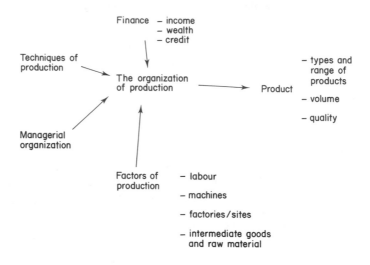

Fig. 1   The firm

The extent of the firm's control of the segments in Fig.
1 will vary. The firm usually owns the factory site and the
machines and, where production is vertically integrated,
direct control may extend backwards into the production of
intermediary goods and raw materials and forwards into the
product market. In these cases, relations internal to the
firm would replace market relations. But this internalization would not necessarily fully remove the constraints
imposed by the market, and new limitations would be introduced in the form of problems with managerial organization
and the need to resolve conflicting sectional interests.

The firm's terms and conditions for employing labour
will be influenced by its need to secure and maintain an
adequate supply of the appropriately skilled labour and to
maintain control in the labour process. But worker organization and legal requirements conditioning the employment
contract and health and safety at work provisions will
constrain the firms and influence wage costs. Thus security
of employment, the wage and employment structure internal to
the firm, organization of the labour process and the firm's

relation to the external labour market will reflect the
methods of production, the efficiency of organization and the
state of the product and labour markets, but will also be
influenced by a bargaining process in which the strength of
workers' organization in the labour market and within the
firms, as well as the legal and political framework for
industrial relations will have a major influence.

The types of products manufactured and the firm's
control of the product market will also have an important
influence on its control over costs. Component manufacturers
and the makers of capital equipment will be confronted in the
market by buyers well equipped with technical knowledge, and
will be more confined to precise product specifications than
the supplier to mass consumption markets where the level of
technical expertise is low and where demand can be
manipulated by mass selling techniques.

The degree of control the firms exercise over the
specification and quality of the product will also depend on
the relative bargaining strength of the buyer and seller. In
this respect small sub-contractors to large firms may lose
all control over product composition whilst at the other
extreme the small assembler faced by large component
producers will be constrained to use intermediary goods over
which no control can be exercised. Between these extremes
product composition will be - to varying degrees - the
outcome of a bargaining process.

The financial constraints on a firm will be a function
of its profitability - the net effect of its control of costs
and prices - its accumulated wealth and access to credit. The
latter will be a function of profitability and financial
resources but may also be influenced by power relative to the
firm's suppliers and those it supplies. Power to dictate the
size of orders, the timing of their delivery and terms and
timing of financial settlement provides a way by which the
firm can shift the cost of holding stocks in raw materials,
intermediary and final products and thereby reduce its
financial constraint (whilst increasing that on the other
firms). Finally, the intensity of this constraint depends on
the firm's financial liabilities relative to its productive
capabilities and the form in which the liabilities are held.
With a large surplus relative to liabilities a high ratio of
fixed interest to equity stock will increase the proportion
of funds over which the managers of the firm have direct
control, whilst the opposite would be the case if profits
were low. In such difficult circumstances a family firm which
derives capital from saving and which depends on family
labour may prove more viable than a firm of similar size
dependent on external finance and wage labour. In the latter

case, the short term needs to finance a fixed bill of wages
and capital charges could bankrupt the firm [7] whatever its
long term prospects, whereas the possibilities of more
flexible cost in the family firm stemming from their greater
dependence on internal resources would give it more survival
value [8].

D. Some Responses of Firms to Change Costs

In the terms of the discussion in the first two sections of
this paper the structure and level of cost have several
dimensions. Unit costs are determined by the type and range
of products, techniques and organization of production, the
volume of output and control in the factor and product
market. The degree of control over cost will depend on
effective decision making in each of these segments and this
will largely depend upon the removal of constraints by the
exercise of power. Within this framework it is possible to
illustrate the process of changing costs by following through
the possible methods by which a reduction in costs could be
implemented and what the consequence of such decisions might
be. Suppose a firm decides to reduce unit labour costs for
one or more of a variety of reasons: to increase profits, to
secure competitive advantage, under competitive pressure or
because of increasing uncertainty about the future. A range
of possibilities are open to it including the redesign of the
product, the adaptation of new techniques of production, the
reorganization of the firm and its structure of production.
But each of these possibilities is subject to a varying
degree of constraint.

The redesign of the product will be constrained by the
product market's acceptance of the change, the technical
capabilities of the firm and the resistance of the workforce
to changes in work organization. A change in techniques can
lower unit labour costs directly by increasing labour
productivity, or more indirectly by facilitating a greater
degree of control over the labour process and the pace of
work by weakening the technological basis for labour
organization. Similar effects could be secured by the introduction of new managerial techniques or by changes in job
content to allow a greater degree of flexibility and
interchangeability in the use of the labour force. Such
strategies will be constrained by worker organization and
possibly by the managerial structure of the firm.

The firm can also cut its labour costs by reducing the
price of labour by either directly cutting the wages of its

labour force or shifting its demand to labour to a different
segment of the labour market by changing hiring rules or relocating production regionally or internationally. The terms
of the contract can also be changed to allow more casual
forms of employment or wage systems more directly relating
wages to output to reduce the fixed elements in the labour
costs. The success of these strategies will depend on the
strength of labour organizations both within the firm and in
the labour market and whether the structuring of the labour
supply provides the firm with easy access to alternative
supplies of labour at lower prices.

Lower labour costs might also be achieved by a radical
reorganization of the firm's structure and operation. One
such strategy is decentralization either within the firm or,
more radically, by putting out production to sub-contractors. The reorganization of the firm into separate profit
centres has been used to subject parts of the company to the
pressure of outside competition, thus changing the balance of
power within the company (both between the firm and its
labour force, and between competing managerial interests).
Similarly, effects can be secured by sub-contracting which
has the dual advantage of delegating the responsibility for
the reduction of unit labour costs to other firms whilst
providing the opportunity to weaken worker organization
within the firm.

Strategies for reducing labour costs thus range from
those designed mainly to cut wages or intensify labour to
those aimed at enhancing labour productivity by the redesign
of products and the innovation of technique and organizational forms. These are not mutually exclusive categories,
and a firm's overall strategy may include aspects of both.
But it is instructive to consider the polar cases separately
because incentives for their adoption, the conditions for
their implementation and their potential for long-term cost
reduction differ widely.

An important determinant of the firm's strategy will be
its financial viability and economic prospects. The latter
will be determined by the overall level of economic activity
and, within that framework, the overall demand for the firm's
particular products and the firm's prospects for securing an
adequate share of its markets. The tighter the financial
constraint and the more pessimistic the firm's expectations
of the future, the greater will be the probability that the
firm will attempt to reduce labour costs directly by cutting
wages and increasing the pace of work within its existing
technical and organizational structure. The less onerous the
financial and economic constraints, the wider the choice of
strategies will be and the greater the possibilities of

investing in new methods of production and new products.

The extent of the possible reduction in labour costs will also be influenced by the strategy adopted. Worker organization, the extent of labour market segmentation, the overall level of unemployment and labour law constrain wage reductions and the intensifications of the pace of work, whilst physiological factors set an ultimate limit. By contrast, improvements made in the techniques of production, products and the organization of the firm will be less subject to such constraint and may well lift them. New methods of production and managerial organizations provide new opportunities to increase control of the labour process and may well serve to weaken the basis for labour organization or the formation of new alliances. Moreover, unlike strategies to reduce wages and intensify work within a given technical and organizational framework (which can only successfully increase profits at the expense of labour), changes in the technical and organizational basis for production may increase the productivity of productive sectors and this may allow both wages and profits to rise. Thus, capital investment and innovation in techniques of production may enhance the possibility of reducing labour cost by reducing the labour content in products, by changing the balance of power in favour of the firm, but also removing any constraints on the lowest limit of labour costs by increasing the productivity of the productive resources it controls.

II. CONCLUSION

The structure and levels of costs of a firm are determined by its products, the techniques of production and the prices of its factors of production. These variables are determined by economic, technical and power relations. the latter can be divided into those within the firm and those between the firm and its factor and product markets and, at a more general level, by the social and political system within which production takes place. These levels are clearly related. The social and political system, for example, determines the role of the state in the provision of social welfare, determining labour and company law and the cohesive use of state power in structuring (or otherwise) the labour and product market. This acts as a general framework for the determination of the power relation both within the firm and the market.

Once the factors above are given, the level and structure of costs are fixed and can only be changed if the economic, technical and power relations are changed. The

degree of flexibility of costs will be determined by the
extent to which the firm can manipulate the variables outlined above at will. However, there are technical limits to
the flexibility of costs set by the available techniques and
the cost of production of the productive factors. But within
these limits the flexibility is determined by relative power.
This can be changed by the adoption of new methods of
production and organization, by changes in the social and
political system or by other factors changing the relative
power in the market, for example, an increase in unemployment. Alternatively, the need to exercise power to adjust
costs may be avoided if productive potential is increased
sufficiently to meet conflicting claims. A survey of history
suggests that the latter is by far the most effective way of
both reducing costs and increasing their flexibility.

NOTES

1. The development of new methods and materials which
    would reduce the technical cost of production does not
    mean that the productive unit would immediately abandon
    existing techniques of production. The replacement of
    existing methods by new means the loss of productive
    capacity embodied in the old, but eventually, if
    techniques continuously improve, the increased
    productivity offsets the cost of scrapping. For example,
    suppose a productive unit consisted of one worker, a
    machine powered by electricity and raw materials (a
    lathe is such a productive unit) and suppose also that
    technical developments have made existing machines and
    the skills necessary to operate them obsolete by
    improving the conversion rate of the other productive
    resources into products. The new lathe would not be
    immediately introduced because of the loss of the
    productive power embodied in the existing machines and
    skills. However, with continuous lathe improvement a
    point would be reached when the productive power saved
    by not scrapping would be more than offset by more
    efficient use of the raw materials, electricity and
    labour (other than the newly obsolete skills) previously
    used by the old technology.
2. In the initial stages of production, for example, more
    human and non-human energy may be needed to produce each
    output than when the machine has reached its most
    efficient operating speed.
3. There will, however, be additional ageing costs because
    by storing its product power, the life of the
    indivisible factor is extended.

4.   The discussion of Taylorism often proceeds as if it only
      had a coercive role. But new methods of management which
      facilitate the more effective use of labour with given
      techniques must be regarded in the same light as new
      techniques embodied in the machine. Both the new
      techniques and the new method of management may allow
      more control of the labour process and an intensi-
      fication of work, but this may only be a secondary
      effect.

5.   This applies equally to the labour provided by the
      owner of an owner-operated firm. This latter case raises
      additional difficulty because the owner of a business
      may be prepared to accept a lower price for labour and
      capital supplied to his own firm than its market price.
      Alternatively, the ownership of these productive
      resources might enhance the bargaining power of the
      owner-operator and the money extracted from the business
      may be higher than the price of the services provided in
      the market.

6.   An important determinant of relative power would be
      the alternative use to which the owner could put the
      productive factor. If, say, workers could find
      alternative employment when not employed productively,
      this would relieve both the workers and original
      employers of the maintenance costs. On the other hand,
      it would mean that labour was not "on tap" to the
      original employer. The importance of such considerations
      would depend on such factors as the length of the
      interruption to production and the prospects of re-
      establishing the previous levels of output and this
      might influence both the level of price and the form
      contracts would take.

7.   This does not necessarily mean that costs are
      inflexible even if firms are bankrupted. The possibility
      of the resale of the firm's assets at prices more
      closely reflecting their economic prospects and the re-
      negotiation of wages with the same aim would allow costs
      and prices to be more flexible downward. But this
      flexibility would be secured by a change of control.

8.   For similar reasons, wages may be more flexible
      downward than the price of other factor inputs because
      of the possibility of substituting family and other non-
      market resources for wages to maintain and reproduce
      labour.

Segmentation, Employment Structures and Productive Structures

F. MICHON

One approach to segmentation analysis is to differentiate
between the various segments of the labour market in
institutional terms: according to the degree of unionization
of the labour force, the legality or otherwise of employment
and working conditions, or even, if possible, as it is in
France, according to the existence of institutional job
security. This procedure provides immediately useful
empirical results and avoids highly abstract theoretical
debates. On the other hand, the segmentation of the labour
market may be explained in terms of the oligopolistic nature
of the productive structures, of large firms dominating small
firms, of the degree of concentration with the sector, etc.
The French example provides a contradiction: in large firms
and highly concentrated sectors there are more jobs without
institutional security and, more generally, more jobs of a
"non-standard" form.

The French example certainly seems to be relatively
specific. Nevertheless, one or other of the above assertions
must provide an explanation. The article that follows uses
the conclusions of an enquiry on the use by French firms of
"non-standard job forms" (NSJFs) in order to illustrate by
means of a few simple diagrams and propositions the

relationship that might link a segmented labour market and an
oligopolistic productive structure. [1].

First, however, it will be necessary to outline and
justify our definitions and hypotheses, which are deeply
embedded in a typically French combination of theory and
empiricism.

I. DEFINITIONS AND HYPOTHESES BASED ON THE FRENCH EXAMPLE

A. A Definition of Segmentation Based on 2 x 2 Assumptions

1. Segmentation: discontinuity and labour flows

For effect, French researchers often describe the segmentation of the labour market in dualistic terms, i.e. in terms
of "good" and "bad" jobs (Salais, 1977) and of certain
categories of workers being condemned to bad jobs. This is a
simplification of the description given by Piore (1978) [2]:

> a division of the labour market into two sectors: a
> primary sector, containing better paying, more stable
> and otherwise attractive opportunities and the more
> privileged members of the labour force, and a secondary
> sector, containing generally poor paying, insecure and
> otherwise unattractive jobs. This second sector is
> manned by women, youths, minority groups, migrants,
> part-time peasants and other groups which we tend to
> think of as marginal or disadvantaged (p. 27).

This description requires two comments. First, the dualistic
aspect is not crucial. It is more important to contrast the
phenomenon of discontinuity between segments of the labour
market with continuous differentiation than it is to debate
the exact number of segments (cf. Berger and Piore, 1980)
[3]. Secondly, particular emphasis must be given to "the
differences between the two sectors with respect to job
security and the stability of employment" (Piore, 1978,
p.27). Indeed, the institutional aspects of job security or
insecurity seem to be absolutely decisive in France. Most
French studies adopt this view of the phenomenon of segmentation. In particular, many of them define them in terms of
labour force flows [4] without even mentioning the question
of wages. This paper does not depart from this position. Our
first two assumptions are, therefore, that segmentation is
defined a priori by (i) discontinuity and (ii) as affecting
labour force flows.

This is of course a rather specific point of view, that is certainly open to debate, even though there is no lack of pertinent theoretical justifications. Ryan (1981), for example, makes a distinction between "strict duality" (discontinuous bi-modal distribution) [5] and "heuristic duality" (a continuous and highly dispersed unimodal distribution). His purpose is to stress that the notion of continuity does not in itself conflict with the idea of segmentation. For Ryan though, only strict duality originates in-market. In our view, statistical dispersion is nothing more than a product of differentiation, and only plurimodality is indicative of segmentation. From this point of view, structuration may be merely differentiation or true segmentation.

The question of wages is usually considered to be inseparable from the question of job security, or even to be much more central: "The existence of segmentation in the labour market, defined as different wages for workers of equal efficiency..." (Wilkinson, 1981). What distinguishes segmentation from mere division is that each segment functions according to different rules, and that as a consequence, wages are different, even if the productive qualities of the labour force are absolutely the same.

The rules by which the segment functions are the procedures for wage determination. But they are also the procedures for allocating the labour force to jobs, which thus control labour force flows. From this point of view, one characteristic of a primary market in comparison with a secondary market is that the two procedures - wage fixing and flow determination - are largely independent of each other: price effects do not regulate a primary market. Labour flows, and any difference in job stability, for example, may be enough to define segmentation.

2. Segmentation: an effect of modern productive structures

Our third assumption is that discontinuity affecting labour flows - the degree of job stability and security - is specific to the present day period. And, fourthly, it is assumed that discontinuity is merely the result of the (modern) characteristics of the productive structures that consist of large firms that dominate small firms. The aim of the following paper is to illustrate to what extent these last two assumptions are indissociable.

The third assumption is quite widely accepted. But it may be, and often is, based on a somewhat mythical reference to a nineteenth century golden age of competition, both in

the labour market and in the market for goods and other
services. Thus a segmented labour market is seen as simply
the result of imperfect competition in the market, which is
hardly a satisfactory explanation.

It is for this reason that the third assumption is
inextricably linked with the fourth. To the extent that
segmentation involves not only the labour market, but is the
direct result of the historical development of productive
structures, the phenomenon cannot be explained as a mere
imperfection in the labour market. At the same time, it
becomes possible to assume that any (waged) labour market is
necessarily imperfect, and cannot and never has obeyed the
canons of the (orthodox) economic theory of the market, not
even in the last century.

Payment by wages necessarily results in an imbalance of
bargaining powers between the "partners" to any exchange in
the labour market (cf. Say, 1972). As a result, workers
compete with each other with respect to the requirements of
employers, they are compared and classified, and categorized
into groups, including the "non-competitive" groups of
orthodox theory. The existence of wage-earning employees
leads necessarily to a heterogeneous and even discontinuous
labour market [6]. Segmentation is an historically new
phenomenon, only in so far as it is a specific form of
heterogeneity and discontinuity.

B. Some Hypotheses on the Structuring of the Productive System and the Segmentation of the Labour Market

When labour market segmentation is closely linked with a
discontinuous productive structure, the latter is usually
described in terms of large firms dominating small firms, or
at least in terms of concentrated and small firms sectors.
This description is quite widely accepted, or is at least
common to different theoretical interpretations.

The theoretical interpretation of such discontinuity may
be based on the relationship of firms to the product market,
their differing powers of negotiation in that market, and
their different abilities to control prices. Other
interpretations, however, stress the internal characteristics
of the firms: the organization of the "internal" labour
market or else the type of labour process. Some stress
manufacturing technologies, and others the hierarchical
social relationships between the members of the labour force.
The usual explanatory variables are the degree of sales
stability and the average level of skill, internal staff
transfers or the size of turnover, and the degree of

unionization or the procedures for controlling the workforce.
    Various elements in the debates on labour market
segmentation can be easily recognized here, such as, for
example, that between "institutionalists" and "radicals" to
make a distinction current in the USA but not always relevant
in France or even Europe.
    With the question of non-standard job forms and the
description of the characteristics of firms that use them,
the French example questions the accepted correlation between
a "secondary" labour market and small firms or less
concentrated sectors. On the other hand, analysis of the ways
in which these NSJFs are used by firms usefully clarifies the
question by shifting the debate.
    The clarification does not lead us unequivocally to
support one or other of the suggested theoretical
interpretations, but serves to sort out the various aspects
of the question.

1. The diversity of the employment structuring processes

The major advantage of non-standard job forms as a means of
controlling the workforce - which is characteristic of the
use of the "secondary" labour market - is their versatility.
Three of their characteristics explain their use in the
pursuit of three different objectives. First, they provide a
form of external labour for firms seeking to specialize their
production unit. Second, they provide a form of temporary
employment for firms seeking to meet the demands of periods
of peak activity known to be temporary. Third, they provide
precarious or insecure employment [7] for firms seeking to
strengthen their control over their workforce, even in the
strictly hierarchical and disciplinary aspects of control.
    Thus, by generalizing from the above, the following
processes can be distinguished:

    i) The process known as the "division of labour"
       in which production units and individual jobs
       become increasingly specialized, the effects
       of which are the decomposition and recom-
       position of tasks at the job level, the
       externalization of jobs and the fragmentation
       of production units.
   ii) The process known as "segmentation", charac-
       terized by uncertainty about rates of activity
       and the level of employment, which leads to
       differential instability in different jobs.
  iii) The process known as the specification of the

wage relationship, a means of controlling the
work-force, of which the hierarchical and
disciplinary aspects account for only a small
part of the effects on the job form (that is,
on the social protections and guarantees
provided by the wage relationship).

2. The effects of structuring and of segmentation

A distinction will be made here between differentiation and
segmentation. Differentiation will be characterized as simple
heterogeneity, and segmentation as discontinuity, similar to
Ryan's characterization: differentiation-heterogeneity-
unimodal dispersion; segmentation-discontinuity-plurimodal
dispersion.

It is no longer sufficient merely to identify the main
job structuring phenomena. The structuring effects of each
phenomenon must be analysed in terms of either heterogeneity
or discontinuity. The main problem is to select, from the
point of view of the labour market, those job structuring
processes that lead to differentiation and those that produce
real segmentation.

Even if the structuring processes are identified by
actual observation, the distinction between differentiation
and segmentation that will be made here remains an almost
totally abstract exercise in pure logic. The question is thus
examined in all its aspects, but no solution is offered here.
Although largely academic, the exercise is nevertheless
useful in that it reminds us that it is impossible to
understand any segmentation phenomenon outside the context of
the competition between individual capital, and the unequal
power relationships and structuring of the productive system
brought about by this competition. Only phenomena of simple
differentiation can be considered outside of this context.

This statement is, broadly speaking, so obvious that
many will conclude that the exercise is a futile one.
Nevertheless, when the consequences for the analysis of
employment and the labour market of over-emphasis of the
macro-economic point of view are examined, it becomes clear
that the obvious is easily overlooked.

3. Some other simplifying hypotheses

First, the productive systems will be reduced to a series of
production units. The processes of competition between individual capital will be symbolized by one of their results,

i.e. the structuring of the productive system into large
production units on the one hand, and small production units
on the other. The aim is not to describe these processes of
competition, but simply to show that no analysis of the
phenomena of segmentation can ignore them.

This very simple aim enables us to overlook the fact
that a production unit is neither a firm (i.e. a legal
entity) nor an individual capitalist (an economic-financial
entity) [8]. The complexity of the relationships between
legal, industrial and financial structures is totally
ignored, as is the problem of the mobility of individual
capital. However, what follows will show that this type of
simplification is untenable when segmentation phenomena in
the labour market are being examined.

Second, Boyer (1981) describes the "rapport salarial" as
"the set of of conditions that control the use and reproduction of the labour force". This French term is much wider
in scope than the simple micro-economic relationship between
employer and wage earner. This relationship is directly
linked to work and to the phenomena of the exchange and use
of the labour force.

In order to indicate the restrictions being used here,
the term "wage relationship" is used to denote these phenomena alone. Moreover, to the extent that job precariousness
and disciplinary control of the workforce depend on job form,
there is an implicit assumption that this job form, whether
standard or non-standard, correctly reflects the type of wage
relationship. In making this assumption, the notion of
control of the work-force is reduced to its micro-economic
aspects (for example, the fact that initial training begins
the process of social control is ignored), and among these,
only the aspect of hierarchy and discipline is considered
(all aspects of the control of qualifications are ignored).

II. UNCERTAINTY AND THE SEGMENTATION PROCESS

Uncertainty in this sense corresponds to what Piore (Berger
and Piore, 1980) describes in terms of variability of
production factors: capital is fixed, while labour is
variable. This can be expressed in another way. One way of
dealing with a fluctuating and uncertain rate of activity is
to reduce average labour costs by increasing the variable
proportion. The most obvious way of achieving this result is
not to pay the workforce as soon as it is under-utilized.
This variation in the quantity of paid work can be achieved
by variations in working hours (provided that wages are

Proportional to hours worked). It can also be achieved by
eliminating and creating jobs, a phenomenon that concerns us
here.

At the macro-economic level, uncertainty leads only to
fluctuations in the level of employment. The problem of job
instability becomes apparent as soon as the fluctuations no
longer affect jobs randomly but in a systematically unequal
way and jobs become equally sensitive to fluctuations, as
measured on the same scale. This does not appear to be
sufficient to define a segmented labour market. In addition,
the sensitivity must be discontinuously distributed over that
scale.

First, unequal sensitivity may arise out of three types
of division:

  i) Division amongst various markets according to
     the stability of demand, i.e. among stable and
     fluctuating markets. Economic activities with
     little fluctuation in demand would offer more
     stable jobs than the others.
 ii) Division within the various markets between a
     stable and unstable part. The same sector
     would contain units offering stable jobs and
     units offering unstable jobs.
iii) Division within each productive unit or
     organization, i.e. a division of workload in
     each one into stable and unstable parts. The
     same unit would thus offer stable and unstable
     jobs.

Figures 1.1, 1.2 and 1.3 correspond respectively to these
three divisions. The difficulty of empirical testing
obviously lies in the fact that each of these diagrams has an
undeniable reality, but that observation may well confirm the
existence of a mixed system (Fig. 1.4).

On a theoretical level, uncertainty appears unaffected
by whatever choice is made between these systems, and seems
compatible with all of them. If there were no other
influences on choice, in a hypothetical situation in which no
structuring process other than uncertainty was operating, the
third diagram would provide the only real area of choice. The
first two presuppose an already existing structured
framework: in the first case this would be a process of
specialization within the productive units in the
manufacturing of a restricted range of products, and
separation with respect to the markets; in the first and
second cases, the instability of the market would be
concentrated on particular productive units. The latter

Phenomenon must of course be linked to the processes of
competition between individual capital and the consequent
inequalities in power.

Figure 1.2 seems to be the only one to presuppose a
close correspondence between true industrial dualism and
possible dualism in the labour market. This emphasizes the
extent to which the phenomena of uncertainty are completely

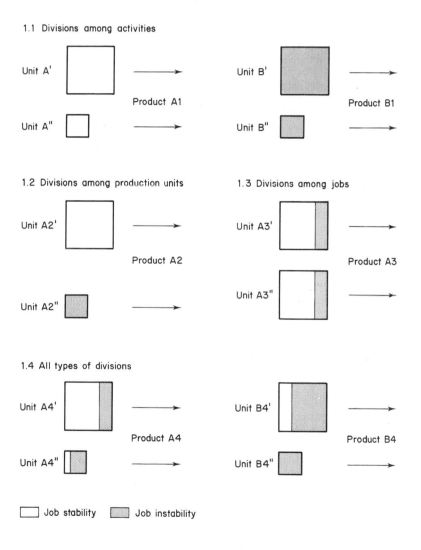

Fig. 1   Economic fluctuations and the distibution
of the effects of instability.

incapable by themselves of causing discontinuities in the
labour market. Thus, the essential point here is that a
specific productive structure, and not phenomena of
uncertainty considered in the abstract, is necessary for
segmentation.

Secondly, however, such diagrams describe only
differences in sensitivity to fluctuations. They do not
necessarily result in real discontinuities in employment
structures, nor, a fortiori, in the labour market. There are
two ways of discovering the source of such discontinuities.
They both involve phenomena other than those of uncertainty.

The first way is to look for these sources in the
obstacles to labour force mobility. the differences in
qualifications between stable and unstable jobs spring
immediately to mind.

But these differences in qualifications may not be the
same for each of the diagrams: in Fig. 1.1 the stable and
unstable jobs do not produce the same goods: thus the
difference between stable and unstable jobs are first of all
differences in occupation, so that the discontinuities
observed are those arising out of the range of qualifications
and occupations.

In Fig. 1.3, the stable and unstable jobs are involved in
the manufacturing of the same product: this still necessarily
involves many different occupations, but this diagram
includes differences which relate to the level of
qualifications and training. Thus, the discontinuities
observed are directly related to the hierarchical structure
of qualifications.

In Fig. 1.2, the stable and unstable jobs manufacture
the same product in separate organizations: the
discontinuities stem from the particular conditions within
each organization and from the specific requirements of non-
transferable training acquired on the job.

In all these cases, whether the differences in stability
are explained in terms of more or less investment in training
of training acquired prior to employment or on the job, or of
transferable or non-transferable training, the existence of
discontinuities is exogenous to labour market phenomena since
it is not caused by them. It is even completely external to
the phenomena of uncertainty. The necessity for various types
of training is always linked to the processes of the division
of labour and to their structuring effect from the point of
view of both productive organizations and jobs.

A second way is to look for these sources of discontinuity in the socio-institutional processes that determine
the nature of the wage relationships,job forms and the
functioning of the labour market. There is a close

relationship between segmentation processes as such and these socio-institutional processes. However, this link is not strong enough to attribute to uncertainty itself the possible discontinuity effects arising out of the various wage relationships.

The figures above seem unaffected by job forms and the ways in which the labour market functions as a result of them, in the sense that they are compatible with all the ways that the labour market might function, from free wage competition to all types of restriction on free wage competition [9].

However, the question is not whether it is possible for the labour market to function in a particular way, but whether it can function simultaneously in at least two ways, since we are concerned with discontinuities. From this point of view, it is obvious that certainty and stability put the workers in the most favourable position for organizing and bargaining, and for imposing restrictions on the processes of competition.

This is a source of division between a market with stable jobs and one with unstable jobs controlled by different rules to the extent that job guarantees, for example, would be offered to the first but not to the second.

This type of division is perfectly compatible with Figs. 1.1 and 1.2. It is not difficult to imagine the relative bargaining powers of employers and wage earners being permanently differentiated from one production unit to the next, and, _a fortiori_, from one firm to the next.

Figure 1.3 presupposes that the relative negotiating powers within the same firm vary from one type of job to another. It presupposes above all that these powers always vary according to the type of job, whatever the firm under consideration. This is not at all unlikely, but requires a much more subtle description of the strategies of the actors than a crude relationship between uncertainty and job instability on the one hand, and relative bargaining powers on the other. In particular, in the present situation, it seems necessary to specify how employers are seeking to re-establish effective control over the labour force by reducing the employment guarantees in certain jobs (see below).

All the preceding systems clearly illustrate that uncertainty does not automatically lead to segmentation, unless all sorts of differentiations between jobs, continuous or discontinuous, autonomous or dependent on the productive structures, are given the label segmentation. In order for segmentation proper to exist, uncertainty must operate in a context of unequal competition between capital, the particularization of skills or qualifications, and diversification resulting from strategies for controlling the labour force [10].

III. SPECIALIZATION AND THE DIVISION OF LABOUR

In contrast to what we have termed "segmentation power", the aim of which is to make working time variable, the processes of the division of labour, whether it be the division of labour "in general" (among the various productive organizations), or "in particular" (the socio-technical division among the various jobs), can be said to be time-saving.
　　Adam Smith reserved the expression "time-saving" for the reduction in the dead time necessary for the worker to proceed from one operation to another, i.e. for the intensification of individual work. The expression may be extended to the collective worker in order to refer to the time required to complete a given manufacturing process. It thus sums up all the procedures by which the division of labour improves productivity: these include not only the intensification of work, but also the increased skill of the worker as the result of the reduced number of operations carried out, the use of the full potential of each worker by avoiding giving simple tasks to skilled workers (the so-called Babbage principle), etc. It is no longer a question of not paying under-utilized staff (the variability principle underlying segmentation) but of using the paid staff to the maximum of their potential and capabilities (the intensity principle).

A. Decomposition and Recomposition of Indiviudal Jobs and Production Units: the Externalization of Jobs and the Fragmentation of the Productive System

In Adam Smith's analysis, the division of labour is a process of specialization with the aim of increasing productivity that generates a process of fragmentation of individual jobs.
　　This unidirectional view of a process of linear fragmentation can be contrasted (Berger and Piore, 1980) with a more contradictory concept of a dual process of decomposition and recomposition, of dissociation and synthesis, that is very similar as far as jobs are concerned to the phenomena of de-skilling and over-qualification (Freyssenet, 1974), as Azouvi (1981) stresses. Moreover, in what follows, we shall assume that the effects of the process on the internal organization of work (in particular on the

division of labour) are, on the one hand, the specialization
of each job in a more restricted range of increasingly simple
operations (ie. the range of jobs increases as they are de-
skilled) and, on the other, the recreation of more skilled
jobs, specializing in a new range of operations that remain
relatively complex.

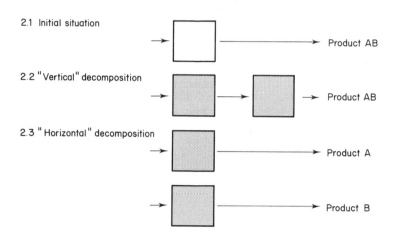

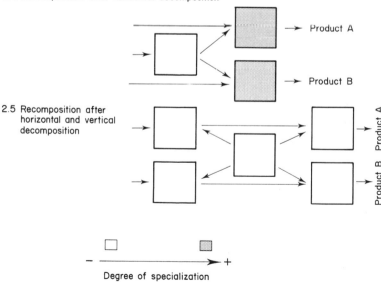

Figs. 2.1 - 2.5 Divisions of labour and externalization.

   Decomposition and recomposition also affect the
organization of the productive system into production units
as much as the internal organization of these units into
jobs, i.e., the division of labour "in general" as much as
the division of labour "in particular". In the process of
decomposition, the range of activities in each unit becomes
more restricted, each one specializing in a certain type of
operation. In the process of recomposition, there is a
regrouping as activities that were previously unconnected and
dispersed are brought together. Greater importance is given
in what follows to this division of labour "in general".

   The process of specialization thus causes an initial
dislocation of the series of tasks that constitute jobs (the
breaking down of jobs into individual operations) and of the
series of jobs that constitute the production units
(fragmentation of the productive system). This can be
represented by the transition from Fig. 2.1 to Fig. 2.2,
during which process the various stages of the same manufacturing process are broken down into several units, that
are themselves organized into more diversified and specialized jobs than the parent unit in 2.1 (vertical decomposition). Fig. 2.3 represents a second, horizontal, type of
decomposition.

   The second phase of this specialization process is the
regrouping of operations or activities previously dispersed
in the various units into separate and external units that
can be reorganized more productively. These units may of
course be a new workshop or service for the production unit,
as well as a new external unit. Fig. 2.4 represents the
recomposition of activities that were all involved in
separate manufacturing processes (recomposition after
horizontal decomposition). Fig. 2.5 represents a process of
recomposition following a double process of horizontal and
vertical decomposition. The case of services for firms and,
more generally, of indirect or peripheral labour (in
comparison with direct labour, involved only in
manufacturing), e.g. transport, handling, maintenance or
administrative services or even workforce management services
(cf. in France, the "interim" contract and the temporary job
agencies) comes to mind immediately [11].

   From the point of view of the division of labour "in
general", which is our main concern here, the phenomena of
decomposition and recomposition proceed in all cases through
successive stages of externalization of series of operations
and of entire sections of the productive process, and then
through the establishment of new specialized production units
and the fragmentation of the productive infrastructure.

B. Externalization, Fragmentation of the Productive Structure and Segmentation

The above figures can be combined and multiplied in an infinite number of ways. One possible combination is shown in Fig. 2.6, the purpose of which is to represent the resumption of processes of horizontal and vertical decomposition, applied to previously recomposed activities, such as indirect or peripheral labour.

2.6 Return to decomposition

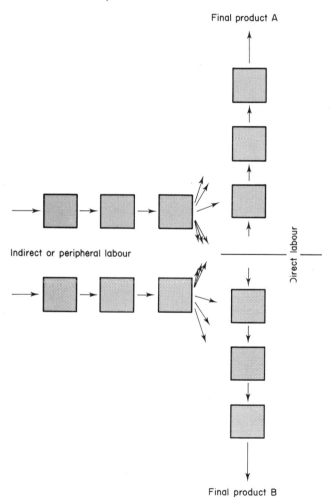

Fig. 2.6   Divisions of labour and
externalization

F. Michon

        The effect of numerous and successive processes of
externalization and specialization ought to be represented by
even greater organizational complexity that in Fig. 2.6, to
the extent that this effect diversifies (from the point of
view of the nature of their activity) and multiplies ad
infinitum the production units. But the consequent extreme
fragmentation tends towards its opposite, the production of
an area with neither polarization nor discontinuity [12].

2.7 Consumer dominates

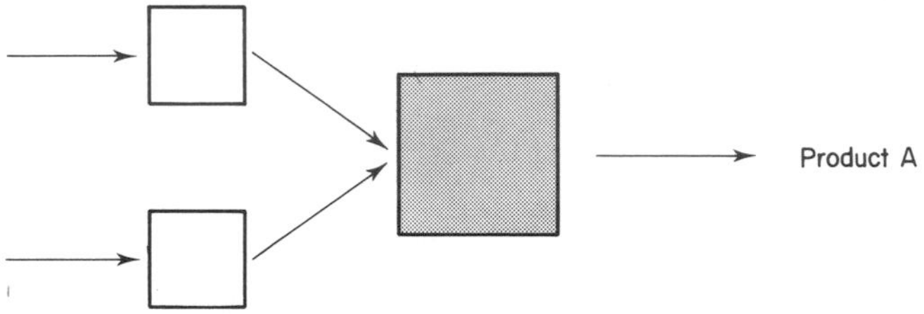

Product A

2.8 Supplier dominates

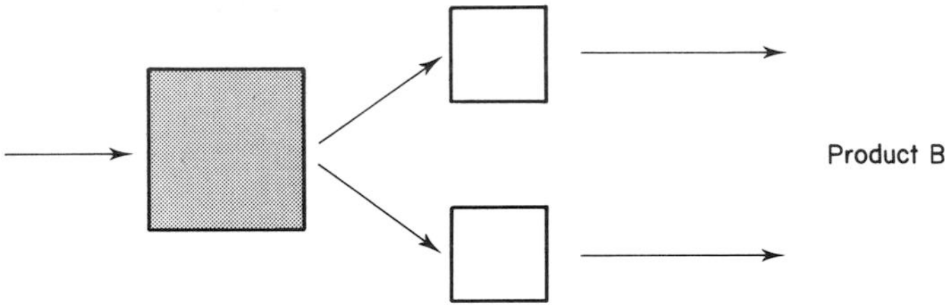

Product B

2.9 Industrial complex

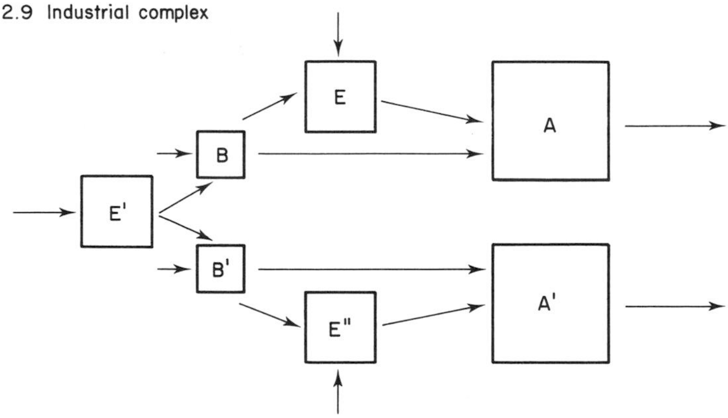

Figs. 2.7–2.9 Divisions of labour and externalization. In
Fig. 2.9, A and A' denote main firms, B and B', subcontrac-
tors; and E, E' and E", firms employing temporary workers.

This seems to be all the more true since the phenomena of externalization and specialization do not in themselves give rise to any specific pattern of domination. Figs. 2.7 and 2.8 represent the alternate situations when either monopolies of supply or monopolies of sales outlets are dominant, but both situations are equally probable, and require much more than the mere effects of externalization and specialization to explain their development.

Figs. 2.7 and 2.8 can be mixed with the preceding ones. The range of possible combinations is almost infinite. Something like Fig. 2.9, for example, would describe the organization of an industrial complex, i.e. a geographically restricted area in which a structured productive organization operates under the orders of, and to meet the needs of, one or several leading firms, for the advantage of a dominant capital [13].

If Figs. 2.7, 2.8 and 2.9 are compared with the preceding ones, and particularly with Fig. 2.6, which represents the type of organization towards which the phenomena of externalization and specialization, the productive system tends towards an atomistic organizational structure with an infinite number of production units, all equal in power, but each one highly specialized and totally dependent on all the others for its supplies and sales. Thus there is a generalized interdependence, without any polarization or domination, and with all possible consequences for the labour market, except the phenomenon of segmentation.

C. The Limits of Fragmentation

1.   The concentration of capital

In reality, the organization of the productive system is obviously not characterized by atomization and generalized interdependence, which would be typical of extreme fragmentation, because the centrifugal dynamic of the social division of labour is not the only influence at work. In particular, to mention a strictly inverse and opposing dynamic, capitalist competition gives rise to concentration phenomena.

Competition between individual capital structures the productive system in the opposite direction to the previous tendencies. It brings about differences of size, oligopolistic or quasi-monopolistic situations and areas of more balanced competition, inequalities and discontinuities affecting the extremely complex network of suppliers and

customers — in short, a polarized, heterogeneous and
discontinuous production system.

   Although both phenomena, the division of labour in
general on the one hand, and capitalist competition and
concentration on the other, are very familiar from the same
economic analyses [14], the link between externalization and
concentration is far from obvious. I shall make only two
observations here.

   First, it will be noted that the precise aim of both
phenomena is not necessarily the same. Conflict is not
inevitable. The difference between capital in the technical
sense of the term — the productive plant — and capital in the
financial sense is well known. It is initially the former
that is subject to fragmentation as a result of the processes
of externalization and specialization. Any possible
consequences for the structure of finance capital come
second. Similarly, the processes of concentration and
centralization concern finance capital, and only have a
secondary effect on productive capital. The legal position
must also be considered. The same financial capital can be
identified with a multitude of legal entities (firms). The
same legal entity may cover various production units
(factories).

   All this is a perfect description of the great structural changes that have taken place in French capitalism in
the past 15 or 20 years: industrial concentration and the
formation of economically and financialy powerful groups (the
five nationalized in 1982) [15]; the spread of the practice
of opening subsidiaries that de-concentrate and multiply the
legal entities dependent on the same individual financial
capital; the multiplication and geographical dispersion of
production units; the sub-contracting of activity and non-
standard job forms. In short, social capital (in the true
sense of the term) has been concentrated, the labour process
has been fragmented and work collectives have been broken up
and destroyed.

   This leads to my second point, that arises out of the
observation that these tendencies are relatively new.
Throughout the first part of the twentieth century [16], that
saw the setting up of a system of mass production based on
Taylorism and Fordism, the same dynamics of concentration and
fragmentation seem to have been linked in a different way
than in recent times, and appear to have taken different
forms. The tendency towards enormous production units that
was characteristic of this period is evidence that the
process of fragmentation did not exclude all forms of the
concentration of productive capital. On the other hand, the
breaking down of tasks into individual operations

characteristic of Taylorian work organization seemed to go
ahead unimpeded. It may be possible to say that "time-saving"
was sought initially at the level of the individual workers,
by the simple process of intensifying his work (Coriat,
1979). If there was any splitting up of the work process and
destruction of the collective within the unit of production
rather than a real break-up, an example of the division of
labour "in particular", concerned only with the internal
organization of the unit of production.

For more than ten years, the processes of externalization and specialization have intensified markedly, or at
least have led to such a degree of fragmentation that the
age-old trend towards the concentration of productive capital
has – at least, on the face of it – been halted, if not
reversed. These phenomena take different forms. In France,
for example, the externalization of indirect or peripheral
labour [17], productive decentralization [18], and the
diversification of the status of the workforce are the most
obvious forms of the fragmentation of the work process. At
the same time, new forms of social conflict (strikes among
assembly line workers, immigrants or women), and the
proliferation of experiments in the recomposition and
enrichment of tasks are evidence of the limits of the
Taylorian breaking down of tasks into individual operations
and the resultant intensification of the work of the
individual. It is at the level of the collective organization of labour as much as – if not more than – at that of
the individual worker that new time-saving efforts (an
increase in efficiency if not in productivity) are being
made.

In this sense, the break-up of the collective
organization of labour has been brought about by a new
organization of the productive system, by a process of the
division of labour within society, between units of
production [19].

The diagrams presented here assimilate by means of a
simplifying hypothesis individual capital (financial) and the
productive unit (productive capital). This is, of course, a
very serious limitation. The diagrams become irrelevant as
soon as the essential point becomes the way in which the
concentration of individual capital of unequal size and power
on the one hand, and the multidimensional [20] fragmentation
of the productive organization on the other are linked. But
they show that if the question of the connection between
financial concentration and the fragmentation of the work
process is not raised, no phenomenon of segmentation and
discontinuity comes to light.

C. The Limits of Fragmentation

1.   The control of the workforce

A collectively organized workforce, once broken up, loses its unity and its ability to defend itself and to fight. This aspect to the fragmentation of work processes underlines the close links between the organizational forms of the division of labour and the control of the workforce.

If, far from conflicting with each other, the need to control the workforce and the search for productive efficiency through specialization and externalization were mutually reinforcing, total externalization of the workforce, i.e. externalization of secondary jobs linked to the use of the workforce - personnel management, supply of labour, training and supervision - could be considered.

The French system of the "interim" contract could well lead to a phenomenon of this kind. It will be necessary to return to the obstacles that might nevertheless prevent the widespread use of the interim contract as a common if not the "normal" job form, and that condemn it to remain a non-standard and relatively marginal job form [21].

I shall limit myself here to the following comment: as soon as personnel management and/or the supply of labour and/or the training and supervision of the workforce are involved, the externalization of activities runs up against some particular difficulties. These difficulties are linked to the control of the labour force (in the widest sense of the word, cf. below), which is thus not always and from all points of view compatible with the phenomena of externalization.

Labour supplied and managed by an outside agency must fit harmoniously into the user's internal organization. This is true from the point of view of qualification: the internal organization must require qualifications to be transferable without any need for on the job training [22]. This is much less true from the point of view of authority and discipline: if the externalized workforce fitted in too easily, collective organization would be re-established and the whole purpose of the exercise defeated.

If the workforce supplied is to be permanent, qualifications are less of an obstacle, but the benefits to be gained from breaking down a collective organization may well disappear also. If the workforce supplied is to be temporary, qualifications may become an insurmountable obstacle, but on the other hand, it is in this case that the collective organization is really broken down.

In short, the processes of the division of labour appear

to be almost universal and without any decisive internal
limits. In fact, the main obstacles appear to be external. It
seems clear, for example, that the need to control the
workforce seriously restricts the use of externally supplied
manpower. More generally, the desire to retain control over
all manufacturing processes, and to avoid any sort of
dependence on other individual capital considerably restricts
the scope for implementing an extreme division of labour. In
other words, the processes in the division of labour seem to
be doubly dependent, first, on the processes of capitalist
competition, and second on the need to control the workforce,
and thus on the processes that determine the "rapport
salarial".

IV. CONTROL OF THE WORKFORCE AND THE DETERMINATION OF THE FORMS OF THE WAGE RELATIONSHIP

The set of phenomena that determine the precise forms of the
wage relationship is obviously too vast to be dealt with
here. Space allows only a few remarks on the relationships
between job insecurity, the negotiating powers of the work
force and the ways in which the labour market functions.
Control of the workforce has been taken as a specific but
basic aspect of the type of wage relationship.

A. Control and Job Insecurity

Control of the labour force is generally understood to mean
the aspects of power and authority within the firm, i.e.
hierarchical and disciplinary control (Edwards, 1979; de
Gaudemar, 1982). This approach is relatively restrictive. We
are more concerned here with the control exercised by
employers over access to jobs, that is, with the freedom to
hire and fire.
    Indeed, it can be assumed that the power of an employer
to hire and fire whom he wants, is fundamental. This power
does not always result in control of the workforce. A
shortage of labour, for example, will hinder the employer in
the exercise of his freedom to hire and fire. But when no
such obstacle exists, the employer controls access to jobs
and the conditions of exchange in the labour market. He also
controls the conditions of use, and has the freedom to
determine disciplinary rules. Even the forms of "passive" and
individual resistance, absenteeism and turnover, are no
longer available to the workforce.
    A labour shortage reduces the freedom to hire and

redresses the balance of power a little. A major
preoccupation of employers, understandably, is to find new
supplies of labour, and to "fix" these new supplies so that
they remain available and dependent.

This, very briefly, was the problem of control as it
presented itself during the industrialization of the Western
countries in the nineteenth century. An industrial
proletariat was formed by the incorporation of the rural
population, and the roots linking the rural population to
agricultural activity had to be cut in the interests of
greater control [23].

The problem today is, of course, very different. The
modern employer is constrained by various legal or
contractual arrangements that considerably restrict his
freedom to hire and fire. The problem of increasing control
over the use of the labour force is one of loosening the
constraints that fix the norms of exchange and of restoring
greater freedom to hire and fire [24].

B. Control and Division of the Labour Force

There are two possible patterns for the evolution of
wage relationships.

i) A simple "transformation" of wage
   relationships, i.e. the reduction of
   protections and guarantees for the workforce,
   and of the limitations standing in the way of
   competition by wages. The first protection to
   come under attack, undoubtedly, would be job
   security — jobs would be made more precarious.
ii) A "diversification" of wage relationships, the
   result of more complex but perhaps more likely
   processes, since this diversification does not
   presuppose that situations and power
   relationships are uniform, since it enables
   employers to benefit from the conflicts of
   interest among the various parts of the labour
   force (a phenomenon stressed by the American
   "radicals"), and also to use the grey areas
   and loopholes in the institutional framework
   designed to protect the labour force. Certain
   jobs would have job guarantees, others would
   be precarious.

If these two broad trends are considered from the micro-
economic point of view, the possibilities for the overall

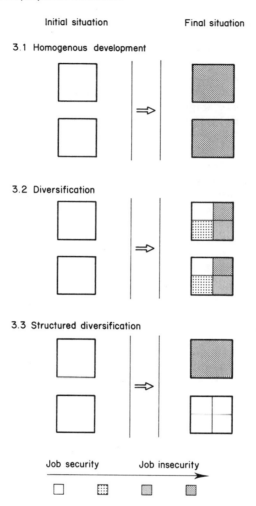

Fig. 3   Control of the labour force and the development
of the wage relationship

social relationship are numerous. Are there similar
possibilities for change based on either the transformation
or the diversification of wage relationships in all
countries? What are the consequences for the overall social
relationship? Does it evolve homogeneously, thus maintaining
the cohesion of the social relationship (Fig. 3.1)? Does the
previous social relationship disintegrate completely,
increasing dispersion without causing real discontinuities,
and largely destructuring the labour market (Fig. 3.2)? Or is

there an ordered diversification along a few broad lines,
which will alone lead to real structuring of the labour
market (Fig 3.3)?

Under these conditions, from the point of view of a
structuring effect on the labour market and on the basis of
a previous single wage relationship, two questions present
themselves that link the processes by which the wage relationship is determined and by which the productive system
is structured. Firstly, is the problem of increasing control
equally serious for all employers? If not, what situations
best lend themselves to the maintenance of protective wage
relationships, and what situations force wage relationships
to be modified? Secondly, do attempts to increase control
meet with the same resistance everywhere? Is this resistance
sufficiently strong to force it to be circumvented by means
of diversification?

The pre-existing institutional situation is also of
considerable importance. The exact nature of this situation,
for example, legislation of general application or
contractual agreements of limited scope, may favour a
particular type of structuring or non-structuring evolution.

In particular, all legislation designed to avoid abuses
and limit the powers of employers - however perfect it may be
- necessarily leaves loopholes. Unless there is a total
upheaval linked to a sudden break-up of the socio-political
balances, it is difficult to see how a change in the "rapport
salarial" would take the form of a total disintegration, or
could develop in a consistent and orderly way. Simply because
of the prior existence of a legal and contractual mechanism,
the most likely evolution seems, at least initially, to be
one of diversification in accordance with the possibilities
afforded by this mechanism.

V. CONCLUSIONS: THE FUNDAMENTAL STRUCTURING PROCESS

Since all the diagrams can be combined with each other, the
number of possible combinations is very large. The most
interesting of them is represented in a simplified way by
Fig. 4.1. It appears to correspond quite well to the
structuring model developed by Piore. It will be noted that
it does not merely presuppose the simple combination of, on
the one hand, a division of the market into stable and
unstable parts between individual capital and according to
the power relationships, and, on the other, processes of
specialization that are separate from this division of the
market. In addition, it assumes two things. First, a
particular combination of these two types of phenomena: the

dominant group will retain those parts of the productive
process that are least sensitive to fluctuations, and
externalize the more sensitive specialisms. This corresponds
very closely to the phenomena of activity sub-contracting.
Secondly, the internal wage relationships of each productive
organization will be uniform, i.e. strategies will be unified
but will vary from one organization to another, leading to a
diversified social relationship at the macro-economic level.

4.1 Segmentation model "according to Piore"

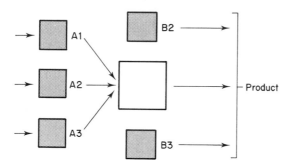

| | Unstable and non-specialized jobs (secondary labour market) | | Secure and specialized jobs (primary labour market) |

4.2 Complete externalization of productive services

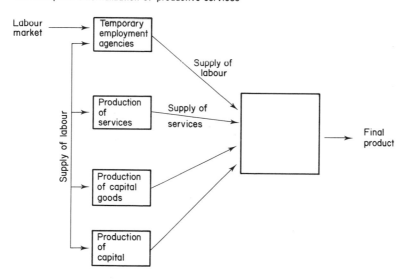

Fig. 4   Two examples of synthesis. A1, A2 and A3; suppliers
        of goods and services; B1; main firm; B2 and B32;
                    subordinate firms.

Very little separates this diagram from the following
one (Fig. 4.2). The latter excludes the processes of
capitalist competition and the inequalities of power that it
causes, but, on the other hand, it stretches to the limit
certain processes already represented in Fig. 1. The
processes of specialization, externalization and recomposition affect all labour that is indirect or secondary
to manufacturing, including all the supply and management of
the productive infrastructures (cf. procedures such as
leasing), and all supply and management of labour. The
diagram even assumes that the phenomenon affects all groups,
including suppliers of services, but this appears only in as
far as it affects the labour force.

The purpose of the diagram is thus to show the outcomes
of the process by which specialisms are externalized: the
firm or productive organization responsible for the final
product tends to become merely an area in which the factors
combine. Its function as a firm is completely broken down
into components specializing in each of the aspects of that
function.

In general, such a situation is characterized by the
formation of a very dense and very complex system of
relationships. But when the aim is only to extend to the
limit the processes of uncertainty and specialization, the
results appear to be characterized by a virtual absence of
structuring, that is, simple and extreme discontinuities.
Here again, the discontinuities appear everywhere and are not
very pronounced. The situation is what Piore would describe
as a continuum.

Such a situation appears utopian and improbable. Thus
the real interest of such a diagram lies less in its content
than in the reasons for it being improbable. It is necessary
to consider the phenomena that it ignores and that may
prevent processes that undeniably exist from being extended
to the limit.

It will be noted that the diagram implicitly assumes
that it is perfectly possible to control the workforce, and
that this control will be identical in all situations, i.e.
that there will be an almost total absence of protections and
guarantees. This is, however, assumed only for the sake of
the illustration: the various forms of resistance adopted by
the labour force stand in the way of perfect control.

But above all, the processes of competition between
individual capitalists introduce a fundamental limitation
that seems to make such a diagram totally impossible, unless
it is assumed that the same capital controls all the productive organizations [25]. This, of course, would represent a
totally balanced whole, with complete co-operation between

the organizations, since each of them would be totally
dependent on all the others. The existence of the processes
of competition appear to encourage each individual capitalist
to avoid such a situation at any price.

In other words, two types of phenomena are able to
explain the whole set of structural discontinuities, both
those in the productive system and those in the labour market
(except for the problems of qualifications): these are the
processes of competition and the processes by which the
"rapport salarial" is determined.

This is, of course, a statement of the obvious. Having
said this however, it is the total effect of these two
processes, the particular way in which they are linked today,
that is the basis for what is termed segmentation - in the
widest sense of the word - of the labour market. Two thoughts
spring to mind immediately, both of which might lead us to
assume that the obvious is not always evident, or at least
that the way in which the two processes are linked today -
and how it might be transformed in the crisis - has not yet
been fully analysed.

It appears quite easy to differentiate studies of labour
market segmentation according to whether they give greater
importance to the procedures of social control of the labour
force (the American "radicals", Edwards, 1979), or to the
oligopolistic structures of social capital (Piore, whose view
is descended from that of Galbraith). The link between these
two arguments is not always easy to make as both types of
study assume, since it is precisely the problem of the link
that largely distinguishes them from each other.

Furthermore, the means by which the growth in
productivity necessary to get us out of recession can be
obtained are considered principally in terms of work
organization within the firm, taking into account the new
technologies, the "time-saving" that they allow, and the
increased control of the labour force made possible by the
new organizations. Moreover, the problems of the competitiveness of competing capital, of industrial re-structuring
and of the role played by labour force problems are also
considered. But the fundamental issue of the way in which
technologies and organization within the firm, the structures
of the productive system and the division of labour within
society, and labour force problems are linked with each other
and interact to determine competitiveness is much less clear.

NOTES

1.   For a detailed analysis of the conclusions of this
     enquiry, a longer account of the broad outlines of the
     French system of job security and a proof of the above
     contradiction, see Michon, 1981. There is an account of
     the empirical research itself in Germe and Michon, 1979-
     80. By "non-standard job forms" we understand any job
     that differs in various ways from the norm. In France,
     this norm presupposes a contract of indeterminate
     duration; this contract is, in fact, established by
     common labour law. This norm excludes any form of
     loaning out of manpower among firms. This is basically
     why the term NSJF is used to describe all temporary
     jobs, all fixed-term contracts and all forms of labour
     sub-contracting. An "interim" contract is used solely
     for the hiring in return for payment of exclusively
     temporary staff. Temporary job agencies are excluded
     from all activities apart from the hiring of staff, i.e.
     from both production activities (the loaning out of
     manpower is not allowed) and from the placing of
     manpower (in which the State has a monopoly). The staff
     hired are employees of the temporary job agency, but
     only for the duration of the assignment with the user
     enterprise. The user enterprise is required to justify
     the temporary hiring of manpower.
2.   In France, segmentation theory is synonymous with
     Piore.
3.   As is well known, Piore uses in turn a minimal
     dualistic version of segmentation and the so-called
     extensive, or compound version (cf. p. 17 et seq.).
     Moreover, there are many models of the segmentation of
     the labour market with three or four segments (cf., for
     example, Bluestone, 1970, Edwards, 1979, Loveridge and
     Mok, 1979).
4.   That is, at the level of empirical tests, in terms of
     mobility chains, of hierarchies or career structures, of
     job precariousness, of different risks of unemployment,
     etc... cf. Michon, 1982.
5.   For Ryan, the distribution of "job opportunities" or
     "rewards".
6.   This was certainly the case in the nineteenth century,
     cf. Germe, 1978.
7.   In contrast to the preceding characteristic of
     temporary employment, there is here a threat hanging
     permanently over the workforce because of the absence of
     institutional job security and not because of actual
     dismissal.

8.   On this notion of "individual" or "private capital",
     cf. Bechtle (1978).
9.   Under free wage competition, all other things being
     equal (that is, primarily, mainly for equal qualifi-
     cations) those who accept the lowest wages are hired and
     the highest paid sacked. The restrictions on this type
     of competition are the contractual determination
     (legally binding or otherwise) of pay, employment
     guarantees and queues for hiring or firing (the
     seniority principle, for example), etc. It is obvious
     that free wage competition is the most unfavourable
     situation for workers and the most favourable for
     employers.
10. Thus Piore (in Berger and Piore, 1980) can put forward
     a "minimal" dualist version of segmentation, based on
     uncertainty alone, and remaining open to orthodox
     interpretation in terms of human capital or even of
     discrimination. For Piore, however, the "minimal
     descriptive" version must be completed by an "extensive"
     version that is more "comprehensive" in terms of the
     capitalist division of labour: for Piore, in terms of
     the content of qualifications, and the extent to which
     they are transferable or versatile, and of the appren-
     ticeship patterns leading to these qualifications; for
     the American radicals, in terms of strategies and
     practices for controlling the workforce by the division
     of interests (cf. Reich, Edwards and Gordon, 1973 or
     Edwards, 1979).
11. The diagrams represent the phenomenon of recomposition
     in a way that is restricted to the question of this
     indirect or peripheral labour. But it is true that there
     is a close relationship with the question of non-
     standard job forms (see below).
12. A continuum, in the same sense with which Piore
     contrasts this notion with that of discontinuity and
     segmentation (cf. above).
13. Cf. in France, the Fos sur Mer complex and the "Solmer
     system" that characterizes it (Broda, Demailly and
     Labruyere, 1978). Fig. 2.9 is only a transcription of
     the diagram proposed by Labruyere (1981) to represent
     the notion of "industrial complex", with two main firms.
14. They are particuarly familiar in Marxist thought. Cf.
     the theme of the division of labour "in general", i.e.
     in society, as the basis of exchange and market
     production ("Capital", Book 1, section 4, chapter XIV);
     the theme of the competition between individual capital,
     the phenomena of concentration as a result of the
     increase of the size of individual capital and centra-

lization as a result of the reduction of the number of individual capitalists ("Capital", Book 1, section 7, chapter XXV).

15. On the strategies of French industrial groups before nationalization, see Freyssinnet, 1982. On the effects of the recession on these strategies, see Soulage, 1981.

16. A period characteristic of the phase of the homo- genization of work according to the American "radical" school (cf. Gordon, Edwards and Reich, 1982), and of the phase of the setting up of a monopolistic "rapport salarial" according to the French "regulation" school (Boyer, 1979).

17. Cf. on Taylorism and time saving, Coriat, 1979. And the parallel growth of a tertiary sector providing services to firms. The phenomenon began before the crisis of the 1970s. In the period of prosperity, the dynamism of this form of tertiarization of employment (cf. Baudelot, Establet, Malemort, 1974) helped to explain the stag- nation in industrial employment and inspired the argument that a fourth sector was emerging.

18. The Italian Emilian model is of course the classic example. In France towards the end of the 1960s, the policy of decentralization and industrialization of traditionally rural regions was markedly, but to a large extent unexpectedly, successful. Today, what little dynamism there is in employment comes from small and medium-sized firms (Didier, 1982).

19. In the hope that the new technologies (computers and robotics) will bring about increases in productivity sufficient to lead the economy out of recession, stress is often put on the implications of these technologies in terms of the organization of work within the firm (Coriat, 1981). But their implications for the organization of work "within society" (productive decentralization) and for increases in efficiency may well be almost as decisive.

20. In the geographical area, the area of activities and products, the legal area, etc.

21. However, Germe (1978b) saw the "interim" contract as "a sort of ideal culmination - for employers - of waged work".

22. Piore would probably contest this, since for him an increased division of labour means specialization and a low level of transferability for qualifications, leading to job stability. (cf. Berger and Piore, 1980).

23. Cf. France, where the maintenance of a strong agricultural sector for a long time provided a fall- back for industrial workers (Germe, 1978a).

24. Edwards, 1979, and De Gaudemar, 1982, have both described the historical forms of control and stressed the relationship with work organization. Taylorist and Fordian organization is symbolized by the assembly line and time and motion studies. On the assembly line, the machine imposes its own law, its own rhythms, and controls the workforce. But control by machines has its limits: unbearable rates of work, absenteeism, turnover, falls in the quality of production. The control thus exercised is so overwhelming that it has been possible to speak of the worker being "modelled" by the machine (Blassel, Germe and Michon, 1979). On the other hand, however, the objective is unattainable, since a man is not a machine (Blassel, Laville and Teiger, 1976). Thus, the current question of control is as much one of a search for more efficient methods of organization as of a reduction of industrial constraints.

25. This shows the limits of a simplification that identifies individual capital with the productive unit. Of course, the processes of competition do not restrict the setting up of a structure like that in Fig. 1.1, with all the units dependent on the same individual capital.

REFERENCES

Azouvi, A. (1981). Théorie et Pseudo-Théorie, le dualisme du marché du travail. Critiques de l'Economie Politique, nouvelle série, 15-16, avril-juin, 3-52.

Baudelot, C., Establet, R. and Malemort, J. (1974). "La Petite Bourgeoisie en France". Maspero, Paris.

Bechtle, G. (1978). Entreprise, procès de production, utilisation de la force de travail: esquisse d'une demarche théorique. Sociologie du Travail, 1.

Berger, S. and Piore, M.J. (1980). "Dualism and Discontinuities in industrial societies". Cambridge University Press, Cambridge.

Blassel, H., Germe, J.F. and Michon, F. (1979). Une nouvelle approche pour l'analyse des conditions de travail. In Economie et Planification (Emploi et System Productif), Commissariat Géneral au Plan, Paris.

Blassel, H., Laville, A. and Teiger, C. (1976). Conditions de travail et analyses économiques. Critiques de l'Economie Politique, 23, janvier-mars, 11-33.

Bluestone, B. (1970). The tripartite economy: labor markets and the working poor. Poverty and Human Resources, v, juillet-août, 15-35.

Boyer, R. (1979). La crise actuelle: une mise au point en
    perspective historique. Critiques de l'Economie
    Politique, nouvelle série, 7-8, avril-septembre.
Boyer, R. (1981) Les transformations du rapport salarial
    dans la crise. Critiques de l'Economie Politique,
    nouvelle série, 15-16, avril-juin.
Broda, J., Demailly, S. and Labruyère, C. (1978). Crise de
    la sidérurgie et recomposition du procès de travail: la
    soustraitance à la Solmer. Sociologie du Travail, 4,
    423-447.
Coriat, B. (1979). "L'Atelier et le Chronomètre: Essai sur
    le Taylorisme, le Fordisme et la Production de Masse".
    Bourgois, Paris.
Coriat, B. (1981). L'atelier fordien automatise.
    Microélectronique et travail ouvrier dans les
    industries de chaîne. Non! Repères pour le socialisme,
    10, novembre-décembre, 90-101.
Didier, M. (1982). Crise et concentration du système
    productif. Economie et Statistique, 144, mai, 3-12.
Edwards, R. (1979). "Contested Terrain". Basic Books, New
    York.
Freyssenet, M. (1974). "Les Processus de Déqualification -
    Surqualification de la Force de Travail". Paris, C.S.U.
Freyssinet, J. (1982). "Politique d'Emploi de Grands Groupes
    Français". P.U.G., Grenoble.
de Gaudemar, J.P. (1982). "L'Ordre et la Production:
    Naissance et Formes de la Discipline d'Usine". Dunod,
    Paris.
Germe, J.F. (1978a). "Emploi et Marché du Travail au 19ème
    Siècle, l'Exemple Français". Université de Paris I
    (thèse de 3e cycle Travail et Ressources Humaines).
Germe, J.F. (1978b). Les nouvelles formes d'emploi: le
    travail intérimaire. Critiques de l'Economie Politique,
    nouvelle série, 5.
Germe, J.F., Michon, F. (1979-80). "Stratégies des
    Entreprises et Formes Particulières d'Emploi". Seminaire
    d'Economie du Travail, CNRS -Université de Paris I,
    Paris, 2 volumes roneo.
Gordon, D.M., Edwards, R., Reich, M. (1982). "Segmented
    Work, Divided Workers". Cambridge University Press,
    Cambridge.
Labruyere, C. (1981). "Le site, lieu d'émergence de nouveaux
    rapports sociaux". Aix-Marseille, Centre d'Etudes sur
    les Relations Sociales.
Loveridge, R., Mok, A.L. (1979). "Theories of Labour Market
    Segmentation: A Critique". Mertinus Nijhoff, La Hague.
Michon, F. (1981). Dualism and the French labour market:
    Business strategy, non-standard job forms and secondary

jobs. In "The Dynamics of Labour Market Segmentation"
(F. Wilkinson, ed.). Academic Press, London and Orlando.

Michon, F. (1982)."La Segmentation du Marché du Travail
Français, Faits et Analyses Economiques 1968-1981".
Seminaire d'Economie du Travail, Paris.

Piore, M.J. (1978). Dualism in the labor market. A response
to uncertainty and flux, the case of France. Revue
Economique, 19 (1), janvier, 26-48.

Reich, M., Edwards, R.C., Gordon, D.M. (1973). Dual labor
markets. A theory of labor market segmentation.
American Economic Review, 63 (2), 359-365.

Ryan, P. (1981). Segmentation, duality and economic
orthodoxy. In "The Dynamics of Labour Market
Segmentation" (F. Wilkinson, ed.). Academic Press,
London and Orlando.

Salais, R. (1977). Une analyse des mécanismes de
détermination du chômage. Economie et Statistique, 93,
21-37.

Say, J.B. (1972). "Traité d'Economie Politique". Calman-
Levy, Paris.

Soulage, B. (1981). L'évolution des politiques sociales des
groupes industriels français avec la crise. Revue
d'Economie Industrielle, 16, 2e trimestre.

Wilkinson, F. (ed.) (1981). "The Dynamics of Labour Market
Segmentation". Academic Press, London and Orlando.

Part II

Labour Market Processes

Flexibility of Labour Costs in Non-Union Firms*

J. RUBERY*

I. FLEXIBILITY OF LABOUR COSTS IN NON-UNION FIRMS

Widespread pressure now exists in most advanced countries to reverse the prevailing trend in the post-war period towards institutional regulation and organization of the labour markets. In Britain in the 1960s the solution to labour problems was believed to be the progressive extension of formal collective bargaining procedures to bring the more informal activities of shop stewards under the direct control of management and unions (Donovan, 1968). In the 1980s the thrust of government policy is towards reducing institutional regulation of labour markets in a whole range

*This paper has been developed out of work conducted jointly with my colleagues in the Department of Applied Economics Labour Study Group. I am indebted to them, and also to the Department of Employment, for sponsoring the original surveys which provided the evidence on which this paper is typed. However, the evidence is here used to address somewhat different sets of questions from those which the projects were primarily designed to answer and the views expressed here are the responsibility of the author alone.

of areas [1] to achieve greater flexibility in the labour
market.

   The intention is to restore to firms the ability to
adjust their labour costs to meet changes in the level of
demand, in technology, in price competitiveness or in labour
market conditions. Institutional regulation of labour
markets has, it is argued, saddled firms with too high fixed
employment costs, rigidities in the organization of
production, and inhibited their ability to vary the
intensity of labour effort and the price of labour to meet
changing conditions in product and labour markets. The
expectations of "supply-side economics" which lie behind
policies to roll-back the union and state controls on
employment are that labour market conditions would be
restored similar to those in neo-classical textbook models
where labour is a variable factor of production, where wages
reflect relative productivities of workers, and firms tend
to adopt best practice techniques of production, unimpeded
by the trade unions.

   Opponents of such measures have tended to concentrate
on the socially damaging effects of deregulating labour
markets resulting from employment instability and the social
divisiveness of passing the burden of economic adjustment
back on to labour. However, it is also essential to develop
an analysis of the kind of labour market organization that
would result from a greater degree of flexibility in their
operation. Would the labour markets conform to a neo-
classical model, or is an alternative framework for analysis
needed?

   This paper argues the case for such an alternative
framework. The next section compares the employment systems
in union and non-union firms. This comparison shows wide
differences in the labour market activities and labour
organization between these types of firms. However, the kind
of employment systems operated in the non-union firms do not
conform to simple neo-classical textbook models. The second
major section of the paper then contrasts the neo-classical
model with the kind of labour market system that exists
currently in sectors outside the direct influence of union
controls, and which might be expected to increase as a
result of the Government's flexibilization policies.

II. LABOUR ORGANIZATION IN UNIONIZED AND NON-UNIONIZED FIRMS

A. Evidence

In this section we compare systems of labour organization

and regulation between firms, using two main dimensions;
size of firm and unionization. Most research has
concentrated on the large unionized firms, but a series of
projects carried out by the Department of Applied Economics
Labour Studies Group has led to an accumulation of evidence
on less well-documented sectors, including small firms and
non-union firms of all sizes. We use, therefore, the
evidence from these surveys, combined with our own and other
research into large unionized sectors, to draw out the main
lines of differentiation between broad categories of firms
[2].

It is essential to consider separately the influence of
size of firm and unionization on the development of
institutionally regulated labour markets. Both factors are
associated with differences in labour organization but
neither factor is independent of industry characteristics:
for example, within an industry the existence and the impact
of unionization will be largely determined by the historical
development of unionization. This is particularly the case
amongst small firms, and only in industries with a long-
established system of unionization - based on organization
at the level of the labour market or the industry - has a
significant degree of union organization in small firms been
achieved. Therefore comparisons of small unionized and non-
unionized firms generally involve contrasting industries
with union organization in small firms (from our sample,
footwear, printing and some stamped or pressed metal-wares
firms) and the rest with only very isolated pockets of
unionization.

B. Labour Organization

Tables I and II outline the main variations in labour
organization between large unionized, large non-unionized,
small non-unionized and small unionized firms. In all
respects the system of labour organization in large
unionized firms conforms most closely to the model of a
bureaucratized and institutionally regulated employment
system, which typifies primary employment sectors in the
labour market segmentation literature (Doerigner and Piore,
1971; Edwards, 1979). Payment systems are usually
formalized, i.e. written down and based on specified grades
of labour, described by jobs or by the characteristics of
the workers, or by both. These payment systems normally
result in an extensive hierarchy of pay differentials within
the firm. Moreover, although there is not necessarily one
integrated payment system for all categories of workers [4],

Table I. Types of payment systems

	Payment System	Pay Differentials
Large firms (unionized)	Formalized system: grading structure based on rate for the job with or without merit seniority pay.	Normally a continuous and extensive pay hierarchy. Minimum rates set at or above industry levels with few workers paid at the minimum.
Large firms (non-unionized)	Generally formalized systems: grading structure based on rate for the job with or without merit/seniority pay. Less formal procedures for determining the latter.	Relatively wide differentials between high and low grades: pay structure may be a continuous hierarchy or be discontinuous between grades. Minimum rates often at or close to industry level, with with many workers paid at the minimum.
Small firms (unionized)	Generally based on industry agreement: degree of internal formality/informality depends on the industry agreement.	Normally a relatively continuous hierarchy of pay but less extensive than in large firms. Minimum rate at or above industry minimum.
Small firms (non-unionized)	Informal payment system: ad hoc individual payments or single rate for broad categories of workers.	Discontinuous pay structure. Narrow differentials between production workers except between men and women or formally qualified workers. Minimum rate often below industry minimum.

Table II. Employment guarantees and training systems

	Large firms (unionized)	Large firms (non-unionized)	Small firms (unionized)	Small firms (non-unionized)
Conditions of employment for manual employees:				
1. Sick pay and pensions	Relatively common: non-discretionary.	As common as in unionized firms: but more likely to be restricted to segments of the workforce.	Pensions uncommon. Sick pay mainly for key employees.	Pensions uncommon. Sick pay mainly for key employees.
2. Holidays	Entitlement either the same as industry agreement or improved upon by local agreement.	Entitlement as industry agreement, or low minimum entitlement increasing with grade or service.	Entitlement usually as industry agreement.	Usually low entitlement for all grades, often below industry agreement.
3. Employment guarantees:				
(a) guaranteed weeks/lay-off/redundancy	Guarantees established through collective bargaining agreement at industry or local level.	Normally no guarantees except for statutory measures: some may follow guarantees in industry agreements.	Normally only industry agreement guarantees in addition to statutory measures.	Normally no guarantees except for statutory measures.
(b) Manning agreements/changes in work organization	Manning ratios/procedure for negotiating changes in technology etc. may be specified in formal agreements or be subject to informal bargaining.	Work organization determined by managerial prerogative.	Formal provisions only usually in industry agreements; but changes may be subject to informal bargaining.	Work organization determined by managerial prerogative.
4. Training systems	Formal training systems, linked to state training systems.	Normally formal training systems, linked to state training systems.	Either recruit externally trained workers or formal training linked to state training systems.	Either recruit externally trained or informal and firm-specific training.

the grades of pay for the different groups usually intersect
and overlap, with management and unions both conscious that
too wide an earnings gap cannot be allowed to develop
between the bargaining groups. When compared with other
firms, large unionized firms tend to have higher pay than
firms in the industries of which they are a part, but inter-
industry variations in pay mean considerable overlap between
the earnings of different types of firms when comparisons
are made on an all industry basis.

      The payment systems of small unionized firms stand at
the opposite end of the spectrum from large unionized firms.
In such firms payment systems are usually informal. In many
cases pay is determined on an individualistic basis, whilst
in others a simple pay rate covers the majority of non-
qualified production workers. There may be some additional
payments based on skill or experience, but these are often
discretionary and their value low. Sizeable pay differentials do exist within small non-unionized firms, but they
are not generally based on a detailed evaluation and grading
of jobs. The major pay divisions are between different types
of employees, for example men and women, or craft and non-
qualified workers. Narrow pay differentials within, and
large differences between, the different categories of
employees have the consequence that the structure of pay is
usually a discontinuous hierarchy with little overlap
between the widely spaced pay bands. Minimum pay levels in
small non-unionized firms tend to be low in all types of
industries but pay levels for some categories of workers can
be comparable to pay levels in large firm sectors.

      The pay systems in the remaining two categories of
firms usually falls somewhere between these two extremes.
Large non-unionized firms normally have some form of formal
payment system including a job grading structure.
Differential payments for merit or seniority are
discretionary in some cases, in others they are included in
the formal payment system, but in both management retains a
higher degree of prerogative than in unionized firms. Pay
hierarchies will again tend to be extensive but managerial
discretion in fixing pay rates, grading workers and making
additional payments produces wide differentials and
discontinuities in payment structures. This is facilitated
by the payment of lower minimum rates than in unionized
firms, or where non-unionized firms follow the industry
national agreement, by the grading of a wider range of
skills and occupations at the lowest wage rates.

      Small unionized firms' payment structures usually
resemble most closely those of the large unionized firms,
with higher minimum rates and continuous pay hierarchies.

Grading structures may be more informal because of the smaller size of the workforce. However, in practice, unionization in small firms is most common in industries with a strong national bargaining framework, which itself serves to establish similarities in payment systems between small and large firms in the industry.

A second important element in the development of institutional regulation of labour markets has been the growth of non-wage employment benefits and wage and other guarantees. These have the effect of separating labour costs from output and increasing the degree of their fixity. Pension schemes are generally found to be most associated with size of firms rather than unionization. The provision of sick pay is related to custom and practice in particular industries although there is some tendency for such payments to be found more frequently in large and unionized firms. Moreover, it is in unionized firms where there is often little or no managerial discretion in the application of such schemes. In holiday entitlement and holiday pay there is a much clearer difference between categories of firms. Large unionized firms provide higher levels of entitlement, above national agreement specified levels in many cases; large non-unionized firms tend to give lower minimum entitlement and provide increased entitlement with merit, grade or service; small unionized firms tend to follow the national agreement entitlement levels, and small non-unionized firms often provide less than the minimum national agreement entitlement.

Guarantees and benefits which protect employees against changes in labour demand are sometimes included in national agreements and even in government regulations, for example, minimum guaranteed week payments. Whether or not non-union firms, large or small, follow national agreement provisions will depend mainly on management attitudes, and will not normally be enforced by employers' associations. Improvements on these national agreement provisions, or substitutes for them where they do not exist, are found mainly in larger union firms with extensive local bargaining power. In some cases procedures for lay-off or redundancy and manning agreements are formally laid down; in other cases they are established by informal shop floor bargaining, usually the only form of control in small unionized firms. However, non-union firms are likely to retain managerial discretion in all aspects of decisions over employment levels and labour allocation, except for those which are legally enforceable.

The system of training is the final area where there is considerable difference in the degree of institutionali-

zation of procedures between these types of firms. All types
of large firms are more likely to have formal training
procedures, linked to the systems of recommended training
established by the Industry Training Boards [5], if only
because large firms are more subject to financial penalties
for failing to provide recommended training, and because
they have more scope for providing training than the small
firms where the disruption to production organization can be
considerable. Large non-union firms tend to have more
flexibility in the use of untrained workers on traditionally
skilled work, even if they normally observe the institutionalized systems of training for skilled occupations.
Small firms are mainly reliant on the external labour market
for recruiting ready-trained skilled workers, but non-union
small firms have a greater tendency to substitute informally
trained workers, who are primarily conversant with the
specific skills required by the firm, for generally trained
craft-type workers, who can only be recruited at high cost
on the external labour market.

C. Sources of Rigidity in Institutional Forms of Labour Organization

Table III summarizes the impact of the forms of labour
organization on the ability of firms to adjust labour costs
to meet changes in the structure or level of production or
to take advantage of opportunities to minimize labour costs.
Formal payment systems based on job grades, or on
workers' characteristics (skill, seniority, etc.) or both,
necessarily limit the firm's ability to vary labour costs.
When the system is primarily job-based, the wage bill for
the production process is given to the firm, and the firm
cannot use cheap labour on high grade jobs. When the payment
system is primarily based on worker characteristics, the
wage bill for the current labour force is given to the firm;
skilled workers, if employed on unskilled work, must be paid
at the skilled rate. Under informal payment schemes there is
usually more scope for redefining the job tasks of workers
without any compensating change in pay. The more experienced
and skilled workers on production work do not necessarily
receive any premia, either for differences in jobs that they
undertake or for differences in their skill; in practice
workers paid at unskilled rates may be used on relatively
skilled work.
However, firms using informal payment systems still
often have to recruit skilled workers with external
bargaining power; and pay the going rate for skilled

Table III. Sources of rigidity

	Formal systems	Informal systems
Payment systems and pay hierarchies		
Rate for the job:	Low paid labour cannot be used on high grade jobs.	More scope for redefining jobs, using workers temporarily on higher grade jobs without pay rises.
Rate for the worker:	Skilled workers must be paid skilled rates when on unskilled work.	
Merit/seniority pay:	When automatic or customary, wage bill increases when labour turnover is low.	Not usually automatic or customary; new payments can be witheld.
Continuous pay hierarchy:	Differentials cannot be easily adjusted to changes in the going rate for different grades of labour.	Pay differentials between "grades" relatively easily adjusted; but only within a "grade" if using individualized payment system.
	High provision	**Low provision**
Employment conditions		
Sick pay/pensions/holidays	High fixed employment costs independent of productivity. High adjustment costs due to workers' absence.	Low fixed employment costs.
Employment guarantees	Either maintain employment in face of demand/technology changes or pay adjustment costs.	Restrictions on employment adjustment only from techno-logical/product market and labour supply considerations.

Table III (cont.)

Training system	Informal system	Formal/state system
Bargaining power	Internal firm-specific training confers no external bargaining power on workers.	Use of general industry or state system confers bargaining power on workers.
Training time	Flexibility in training time; shortages made good more quickly.	Little flexibility in training time.
Labour hoarding	Low grade workers may be informally trained to replace skilled, high grade workers; less need to hoard high paid workers.	Training and payment systems are normally integrated. Only high grade workers can do all jobs, so these have to be hoarded.

Collective bargaining systems	Local regulation	Industry regulation	Independent
Adjustment to changes in product market/technology	Restricted by existing detailed framework/ procedures. Committed to annual wage bargaining. Committed to procedures for negotiating changes in work organization/ technology: may involve maintaining manning levels and/or increasing pay levels.	Committed to annual pay rises negotiated externally. Only restricted if industry agreement includes provisions on manning/ new technology. Less detailed than local agreements.	Committed to existing pay levels and usually to pay rises by workers' expectations. Few restrictions on changes in technology/ work organization/ manning levels.

workers. The share of skilled workers in the labour force is
likely to increase in the recession, either because these
are the more flexible workers on which to base a smaller
production system, or because the less skilled workers can
be more readily re-hired. Firms with a wider differential
between skilled and unskilled workers - usually those with
informal payment systems - will suffer more than a
proportional rise in labour costs as a result. However,
firms with formal payment systems can also face increased
labour costs in a recession because the decrease in labour
turnover increases the level of merit and seniority
increments in firms where these are awarded automatically
for long service. Merit and seniority pay under informal
systems is usually discretionary and new payments can in
fact be withheld from all workers in a recession or even
existing payments withdrawn.

The continuous and integrated hierarchies of pay found
in formal payment systems necessarily limit firms' ability
to respond to changes in labour market conditions for a
particular grade of worker without having to make similar
adjustments for all grades. Restructuring of the graded
payment system is not a task to be undertaken frequently as
it requires renegotiation in unionized firms, and even in
non-unionized firms arbitrary changes in differentials are
liable to worsen industrial relations. In firms without
formal payment structures changes in differentials between
categories of workers can be more easily affected. Firms
using ad hoc merit payment systems may also be able to take
advantage of the availability of labour at low wage levels
by paying new recruits low wages. This opportunity is not
readily available to firms with informal payment systems
which use a single wage rate for a wide range of workers,
because the existing workforce would not be happy to see
changes in this rate even for new recruits. Firms using
informal payment systems are also subject to resistance from
their labour force to cuts in money wage levels in the same
way as are those using formal systems, except that it may be
more possible to cut bonuses, overtime, merit pay and the
like in the more informal systems [5].

Non-wage benefits and employment and earnings
guarantees all tend to reduce firms' abilities to link wage
bills to current output and productivity levels. In the case
of employment and earnings guarantees firms must either
maintain employment and wage levels at a high level relative
to current production, or face high fixed adjustment costs
such as redundancy and lay-off pay. However, firms that do
not provide formal employment guarantees are not always in a
position to adjust labour costs to demand. Their employment

levels will be influenced also by the technology in use and the range of products produced, which determine the range of skills and the minimum number of workers necessary to operate the production process. However, the more flexible the workforce, i.e. the wider the range of skills that each worker can provide, or the greater the possibility for sub-contracting parts of the production process, the easier it is to reduce employment costs in line with output. As we have argued above, these conditions may be more usually associated with the use of informal payment systems.

The use of institutionalized training systems instead of informal systems designed primarily to meet firms' specific skill requirements imposes several types of limitations on the firms involved. First of all, the acquisition of general industrial skills, and a generally accepted certificate of skills, tends to increase workers' opportunities in the labour market, and therefore to increase their external bargaining power. Workers who acquire only very specific skills are not able to transfer their skills elsewhere, and therefore they only have improved bargaining power within the firm in which they are currently employed. Secondly, the use of institutionalized systems reduces flexibility in the training time necessary to make good a shortage of skilled labour. Thirdly, the use of formal training systems are much more likely to have a graded payment system incorporating grades and skill classifications which are linked to the training system. In these circumstances the training system helps to reinforce the rigidity in the pay structure and system of labour allocation; for example, only apprenticed labour is permitted to be trained on certain tasks, and therefore, non-apprenticed labour does not acquire the skills. Apprenticed labour therefore has to be retained to carry out these functions even if there is a major reduction in output, and moreover, they must be paid at the skilled rates even when allocated to other work. In firms with less formal training systems, informally trained workers can in some cases be used as substitutes for highly paid formally trained workers.

Many of the differences in forms of labour organization which we have discussed are related to the system of collective bargaining in operation in the firm. Collective bargaining also limits the scope for changes in the employment system in a more general sense. Local collective bargaining usually results in formal written procedures and agreements, or in similar procedures established through custom and practice. These limit the firm's room for manoeuvre, usually committing the firm to annual

negotiations over pay increases irrespective of labour
market conditions and to negotiating the introduction of new
technologies or new forms of work organization which involve
commitments either to at least maintaining the existing
labour force, with jobs lost only through natural wastage,
or to paying for adjustments to employment through higher
wage levels. Firms which have no local negotiations are much
less likely to be subject to constraints on their freedom to
introduce new working arrangements: few national agreements
include such restrictions and these would in any case be
likely to be ignored in non-union firms. The main way in
which non-union firms are limited in their employment
options is by workers' expectations which may include the
maintenance of existing pay levels, and the provision of an
annual pay rise. Non-union firms often follow national
agreements in determining wage increases, and in these cases
their freedom to decide the actual size of the increase is
again constrained. Some of these firms believe that
following a national agreement legitimizes their payment
system and protects them from unionization, but if the
likelihood of unionization diminishes, so does the incentive
to use this form of wage regulation [6].

D. The Origins of Different Forms of Labour Organization

The early labour market segmentation literature attributed
the growth of institutionalized labour markets in primary
employment sectors to changes in the labour market
requirements of large oligopolistic-type firms towards a
more permanent, stable labour force which would acquire
firm-specific skills. Secondary employment sectors could
operate with the casual labour forces associated with
competitive labour markets as low levels of skill were
required. Even the skilled workers employed were assumed to
be mainly craft workers with high levels of general skills
and low firm-specific skills so that they were mobile
between firms. In contrast, our analysis finds little
evidence to support the view that the origins of different
forms of labour organization, for example, between large and
small firms, and between unionized and non-union firms, are
to be found in their respective technological and production
requirements. Instead we found that most types of firms
required a core stable labour force to operate efficiently,
and that this labour force usually required both firm and
job-specific skills. The difference between firms lay more
in their ability to achieve similar technological and
production targets through different employment strategies.

Size of firm, the system of collective bargaining within the
firm and industry, and the opportunities for recruitment of
workers from relatively disadvantaged or advantaged groups
all had significant effects on these strategies.

It is not only that the achievement of, for example, a
skilled and stable labour force can be sought through
different strategies, but that the application of similar
strategies in different types of firms can have variable
consequences. For example, firm-specific training in a large
firm with established union organization is likely to
increase the bargaining power of the employed labour force,
a power which can be used collectively to improve their
employment position. Firm-specific training in non-unionized
firms is less likely to improve bargaining power. The
individual has not improved his or her external labour
market opportunities. The firm may recognize the strategic
value of the worker to the firm and decide to compensate the
worker according to their current worth, but if their
external opportunities are poor there is no compulsion on
the firm to do this. Clearly an individual may be able to
exercise his or her strategic power within the production
process, but in a non-union firm this is not an automatic
process; nor would it necessarily be effective. Secondary-
type firms can employ workers with weak bargaining power,
train them in job-specific skills, and because of their weak
bargaining power, still retain them at low wage levels.
Moreover, this kind of strategy could be used for jobs
normally carried out by formally qualified workers, such as
craftsmen, provided the firm has the resources to train the
workers, whereas large firms are under pressure from the
state to provide formal training, as are unionized firms
from the trade unions. The emphasis on primary firms using
job-specific training and secondary firms using craft-
trained workers may therefore be misplaced, except in so far
as small firms cannot spare the resources for training.

These strategies require the existence of a supply of
relatively stable secondary-type labour. Our survey work
suggests that such a supply is readily available, and that,
again, the emphasis in the segmentation literature on an
unstable secondary labour force is misplaced. In fact it is
now widely recognized that these early studies failed to
differentiate between stability of jobs and stability of
workers. A good example of the need for such a distinction
is found in the practice of labour hoarding. Employment of
relatively skilled secondary-type workers (for example,
married women or immigrants) in secondary-type firms is
likely to be relatively unstable as firms believe they are
able to lay-off these workers and to re-employ sufficient

numbers of ex-employees when demand rises again. This is
true, for example, for homeworkers who are often expected to
be amongst the most casual of workers. Most firms fail to
provide their homeworkers with work for long periods of
time, but find that most are still available for work when
needed (Rubery and Wilkinson, 1981). Moreover, many firms
only use ex-employees as homeworkers, as these are the only
people with the necessary skills. The practice of hoarding
workers may therefore be more related to their external job
opportunities than to the level of their firm-specific
skills. Unstable employment may therefore be wrongly
associated with casual employment relationships.

Although secondary-type firms are able to take
advantage of the existence of weaker labour market groups,
their reliance on the skills of their workforce limits their
ability to pursue employment strategies where labour costs
are automatically adjusted to changes in demand. Secondary-
type firms also have to take into account the need to
motivate and control their labour force and are not able to
assume, as in neo-classical theory, that the wage-effort
relationship is determined for the firm by the impersonal
relations of the exchange labour market. Firm-specific
skills are embodied in individuals and in the work-group as
a whole, and the firm has to take account of motivation and
control in organizing its payment systems and methods of
work organization as well as in the permanence of its
employment contracts.

Our description of the forms and origins of labour
organization in secondary-type sectors differs in certain
important respects from those of the standard labour market
segmentation literature. The latter concentrates on supposed
differences in the nature and level of skills or in the
stability and work-commitment of the labour force whilst our
research points to the centrality of differences in
bargaining power. Differences between our analysis of
secondary sectors and that of neo-classical theory have
already been hinted at, but it is to a more direct
comparison of the reality of labour organization in
unregulated firms with that in neo-classical models that we
now turn.

II. LABOUR ORGANIZATION IN NON-UNION FIRMS AND COMPETITIVE LABOUR MARKET MODELS

Comparing the systems of labour organization that we have
observed in non-union firms with the practices of
competitive labour market theory raises major difficulties.

There are three main reasons why the simple text book neo-classical model cannot be used for comparative purposes. First, it is assumed that the labour market is in equilibrium and this may not be the case. Observed cross-sectional employment patterns which do not conform to conditions expected under equilibrium may still be compatible with disequilibrium in a neo-classical model. Second, modern neo-classical economics has progressively incorporated into its framework "imperfections" which are used to explain the differences between empirical observation and the predictions of the simple equilibrium model [7]. The impact of these developments is to reduce the predictive power of neo-classical labour market theory as adjustments of supply and demand to equilibrium conditions are much more long-term, and the nature and rate of adjustments depends on a whole set of costs and other factors associated with uncertainty and imperfect information. Third, neo-classical theory admits the likely existence of social and institutional influences on labour markets, other than those associated with trade unions, so that the results that indicate the predominance of non-competitive wage structures could be attributed to exogenous social influences rather than to the failure of neo-classical theory.

However, these problems become less severe when the purpose of this comparison is recalled. We are mainly concerned with establishing whether or not the impact of reducing institutional controls will be to establish a more competitive labour market, with lower fixed employment costs, with wage levels more directly related to workers' relative productivities, and with greater flexibility for firms to adjust to product market and labour market conditions. If, for example, we find that instead wage differentials in the absence of union controls reflect primarily the social advantage/disadvantage of the worker employed, or the product market position of the firm, this would imply that instead of firms facing more equal labour costs, adjusted for the relative efficiency of the workers employed, they will be faced with increased opportunities to exploit socially disadvantaged groups. In these circumstances, the labour market would be in neo-classical terms _less_ competitive, and institutional and social controls would need to be established in the labour market to create the conditions for competitive labour markets where a worker's potential productivity has more impact on earnings than his social background or position. Likewise if we find that there are reasons other than those associated with union controls, why firms enter into relatively

Table IV. Labour market models and DAE survey findings

	Neo-classical	Dual labour market (i)	DAE survey findings
(a) Pay structure	Differentiated pay, directly related to skills and productivities of workers.	Primary: wage hierarchies, not directly related to and in excess of differences in skills and productivities of workers. Secondary: homogeneous pay directly related to low skill and productivity of workers.	Primary: differentiated pay, not directly related to skills and productivities of workers. Secondary: homogeneous pay but differentiated productivities and skills of workers.
(b) Skills and employment stability	Firm-specific skills a special case; workers are still relatively mobile and pay determined by external as well as internal factors.	Primary: high firm-specific skills, employment stability, firm-specific pay structures. Secondary: low firm-specific skills, employment instability homogeneous pay structures.	Primary: relatively high firm-specific skills, relative employment stability and firm-specific pay structures. Secondary: relatively high firm-specific skills, relative employment stability, homogeneous pay.
(c) Systems of work organization	Technology and job structure determined by best practice technique; wage-effort relationship determined by market forces.	Primary: firm specific influences on job structures; control strategies structure pay and labour organization. Secondary: technology, job structure and wage-effort relationship ensured by market forces.	Primary: firm-specific influences on job structures; trade union and managerial control strategies structure pay and labour organization. Secondary: firm-specific influences on job structures; workers' disadvantage in labour market minimises need for control strategies.

(i) This characterization of the dual labour market model cannot necessarily be directly attributed to specific authors, but in our view summarizes the standard dualist model used in the literature.

permanent employment contracts and incur fixed employment
costs, then evidence that firms were moving towards more
casual forms of employment might not imply a move towards
more competitive and efficient forms of labour market
organization. Instead, firms under pressure from
recessionary conditions may be trading their long-term
interests for the sake of short-term gains, or simply for
survival; or they may be taking advantage of social
divisions in the labour force to acquire for themselves a
permanent labour force without providing permanent income
and employment. If the reason for an increased tendency to
lay workers off relates to the certainty that these workers
will remain unemployed until they need to be re-hired, then
these practices again have little to do with increasing
efficiency in the allocation of labour.

   With these considerations in mind, we will attempt to
specify the characteristics of labour organization which we
would expect to be associated with a competitive labour
market and to compare our own findings to these predictions
and to those of the dual labour market model. Table IV
summarizes the different labour market structures that these
"models" give rise to, with respect to pay structures,
skills and employment contracts, and systems of work
organization.

A. Pay Structures

In neo-classical theory wage levels reflect the relative
skills and productivity of the workers employed. However,
whether this implies relative homogeneity or dispersion of
earnings depends in part on the range of productivities of
the workers. This fits with Marshall's proposition:

> instances of unequal time wages tend on the whole to
> support, and not to weaken, the presumption that
> competition adjusts earnings in occupations of equal
> difficulty and in neighbouring places to the efficiency
> of workers (Marshall, 1946, p. 548).

However, Marshall himself points out that in practice, wage
levels relate to the normal expected productivity of the
workers employed and not necessarily to the productivity of
specific individuals. This aspect has been taken up in more
recent neo-classical work on information costs, and in
particular in the job signalling literature, to suggest that
costs of identifying differences in workers' productivity
may lead to great homogeneity of pay than of productivity

(Spence, 1973; Phelps, 1972). The overall prediction of neo-classical theory nevertheless remains that pay differentials are related to real differences in workers' productivity whether measured as a group or on an individual basis.

This position can be contrasted to the dual labour market model, for although the acquisition of firm-specific skills provides the rationale for the development of internal labour market systems, there is no presumption of a direct correspondence between wage differentials and workers' productivities in the primary sector. Hierarchical pay structures are established to provide a general incentive to stability, and are then maintained through custom and practice, with no direct attempt to relate pay to individual productivity. In the secondary sector pay is expected to be relatively homogeneous, reflecting the low demands made by secondary jobs and the low productivities of secondary workers. In this sector, then, pay is again taken as already linked to workers' skills and productivities.

Our research suggests that pay structures are generally more differentiated in primary sectors (i.e. large unionized firms) and that these differentials do not necessarily relate directly to workers' productivities. Indeed it is not really possible to talk about technical skill and worker expertise as exerting an independent influence on pay structures, as it is the processes that led to the recognition of these skills which appear crucial: these processes include managerial control strategies, trade union and individual bargaining strategies, and the force of custom and practice. These findings, in practice, also account for the pattern of relatively homogeneous pay found in the secondary-type sectors. Again the pay structures bore no direct relation to the skills and productivities of the workers, but instead reflected the relatively disadvantaged social and labour market position of the type of worker employed. In this sector real differences in skills and experience went unrewarded as pay for all employees was related to norms associated with casual and unskilled work. The "artificial" hierarchy of the primary sector is thus counterbalanced by an "artificial" homogeneity in the secondary sector.

B. Nature of Skills and Employment Relationships

Neo-classical labour economics has traditionally considered firm-specific skills to be a special case of human capital acquisition but which is sufficiently limited in its applicability not to disturb predictions for tendencies

towards equalization of wages for workers with the same
basic capabilities. A more widespread phenomena of firm-
specific skills would disturb such predictions as workers
would be unable to market their skills and would be locked
into specific firms, with firm-specific pay structures. The
existence of a low paid homogeneous sector, where no returns
to firm-specific skills are apparent, would be taken to
imply the absence of such skills. The dual labour market
model makes similar predictions to that of neo-classical
theory, except that it assumes that within the primary
sector firm-specific skills are both widespread and significant, leading to the development of horizontal as well as
vertical divisions in the labour market which impede
mobility and result in structured and relatively stable
employment relationships.

Our survey evidence contradicts these assumptions with
respect to the secondary sector and considerably qualifies
the assumptions about the primary sector. The overall
finding was that firm-specific skills (including skills
associated with the organization of work as well as with
specific techniques) were found in most types of jobs but
that these types of skills did not automatically lead to the
establishment of either employment security or hierarchical
pay structure. These developments depended on whether the
workers with these skills could exert some leverage, through
intra-firm organization, or through external bargaining
power (so that the mobility threat has some force). Thus
there was no real difference in the production, technological and skill requirements of secondary and primary
firms. The former often obtained a stable and committed
labour force by recruiting from disadvantaged workers. These
workers were generally stable, and indeed such firms could
often vary employment without risk of skill loss as they
could expect to re-hire the same workers when demand
increased. Some firms, of course, had to operate with a
relatively casual labour force because of demand conditions
rather than because of production requirements, with a
consequent loss in long-term efficiency. Thus it is the
firms' position in the product market, and the strategies
that they adopt which explain differences in employment
relationships between firms, and not primarily differences
in their technological and production requirements. These
findings also contradict the simple neo-classical model,
where the norm is an essentially casualized labour market,
in which firm-specific skills are relatively unimportant,
workers are assumed interchangeable and their employment
relationships short term.

C. Systems of Work Organization

Again, a traditional neo-classical model would predict a
relatively weak influence of firm specific factors on labour
organization. The firm is essentially both a wage taker and
a recipient of best practice techniques, which in turn
determine best practice systems of labour organization.
Maintenance of labour productivity levels is assured by the
operation of a competitive labour market. In the dual labour
market model the emphasis on firm-specific skills leads to
the redefinition of the primary firm as a wage-maker, and
later work identifies the control of the labour process as
one of the objectives influencing management's pay and
employment strategies. Technology and market forces are not
considered the only factors to influence work organization
in the primary sector, although the labour process in the
secondary sector is still taken as both relatively simple
and as determined by market forces, thus minimizing inter-
firm variations.

Our research found no tendency towards standardization
of systems of work organization or technology in use even in
highly competitive industrial sectors. There were significant inter-firm variations both in type of technology
employed and in the system of work organization used with
any given technology. Moreover, some of the differences in
work organization were related to firm-specific pay
structures. Thus firms using informal payment systems were
likely to use more flexible systems of work, with the same
workers deployed on unskilled and skilled tasks. Motivation
and control of labour were significant issues for all types
of firms but different strategies were deployed to resolve
these issues. Secondary firms seemed to require as high if
not higher commitment from their employees as primary firms
because of restricted resources for supervision, and the
importance of labour quality in many relatively non-
automated processes. However, this requirement did not
necessarily show itself in hierarchical payment systems
because relatively disadvantaged labour could be relied upon
to be self-motivated because of restricted job opportunities. Thus the apparent absence of control mechanisms
did not indicate the perfect functioning of the market, but
the absence of good employment opportunities for significant
parts of the labour force.

III. CONCLUSIONS

The dual labour market model departed from the neo-classical model by assuming that wage hierarchies in the primary sector are more extensive than the real differences in job content or productivities between workers employed, as their function is to secure a stable labour force and not to reward current productivity. Our findings mark a further departure from neo-classical theory by suggesting that in the secondary sector there is an extensive hierarchy of jobs and of productivities of workers that are rewarded at a relatively homogeneous and low pay level. The factor that workers most have in common in this sector is social and economic disadvantage, not low skills or lack of work commitment.

The most probable effect of a progressive reduction in institutional constraints on the labour market would be to intensify the exploitation of disadvantaged groups and as a consequence to increase the competition between high and low paid segments of the labour market. Neo-classical economists may be prepared to accept that in the short run the effect would be to make more visible the impact of non-competing groups in the labour force and to widen the divergence in wage rates, but they would probably believe that the long-term effect would be to eliminate these social divisions by bidding down the bargaining power of the high paid groups and establishing a competitive labour market in which wages reflected workers' productivities. This result depends on the possibility of a floor to wages being established through the operation of supply and demand in the labour market. The reasons for rejecting this view have been outlined elsewhere: in short, labour is not a scarce commodity, so that competition tends to depress rather than equalize wage levels (Craig et al., 1982, 1985a, 1985b; Humphries, 1977). The impact of policies to deregulate the labour market would therefore be primarily to destabilize the market and to lower wage levels for the already most vulnerable and low paid workers. Higher paid workers could be affected by the destabilizing policies but the roots of pay inequality are to be found deeply embedded in the social, family and economic system and cannot be attributed to "imperfections" such as trade unions, which are in fact only one element in the set of institutional and social factors that structure labour markets.

Paradoxically, the impact of removing social divisions in the labour force would be to reduce the extent to which secondary sectors at present apparently conform to simple neo-classical models of labour markets. Instead of being

able to employ disadvantaged workers at a relatively
homogeneous wage rate, and yet secure their stability, and
loyalty to the firm, employers would have to devise other
strategies to secure a permanent employment relationship
with its workforce, which is as necessary in secondary as
primary type firms to acquire the firm-specific skills. The
divergence in employment systems between primary and
secondary sectors at present stems more from the ability to
exploit social differentiation due to the lack of union
control, than to fundamental differences in production
requirements. If social differentiation were reduced, labour
markets in secondary sectors would be likely to become more
overtly structured and segmented with differential payments
based on formalized systems of job grading, merit and
seniority.

NOTES

1.   For example, by introducing restrictions on closed
     shop, reducing trade union immunities and minimum wage
     protection, removing obligations for industrial
     training, encouraging nationalized industries and
     private companies indirectly, to narrow the scope of
     issues for collective negotiation, and re-introducing
     casual forms of labour organization in the public
     sector through its "privatization" policies.
2.   The results of the two main projects on which this
     analysis is based have been published in Craig et al
     (1982) and Craig et al (1985b). Between them they cover
     12 industrial sectors, nine in manufacturing. To
     simplify the analysis we will concentrate on the main
     differences between these broad categories that often
     relate to specific characteristics of the industry in
     which the firm is located. For the inter-industry
     analysis and the detailed survey results, readers are
     referred to the above two publications.
3.   For example, there may be separate bargaining groups
     and different types of grading and payment systems for
     craft workers and non-craft or for maintenance workers
     versus production workers.
4.   The majority of these Industry Training Boards were
     abolished under the first Thatcher administration but
     they were still in existence when most of these surveys
     were carried out.
5.   It is clear that many firms using formal payments
     systems have cut bonuses and overtime in the recession,

without active resistance by workers. Nevertheless,
firms with informal payment systems are likely to take
action sooner to reduce wage costs.

6.   A more recent survey has shown that small firms and
      non-union firms were the least likely to provide a pay
      rise to their employees in 1983. (Daniel, 1984).
7.   See, for example, the work on information costs,
      implicit contract theory, search theory and work on
      firm-specific skills (Phelps 1970, 1972; Spence, 1973;
      Azariades, 1981).

REFERENCES

Azariades, C. (1981). Implicit contracts and related topics:
    a survey. In "The Economics of the Labour Market" (Z.
    Hornstein et al, ed.). HMSO, London.
Craig, C., Rubery, J., Tarling, R. and Wilkinson, F. (1982).
    "Labour Market Structure, Industrial Organisation and
    Low Pay". Cambridge University Press, Cambridge.
Craig, C., Rubery, J., Tarling, R. and Wilkinson, F. (1982).
    Economic, social and political factors in the operation
    of the labour market. In "New Approaches to Economic
    Life" (B. Roberts et al, ed.). Manchester University
    Press.
Craig, C. Garnsey, E. and Rubery, J. (1985b). "Payment
    Structures in Smaller Firms: Women's Employment in
    Segmented Labour Markets". Department of Employment
    Research, Paper No. 48.
Daniel, W.W. (1984). Who didn't get a pay increase last
    year? Policy Studies, 5, part I.
Doeringer, P. and Piore, M. (1971). "Internal Labour Markets
    and Manpower Analysis". Lexington, Mass.
Edwards, R.C. (1979). "Contested Terrain: the Transformation
    of the Workplace in the Twentieth Century". Heinemann,
    London.
Humphries, J. (1977). Class struggle and the persistence of
    the working-class family. Cambridge Journal of
    Economics, 1, September.
Marshall, A. (1946). "Principles of Economics", Eighth
    Edition. Macmillan, London.
Phelps, E.S. (ed.) (1970). "Microeconomic Foundations of
    Employment and Inflation Theory". Norton, New York.
Phelps, E.S. (1972). The statistical theory of racism and
    sexism. American Economic Review, 62 (4), September,
    659-661.
Rubery, J. and Wilkinson, F. (1981). Outwork and segmented
    labour markets. In "The Dynamics of Labour Market

Segmentation". Academic Press, London and Orlando.

Spence, M. (1973). Job-market signalling. Quarterly Journal of Economics, LXXXVII, 355-374.

Working Hours and Workforce Divisions

E. GARNSEY

In recent years innovations in working arrangements [1] have been in the news. There are frequent reminders in the press of widespread changes taking place in the distribution of working time. And yet full-time employment, uninterrupted after completion of education and training, remains the norm. Changes are taking place on the fringe, but the principle of full-time uninterrupted employment holds strong. In this paper an attempt is made to show why innovations have not made more impact on normal working arrangements for the majority of employees. The aim of this paper is to identify and examine constraints on radical innovations in working arrangements and to assess the ways in which traditional patterns of work help to segment labour markets.

Innovations in working arrangements have aroused a new level of interest under conditions of high unemployment. They are now viewed not only as a way of meeting individual needs and preferences, but also as a means of sharing out paid employment. Recent evidence indicates that many employees would be prepared to forego some of their earnings in order to reduce their hours of work (OECD 1982). However, employers have no direct incentive during a recession to accommodate the preferences of employees regarding hours of work. Some policy-makers believe that state subsidies may

create the necessary incentives. A number of governments
have attempted to encourage flexible working time and to
promote work and job sharing (IDS 1982). It often appears
that conventional attitudes and customs constitute the main
obstacles to change in this area and that the promotion of a
more enlightened outlook among managers and unions would
increase innovation and adaptation of working arrangements.
But in practice the economic and institutional constraints
on any radical and widespread change in working arrangements
are deep seated. These obstacles have not yet been
systematically analysed and the connections between them
remain to be traced out.

Standard hours of work form part of a network of social
and economic arrangements which interact closely with one
another and which together constitute a very powerful brake
on innovation. Widespread radical change in working
arrangements would challenge accepted ways in which work is
co-ordinated, control exerted and protection afforded.
Moreover, jobs are allocated and payments structured under
the influence of divisions in the workforce promoted by
rigid working arrangements. This can be seen when the
benefits conferred by standard working arrangements and the
reason for vested interests in their retention are examined.
The strength of existing arrangements must be recognized if
the limitations and potential of measures aimed at altering
rigid working arrangements are to be assessed realistically.

I. THE REDUCTION OF STANDARD WORKING HOURS AND JOB CREATION

During periods of economic expansion some of the benefits of
productivity gains can be made over to the workforce through
shorter hours of work, in addition to or instead of higher
wages. Over the long term there has been a steady decrease
in the hours of work. In the short run, periods when hours
of work loom large as an issue in industrial relations have
tended to alternate with periods when negotiations centred
on pay issues, as during the Social Contract of 1974-5 in
the UK. Since that time a reduction in standard working
hours has been a central objective of British trade unions.
However, in periods of recession the issue of shorter hours
of work may arouse as much conflict as do pay disputes in
more prosperous times.

The potential for job creation offered by reductions in
standard working hours is limited by employers' reluctance
to take on new workers in a recession and by unions'
insistence that shorter standard hours should not entail a
loss of earnings. Both conditions favour the use of regular

or intermittent overtime in place of the creation of new
jobs [2]. Reductions in hours of work of a few hours per
week cannot completely offset the influence of increasingly
capital intensive production methods and the growth of the
labour supply in many economies. Empirical evidence suggests
that reductions in hours of work are only absorbed by firms
without raising costs if there are productivity gains which
remove the need for new hirings.

Case studies indicate that reducing the standard
working week has not resulted in job creation in the firms
investigated (White, 1981). In many cases there are
practical difficulties which prevent marginal reductions in
standard hours from being parcelled up to form new jobs.
These constraints are not usually taken into account in
macro-economic forecasts of the effects of shorter standard
working hours on employment. More radical measures,
involving the splitting up of existing jobs, are required to
make any significant impact on the numbers out of work.
Recognition of the need for more than marginal change in
hours of work led to the introduction of subsidies for
employers creating jobs through job-sharing schemes in both
France and the UK in 1982 (IDS International Report Nos. 160
and 162). These measures have had no significant impact on
unemployment. Policy initiatives of this kind are limited in
their impact by the network of arrangements which support
and maintain standard full-time working as the prevailing
norm for employment. In neo-classical economic theory,
workers subject to the standard working week are described
as "rationed" in relation to the hours of work they may
supply and this is treated as a market imperfection (Ham,
1977). But standard working arrangements are not arbitrary,
nor simply historically determined conventions with no
particular rationale, as is suggested by the practice of
relegating them to the status of market imperfections. In
the following section we discuss the ways in which these
arrangements interact with other institutional and economic
practices and operate to serve the interests of important
groups.

II. CO-ORDINATION OF WORK

Regulations governing hours and conditions of work
presuppose interaction among employees and the need for co-
ordination of their activities. Constraints on possible
hours of work stem in part from the nature of the product or
service and the type of production process. It must be
emphasized that the impact of the production process on

working arrangements is not direct, but is mediated by the system of work organization in use.

Clearly, industries with continuous production processes, or where there is a 24-hour demand for services, cannot phase out shift work. Teams of workers on shifts may complement each other and their work will need to be synchronized in a daily or weekly routine. Through the influence of custom and practice, production methods are geared to manning by full-time workers and routines making use of part-time workers are seldom developed in manufacturing except in conditions of labour shortage. A survey of 800 employees revealed that:

> part time work mainly exists to suit employers
> rather than to produce a more varied range of
> employment opportunities for workers,
> especially for women. Employers' reasons for
> taking on part-time workers almost always
> relate to the difficulty of getting full-time
> workers or to peak load needs rather than to a
> settled role for part-time work (as for
> example in twilight shifts) on the total
> pattern of employment (McIntosh, 1980, p.
> 1145).

This was confirmed in a survey of small firms where it was found that prolonged shortages of skilled female labour were associated with the settled provision of part-time employment (e.g. for experienced female machinists in the footwear industry) but in many firms when labour was abundant part-time work was often eliminated, except to meet peak load needs (Craig et al.,1985; see also EOC 1981).

The reason for the elimination of part-time jobs was only partly related to cost considerations and these were not precisely established. Often a firm's authority over structure depends on senior staff exercising control over their subordinates on a full-time basis. The system of job demarcation may further reduce the possibility of using part-time workers, or workers on individualized work schedules in place of full-time staff, because specialists have to be available at all times. In general, the more flexible the division of labour, the less rigid the demarcation of jobs and the greater the autonomy of the workforce, the less necessary it is for all employees to work precisely the same hours. But by the same token, individualized working arrangements challenge the

prevailing authority structure and system of work
organization.

III. COSTS AND BENEFITS OF PART-TIME EMPLOYMENT

Many employers are reluctant to allow part-time work, except
in special circumstances, because they believe that part-
time workers entail additional costs. In some countries,
payroll taxes do raise the cost of part-time employees, but
even where contributions are scaled to hours worked
employers may be deterred by the internal administrative
costs of having part-time workers. Systematic analysis of
the cost and benefits of part-time work, taking into account
the higher productivity often achieved by employees working
reduced hours per week and the time wasted by full-time
employees, are not always carried out. Employers often base
their policy towards part-time work on impressions rather
than detailed costings. Their impressions may be influenced
by customary procedure and do not usually incorporate a
willingness to re-assess working arrangements and job
demarcations; indeed it may not be within their power to do
so unilaterally where there are industry wide regulations,
often established on the basis of collective bargaining
agreements.
     In some industries patterns of activity vary in such a
way as to make part-time employment attractive to employers.
But the provision of seasonal or part-time jobs in
agriculture and retailing is not designed to meet employee
preferences. In retailing, for example, the widespread
extension of part-time employment has been aimed at meeting
peaks in customer demand. Moreover, the authority structure
dictates that supervisory and managerial positions continue
to be held on a full-time basis in retailing and part-time
work remains at a subordinate level. The attraction of part-
time work to employers lies not only in adjusting wage costs
in line with patterns of activity, but in institutional
arrangements which make it possible to evade protective
legislation by taking on part-time workers. During periods
of labour shortage, job protection and rewards for seniority
were used to retain labour and cut down on recruitment and
training costs. For the core workforce these working
conditions have been institutionalized, partly through trade
union pressure, and they persist under conditions of
recession. But these benefits have been reserved for jobs
carried out on a full-time basis, regardless of how
adequately the work could be performed by part-time staff.
Thus, for employers, part-time jobs provide a category of

work in which they can minimize their commitments to a
sector of the workforce. This affords employers flexibility
and the possibility of making wage costs variable while
reinforcing the divisions in the workforce discussed below.

IV. CONTROL AND COMMITMENT

Standard working arrangements have not only a co-ordinating
function but are also used to control the workforce.
Management may be reluctant to give up the disciplinary
powers which rigid working arrangements afford. More
sophisticated and individualized ways of controlling time-
keeping have to be evolved. The issue is not only control
during working hours, but the degree of commitment of the
workforce. It is widely believed that only full-time workers
show commitment and that part-time workers are less
reliable, though there is no systematic evidence on the
subject. Managers tend to oppose changes in working
arrangements which affect their status as sole employers of
their employees. Not long ago, a publication by the CBI
represented work-sharing as a defensive and negative response to unemployment and pointed to the danger of dual job
holding: "Increased leisure could encourage people to take a
second job, thus reducing job opportunities for the unemployed. There is then the danger that the cash economy could
spread and with it tax evasion." (CBI 1981, p. 42) [3].
    Those who are permitted to combine several jobs are
frequently found at the top of occupational hierarchies.
Elite part-time positions, as company director, head of a
commission, professional consultant, etc., almost always go
to multiple job holders. Flexible arrangements are tolerated
to a greater extent where the control function of working
arrangements is less central either because payment is for
end product or service rendered rather than on a time basis,
or because the work is done by a person who is above the
ordinary exercise of control by virtue of his social or
economic position.

V. THE PROTECTIVE ROLE OF STANDARDIZED WORKING ARRANGEMENTS

Standardized hours of work were not imposed on a passive
workforce; on the contrary, they represent important gains
achieved by labour in the course of development of
industrial relations. Employment contracts guaranteeing
full-time work ensure a much higher and more reliable level
of income than can be achieved where working hours vary

unpredictably [4]. Further gains were made by labour in regularizing earnings premia for overtime work, which in some countries make up a sizeable proportion of male manual workers' earnings. The earnings guarantee implied in full-time employment contracts constitute a major objection to the extension of part-time work. Unions see a danger of part-time employment and ensuing wage cuts being imposed on members on an involuntary basis. For many members this threat outweighs possible advantages of extending part-time employment to those who want reduced hours of work at reduced levels of earnings.

Standard working hours have other protective functions in ensuring against excessive or arbitrary hours of work and also in establishing common periods of time off work for families and communities. Hence alternative working arrangements are often viewed as a threat to existing rights and customary benefits. Many union members have regarded a unified campaign for a reduced working week for all as their priority. There are recent indications of a modification of this position among union officials; there is, however, a diversity of interests among members, the majority of whom would not benefit from radical changes in working arrangements because this would entail a loss of earnings.

Most part-time jobs are so badly paid that at least one adult must work on a full-time basis to keep the family from poverty. Social security legislation provides a floor to family income levels and many part-time jobs pay at rates below this floor; in many countries part-time earnings reduce eligibility for social security or unemployment benefits. Part-time earnings can normally be used to supplement the income of the primary wage earner without prejudice to the family, but they cannot replace the earnings of the main full-time wage earner and in practice may leave a family no better off than dependence on social security provisions [5].

For example, in the UK, workers earning at the average wage rate for male full-time employees (£125 per week in April 1981) who took a half-time job at the same hourly rate would obtain less than the equivalent of supplementary benefits for which a family with two children were eligible (approximately £81.00). In addition, eligibility for Family Income Supplement depends on the claimant working more than part-time hours.

VI. THE DIFFERENTIATION OF THE LABOUR SUPPLY

A. The Division of Labour in the Family

We have examined standard working hours in relation to the
co-ordination and control of work and the respects in which
they have been used by workers to achieve earnings
protection. A further implication of the institution of
standard working hours is the way in which it serves to
differentiate the labour supply into groups which are
dissimilar in the extent to which they are able or willing
to supply their labour over specific periods of time.

The norm of full-time uninterrupted employment assumes
that workers can devote the bulk of their lives to paid
employment. This is only possible for those in good health
who can avoid such responsibilities as the care of the old,
the young and the sick. Full-time employment depends on
social arrangements which release workers from outside
commitments. Since state provisions for the care of
dependants are on a limited basis, in practice the
traditional division of labour between men and women is
reinforced by rigid working arrangements and full-time
requirements. Most women supply their labour subject to
responsibility for the care of family members, whilst most
men supply their labour subject to the enabling services of
others. For this reason, many women are unable to work on a
full-time basis, given socially determined requirements for
the care of dependants within the family. The standard of
care required varies with prevailing customs and income
levels. More rudimentary standards of care may be
unavoidable in societies where able-bodied women must engage
in economic activity to avoid starvation or penury for
themselves and their children. The inability to work full-
time is not absolute but culturally relative; it is
nevertheless a sufficiently binding constraint to limit job
seeking and activity rates in Western societies. Surveys
indicate that the lack of alternative child care provision
prevents women who would otherwise look for jobs from doing
so (Elias, 1980, p.77).

The division of labour in the family is reflected not
only in well-known differentials in male and female economic
activity rates, but in the difference between the proportion
of men and women working part-time. To take the case of the
UK in 1981, when 41.7% of women worked part-time while only
5.8% of men did so [6]. Responsibility for child
care is closely related to part-time work, and the age of
the youngest child is an important factor determining
whether women in employment work full- or part-time. In

recent years in the UK nearly three quarters of women
without dependent children who were in paid employment have
worked full-time. But in 1982 only 12% of employed mothers
with a youngest child under ten years of age, and 6% of
those with a child under four years of age worked full-time
(GHS, 1982).

Mothers with young children find it difficult to obtain
suitable work, while fathers of young children frequently
work very long hours to support the family in the absence of
earnings by the wife. Systematic information on hours of
work of men in relation to the number and age of dependent
children is not provided in the official statistics, but a
number of studies have shown that paid overtime is most
common among younger married men, especially those with
young children. In a 1972 sample survey it was found that
married men under 30 with children worked four times as much
paid overtime as childless married men of the same age
(Young and Wilmot, 1973).

Mainly as a result of the recession, the proportion of
male manual workers on overtime has dropped in recent years
from 60.7% in 1974 to 58.5% in 1979 and to 49.3% in 1982. In
1982 average weekly overtime for male manual workers was 4.9
hours per week as compared with 6.5 hours in 1974. But for
those doing overtime work, average hours fell relatively
little (from 10.6 hours in 1974 to 9.4 hours in 1982). It
seems likely that fathers in a single income household
remain especially liable to work overtime. Basic weekly
hours of work have been falling, but in 1982 average total
weekly hours of manual men were still 44.3 hours (New
Earnings Survey). Non-manual men have shorter official hours
of work but unpaid overtime increases total hours especially
in professional or managerial jobs. Often long hours of work
prevent fathers from providing any of the practical
assistance which is necessary if mothers are to work even
part-time when their children are young. These circumstances
further reinforce the traditional division of labour,
preventing many men who do earn a "family wage", i.e. a
single wage sufficient to support a family, from taking part
in family life [7].

B. Rigid Working Arrangements and Disadvantaged Groups

The difficulties of combining domestic commitments with paid
employment under rigid working arrangements do not only
apply to women. This can be illustrated from a UK survey of
nearly 400 families with young children where the wife had
died or departed. A fall in earnings (in addition to further

earnings foregone) was common in these households. In only
12% of cases was this the result of the loss of the wife's
earnings: 35% of fathers experiencing loss of income could
not find work compatible with child care; 10% had to change
to less well paying jobs (e.g. with more suitable hours);
18.5% suffered from loss of overtime earnings. As the
authors of the study explain:

> For many, a new and overriding criterion
> asserts itself - the compatibility of work
> with the care of children.

The difficulties faced were much greater for men in manual
than non-manual jobs because employers are much more
flexible over hours of work, punctuality and time off for
emergencies for staff than for manual workers.

> These privileges and inequalities (in working
> conditions) can be of crucial importance for
> the father struggling to combine work with the
> care of children
> (George and Wilding, 1972, p. 87)

Rigid working arrangements were a crucial factor, quite
independent of experience and training depriving many of
these men of access to better paid jobs [8]. There is also
evidence of disabled men being confined to low paying part-
time jobs where their health does not permit them to work
standard hours (Buckle, 1971).
    Thus, in a variety of ways, rigid working arrangements
have the effect of depriving certain social groups of access
to "good jobs". Desirable jobs are not available, especially
for manual workers, on a part-time basis. Working
arrangements act as a stratifying agency and serve to
differentiate the labour force, providing a basis for labour
market segmentation.

VII. PART-TIME WORK AND LABOUR MARKET SEGMENTATION

Part-time status is often treated as a feature of jobs in
the secondary labour market similar to such characteristics
as low pay and insecurity. But part-time working
arrangements are not in themselves disadvantages, though
they may be an unacceptable alternative to those seeking
full-time work and higher earnings. It is specifically the
unfavourable terms on which work is available other than on
a full-time basis which is conducive to labour market

segmentation. The rationale for these unfavourable terms is
seldom questioned or included in the problematic in much
economic analysis, and this narrows the scope of analysis of
labour market segmentation and of women's employment
position. Part-time work entails disadvantages where the
following conditions prevail:.

   i) The provision of part-time jobs is very limited
  ii) These jobs are usually at the base of occupational
      hierarchies
 iii) They are usually excluded from the internal career
      ladder
  iv) Part-time workers are not eligible for fringe benefits
      and lack security
   v) Pro-rata, pay rates are often lower than for full-time
      workers

These features also summarize the benefits to employers of
having a section of the workforce to whom they can minimize
their commitments. The earnings and status of part-time
workers are directly affected by these conditions, and
household income levels suffer where full-time earnigs are
not available. These conditions also have important indirect
effects on the employment prospects of those workers, mainly
women, who are unable to work on a full-time basis.

VIII. PART-TIME WORK AND WOMEN'S EMPLOYMENT; CAREER CHOICE
AND JOB SEGREGATION

Working arrangements which apply to various occupations have
a major influence on women's career choice, given the
current division of labour in the family. There is little
incentive for women to acquire training and qualifications
for jobs which are known to have long and rigid hours of
work, and these areas have remained male preserves. This is
a self-reinforcing process, since in industries and
occupations in which women predominate employers may provide
part-time working conditions even for highly qualified
personnel in order to attract married women, usually in
place of offering higher pay rates. This option is used in
particular by small firms which provide the bulk of job
openings for women and in which there are few prospects for
advancement (Elias, 1982).
      Occupations become feminized for a variety of reasons
in the course of their development, but jobs done mainly by
women are almost always characterized by low pay (Craig et
al., 1985). Certain industries are dependent on low-paid

female labour and part-time work is more common in
predominantly female industries (Employment Gazette, July
1979). It is often assumed that this is because the jobs
done by women are better suited to part-time work [9], but
men's jobs may be no less amenable to part-time arrangements. Proportionately more highly qualified women do part-
time work than do unqualified men (Social Trends, 1983). At
present 95% of men work on a full-time basis, but this is
not necessary from the purely functional standpoint.

The limited availability of part-time work and its
concentration in specific occupations and in particular
sectors is a major cause of occupational and industrial job
segregation. In the case of the UK the three industries
which had the highest level of female employment -
distributive trades, professional and scientific services
and miscellaneous services - accounted for 58% of female
employees in December 1978; in 1976, 73% of part-time women
were employed in these industries and the concentration of
part-time jobs for women was on the increase (Moss, 1980).
Vertical segregation is also considerably more pronounced
for women in part-time jobs than for women in full-time
jobs, as is to be predicted from the concentration of part-
time jobs at the bases of occupational hierarchies.
Restricted job opportunities associated with part-time work
are described by Hunt (1975), McIntosh (1982) and Leicester
(1982) among others, and more recently in some detail by
Martin and Roberts (1984).

Rigid working patterns have been modified by flexitime
and other arrangements which make it easier to vary starting
and finishing times, but when total hours of work are only
slightly reduced these arrangements do not make a significant difference to groups disadvantaged by long working
hours (Stoper, 1982). Traditional working arrangements are
not a primary but a contributory cause of segmentation.
Hours of work requirements operate in conjunction with other
job requirements which most women cannot meet - and which
are not always essential for competent job performace - to
restrict opportunities.

IX. CAREER INTERRUPTIONS

The shortage of part-time jobs enforces complete withdrawal
from the labour market for many women who would be able and
willing to work part-time during the early stages of family
formation. In many cases part-time employment would suffice
to maintain competence and update skills, preventing the
"deterioration of human capital" to which women's low pay

and subordinate status is often attributed. But the loss of
pay and position which women experience following a period
of family formation is usually out of proportion to the loss
of proficiency directly attributable to their breaks in
employment. As Greenhalgh and Stewart have shown these
breaks are usually few in number and their total duration is
small in comparison with the total length of working life
(Greenhalgh and Stewart, 1982). In many cases there is no
significant deterioration in job performance after a break
in full-time employment. Many employers are eager to re-
engage experienced women who have left their employment to
have children (Craig et al., 1985). In many jobs in the
caring professions this break may actually increase
professional awareness and competence. In other cases the
amount of re-training required would be relatively rapid and
inexpensive. A problem no less significant than the loss of
skills through withdrawal from the labour market is the
subsequent non-utilization of women's skills. Women are
frequently unable to obtain jobs which do make use of their
training and qualifications. Instead they take on work for
which they are over-qualified but which provide suitable
hours of work. Part-time work in particular is the domain of
labour market re-entrants (Elias and Main, 1982, p. 17). It
is significant that women with teaching and nursing
qualifications accumulate more work experience than women in
most other occupations; as Elias and Main point out, these
professions have allowed women continuity of experience by
providing part-time work (1982, p. 27). In general, net
downward occupational mobility or skill downgrading is
experienced by women as they grow older (Greenhalgh, 1982;
Elias and Main, 1982).

Women who interrupt full-time employment do not
universally experience a loss of skill or professional
competence but they do almost invariably lose their place in
any internal job structure and forfeit promotion rights.
They are seldom able to return to jobs at their previous
level if they outstay statutory maternity leave, more
especially if they return to part-time work. Internal career
structures often depend on short-term female employment and
part-time jobs are usually excluded from the promotional
ladder. This practice is justified on the grounds that
senior positions are not suitable for part-time work [11].
However, senior positions often involve distinct and separate areas of responsibility which could be split up. As we
have seen, several senior posts are often held on a multiple
basis by the same person suggesting that these positions
could be divided among several people working part-time.
Employers do not usually reassess their authority structure

and work organization when ruling out part-time positions.
Managers often assume that women want to avoid responsibility because they fail to apply for senior posts (Hunt,
1975). However, many women would gladly assume greater
responsibility in their work. What they are less likely to
tolerate than men are the very long hours of work attached
to senior positions. Long hours of work at this level are
seldom questioned, but they may not be conducive to greater
efficiency than the systematic division of responsibilities
among two or more persons on proportionately lower salaries.

  Standardized working arrangements are only one factor
contributing to labour market segmentation. The connection
is emphasized here because their importance has not been
sufficiently acknowledged. The shortage of part-time work
weakens the bargaining position of those unable to work on
the traditional full-time basis, creating a buyers' market
for part-time labour even in prosperous times, and enabling
employers to fill jobs at the base of their employment
structure, despite poor pay and conditions, with
disadvantaged workers. Employers do not deliberately ration
the supply of part-time jobs with this aim in mind, but this
"rationing" is a consequence of prevailing work patterns.

X. CONCLUSION

We have seen that it would require a major social upheaval
to remove the constraints which now prevent radical change
in work patterns. Moreover, the prospect of employers
reorganizing work flow and restructuring working arrangements to create more favourable conditions for those unable
to conform to traditional working patterns is remote.
Indeed, the possibility is seldom even acknowledged. Instead
we find it argued that the provision of more part-time jobs
cannot be expected to improve women's employment position
(Elias and Main, 1982). Those who treat the demand for part-
time labour as given often argue that women's employment
position can only be improved through marked changes in
female labour supply conditions. The type and conditions of
work made available on a part-time basis are not in question
in this line or argument. There is, however, an element of
circularity in arguments to the effect that women must cease
to interrupt full-time employment and must enter currently
male-dominated skilled occupations in order to improve their
employment position (Nickell, 1977, p. 206). This type of
"solution" could only work for some limited number of individuals under present circumstances.

  In reality, significant improvements can only come

about as a result of changes in both supply and demand. The
shortage of jobs available to women which are sufficiently
well-paid to meet child care costs is a basic constraint on
female activity rates. An improvement in the relative position of women requires a fundamental change in the family
division of labour and the family wage system. Neither
changes could occur as a result of autonomous developments
on the supply side. Institutional facilities can never more
than partially relieve domestic duties. The division of
labour in the family is not immutable but it is deeply
ingrained in culture and tradition and strongly reinforced
by the family wage system. On the other hand, a radical
improvement in the type of work and level of earnings
available on a part-time basis could be an engine of change.
Over time a marked improvement in the amount and quality of
part-time employment could alter both the family division of
labour and the family wage system. The necessary changes in
demand would involve a large absolute increase in the number
of well-paid and well-integrated part-time jobs. Applying
primary sector conditions to only a restricted set of part-
time jobs would be insufficient to alter the self-
perpetuating features of the present division of labour.

Improvements of this kind would not be a panacea, but
reference to the scope for change is frequently left out of
account entirely in discussions of women's employment
position. The causes of the shortage and inferior status of
part-time jobs have not been adequately investigated and
must be included in any full analysis of these issues. There
are certainly limits to the range of alternative work
patterns compatible with industrial efficiency, but these
cannot be established without systematic experiment and
research.

What is already clear is that many of the factors which
maintain traditional working patterns and stratify jobs
according to full- and part-time status are not directly
related to the requirements of productive efficiency.
Instead they are related to current methods of co-ordination
and control of the workforce: traditional patterns of full-
time employment often help maintain the existing authority
structure. Moreover, groups of employees have played a
major part in the development of these arrangements which
they have used for their protection. The prospect of a
radical change in work patterns presents what appears to
be a threat to the earnings and status of many established
employees. New patterns of work in recession conditions
might lead to job sharing at low rates of pay, so undermining
the benefits which some now gain from the family wage system,
without providing other safeguards to living standards. Under

providing other safeguards to living standards. Under
conditions of recession the total amount of employment
available would not be increased by creating part-time jobs
at the expense of full-time work. The unions have not
established a common viewpoint on job sharing and official
organs prefer to pursue the campaign aimed at reducing the
working week for all to 35 hours (TUC, 1983). Thus, both
employers and unions in key sectors have reason to limit the
spread of innovative working arrangements. Those who might
benefit from innovations in working patterns have no direct
representatives to make their viewpoint known; they have to
await a coincidence of their needs and employers' self
interest.

Policies designed to encourage employers to introduce
job-sharing schemes by providing government subsidies [12]
are the direct outcome of high levels of unemployment. They
were not proposed to deal with inequalities of opportunities
in more prosperous times. It is likely that attempts will be
made by employers and unions to limit the provision of
"shared jobs" and to prevent the practice from improving the
position of part-time workers as a whole [13]. Nevertheless,
these measures raise possibilities for a break with
tradition that were not even conceived of in official or
academic circles in Britain before the recession. For years
advances in technology have been associated with job
displacement and the retention of traditional working
patterns for those who remained in employment (TUC, 1983).

It may be that the social upheaval entailed by
unemployment will, for better or worse, alter the relative
strength of interests supporting traditional working
arrangements and unloosen the existing structure of
constraints still impeding widespread innovation in patterns
of work.

NOTES

1.   By working arrangements is meant regulations and
      practices governing the time devoted to paid employment
      and intermissions between periods of work, including
      those occurring over the entire working life. The
      location of work and entitlement to job security and
      benefits may be included in the term.
2.   Trade union campaigns for shorter working time now
      include objectives for the reduction of overtime
      working (see, for example, TUC, 1983).
3.   There has been a change in the official CBI viewpoint
      which now favours job sharing, with the rise in

unemployment levels (see CBI, 1982).

4. This is recognized where government subsidies are provided during periods of economic difficulty in firms and industries where workers are short-time.

5. This may help to account for the fact that in the UK in 1970, 43% of disabled females worked part-time, but only 6% of disabled males did so (Hurstfield, 1980).

6. Forty per cent of male part-time workers were over retirement age, as compared with 10% of female workers (1981 Census of Population).

7. Large numbers of men in full-time employment earn so little that the earnings of their wives are essential to keep the family from poverty (Layard, 1978).

8. See also Schaffer (1968, p. 34) for cases of men losing their jobs when their wives were in hospital because they needed to take over domestic duties incompatible with job requirements.

9. Services have to be fitted around normal full-time working hours, which results in peaks in demand. Part-time jobs in the services are therefore partly the outcome of rigid hours of work elsewhere. Many women in low-paid service jobs work unsocial hours, evenings and weekends (Moss, 1980).

10. Often minor changes in work organization would also make such requirements as physical strength or geographical mobility unnecessary for efficient job performance on responsible jobs.

11. See, for example, the CBI and IPM comments on the EEC draft directive aimed at removing discrimination against part-time workers (IDS No. 267, 1982).

12. See Department of Employment, Job Splitting Schemes (HMSO, 1983).

13. See The Guardian, October 8, 1982.

REFERENCES

Bekemans, L. (ed.) (1982). "The Organisation of Working Time". Maastricht (European Centre for Work and Society).

Buckle, J.R. (1971). Work and housing of impaired persons in Great Britain. In "Handicapped and Impaired Persons in Gt. Britain". Pt. II, OPCS, HMSO.

Confederation of British Industry (1981). "Unemployment - A Challenge for Us All". First Report of the CBI Group on Unemployment, October.

Confederation of British Industry (1982). "Jobs - Facing the Future". A CBI Staff discussion document.

Craig, C., Rubery, J., Tarling, R. and Wilkinson, F. (1982).

"Labour Market Structure, Industrial Organisation and
Low Pay". Cambridge University Press, Cambridge.

Craig, C., Garnsey, E. and Rubery, J. (1985). "Payment
Structures and Smaller Firms: Women's employment in
segmented labour markets". Department of Employment:
Research Paper No. 48.

Elias, P. (1980). Employment prospects and equal
opportunity. In "Work and the Family" (P. Moss and N.
Fonda, eds.). Temple Smith, London.

Elias, P and Main, B. (1982). "Women's Working Lives".
Evidence from the National Training Survey, University
of Warwick, Coventry.

EOC (1980). "The Experience of Caring for Elderly and
Handicapped Dependents: Survey Report". EOC.

EOC (1981). "Job Sharing; Improving the Quality and
Availability of Part-Time Work".

EOC (1981). Women and under-achievement at work. EOC
Research Bulletin, 5, Spring.

George V. and Wilding, P. (1972). "Motherless Families".
Routledge and Kegan Paul.

General Household Survey (1977). O.P.C.S.

Glucklich, P., Povall, M., Snell, M.W. and Zell, A. (1978).
Equal pay and opportunity. Department of Employment
Gazette, 86.

Greenhalgh, C. and Stewart, M. (1982). "Occupational Status
and Mobility of Men and Women". Warwick Economic
Research Papers No. 211.

Ham, J.C. (1977). Rationing and the supply of labour.
Industrial Relations Section Working Paper No. 103,
Princeton University.

Hunt, A. (1975). "Managerial Attitudes and Practices towards
Women at Work". London, HMSO.

Hurstfield, J. (1980). "Part-time Pittance". Low Pay Review.
June 1980.

Incomes Data Services (1982a). "Part-time Workers". Study
No. 267.

Incomes Data Services (1982b). International Reports. Nos.
160, 162.

Jallande, J.P. (1982). "L'Europe a Temps Partiel". Paris,
Economics.

Layard, R. et al (1978). The Causes of Poverty, Background
Paper 5. Royal Commission on the Distribution of Income
and Wealth, London, HMSO.

Leicester, C.(1982). Le travail a temps partiel en Grande
Bretagne. "L'Europe a Temps Partiel". (J.P. Jallande,
ed.). Paris, Economics.

Martin, J. and Roberts, C. (1984). "Women and Employment; A
    Lifetime Perspective". Department of Employment,
    O.P.C.S.
McIntosh, A. (1980). Women at Work: A Survey of Employers.
    Employment Gazette.
Moss, P. and Fonda, N. (eds.) (1980). "Work and the Family".
    Temple Smith, London.
Moss, P. (1980). Parents at work. In "Parents at Work" (P.
    Moss and N. Fonda, eds.).
Nickell, S.J. (1977). Trade Unions and the position of women
    in the industrial wage structure. British Journal of
    Industrial Relations, XV (2).
OECD (1982). "Labour Supply, Growth Constraints and Work
    Sharing". Paris.
Robertson, J.S. and Briggs, J.M. (1979). Part-time working
    in Great Britain. Department of Employment Gazette,
    July.
Schaffer, H.R. and Schaffer, E.B. (1968). "Child Care and
    the Family". Occasional Papers in Social
    Administration. Number 25.
Stewart, M. and Greenhalgh, C. (1982). "Work History
    Patterns and the Occupational Attainment of Women".
    Warwick Economic Research Papers No. 212.
Stoper, E. (1982). Alternative work patterns and the double
    life. In "Women, Power and Policy" (E. Boneparth, ed.).
    Pergamon Press, New York.
T.U.C. (1983). "Campaign for Reduced Working Time". T.U.C.
    Progress Report No. 9, (January).
White, M. (1980). "Shorter Working Time Report", No. 589.
    Policy Studies Institute.
White, M. (1980). "Case Studies of Shorter Time". Report No.
    597. Policy Studies Institute, London.
White, M. (1981). Effects of reductions in working time.
    Employment Gazette, (October).
Young and Wilmot (1973). "The Symmetrical Family". Routledge
    and Kegan Paul, London.

Mobilization Networks and Strategies in the Labour Market

J.-P. DE GAUDEMAR

I. ECONOMIC ANALYSIS AND THE LABOUR MARKET

One element appears to be common to all notions formulated by economists about the "labour market" [1]: the subordinate role of the supply of labour, or rather, of the behaviour of those seeking employment in the determination of the level of employment. In short, wage earners, or those applying for jobs must adapt their behaviour to the laws that balance the economic markets, notably through wage adjustments.

In the basic neo-classical model, for example, only the level of the real wage is considered to determine the behaviour of supply and demand, and the economic and social factors that condition these relationships, such as career and social aims, methods of organization and the conditions of competition are deliberately ignored. As a result, no thought is given in such a context to the behaviour which is likely to define the ways in which changes of job are made, except in so far as this relates to the stochastic variations in the real wage. Moreover, the probabilities of being unemployed are by definition nil, since, with the exception of frictional unemployment, this theory is incapable of conceiving of involuntary unemployment because of the supposed flexibility of the real wage. Thus, it is

only when neo-classical theory takes into account, for
example, certain rigidities in the real wage that it
rediscovers the significance of social systems.

The upheavals caused by Keynesian theory can be
interpreted in these terms. Instead of a mechanism for
balancing the "labour market" by adjusting the real wage,
Keynes introduced the idea of incompatibility between full
employment and the level of employment needed to balance
savings and investment or for consistent financial
decisions. As a result, Keynesian theory upset the order in
which the macro-economic variables were determined, by
making the actual level of employment the result of the
balances in the product and money markets. Unemployment is
thus the result of a process, external to the "labour
market" itself, which determines the supply of jobs and
which is influenced still further by the institutional
rigidity of the nominal wage. The sequence of the processes
of determination is basically as follows:

	I		II		III	
Demand	–	Production	–	Employment	–	Unemployment

This theory makes the situation in the labour market the
direct effect of the state of overall demand.

Processes I and II can thus be interpreted as the
economic formulation of the relationship between firms'
situation and their employment strategies. Similarly,
Process III can be interpreted in terms of power
relationships so that it is possible not only to identify
the ways in which the demand for labour is satisfied, but
also to identify social categories most likely to have a
high rate of unemployment.

This, moreover, is the reason for one of the
immediate effects of Keynesian theory. In describing
employment, it is possible to introduce more realistic
stochastic assumptions, such as, in particular, that the
probabilities of being unemployed are not zero. This
interpretation seems to be confirmed by several recent
studies, in particular that of Edmond Malinvaud (1980), in
which the author, on the basis of a "fixed prices" model of
general equilibrium with rationing [2], attempts to develop
a composite typology, distinguishing in particular between
"classical unemployment" and "Keynsian unemployment"
according to the distinctive features of rationing on the
labour and product markets (Malinvaud, 1980). This is a good
example of the widening of the "neo-classical synthesis" in
which the introduction of the concept of rationing
(purchases lower than demand, sales lower than supply) is an

indirect indication of the importance of the social
constraints that affect the free play of market mechanisms
and of their stochastic effects on the development of the
"labour market". It is obvious that, as for Keynes, the
problems are considered basically from the point of view of
the supply of jobs (or the demand for labour). In other
words, it is the dominant effects that are analysed. The
demand for jobs (the supply of labour) is always assumed to
adapt. This assumption is often based on very crude
hypotheses. Thus Malinvaud, using the results of econometric
studies utilizes a hypothesis that regards the demand for
jobs (the supply of labour) as an increasing function of the
nominal wage! (Malinvaud, 1980).

These processes of determination are thus one-way
processes. They recognise that firms' strategies are rooted
in a general economic situation but take no account of
mechanisms specific to the behaviour of those seeking jobs.
Moreover, it is only because firms' strategies are rooted in
the general economic situation, and because of the need to
establish short-term equilibrium, that changes in employment
systems can be described in terms of "egodic" Markov chains.

The dualist theory lends itself in part to the same
kind of interpretation. It is central to dualist theory that
the heterogeneity of the economic structures which it
attempts to analyse (such as large oligopolistic firms/small
peripheral firms, traditional sector/ modern sector and
primary/secondary sector) is reflected in the heterogenous
strategies adopted by the agents. This is particularly the
case at the micro-economic level, but it is also true, in
the latest presentations of the theory, at the macro-
economic level [3]. In other words, dualist theory seems to
be well and truly based on analysis of a relationship
between agents' strategies, determined both by a desire to
guard against uncertainty and by the processes of the
division of labour [4], and forms of segmentation in the
labour market. Thus firms wishing to guard against these
uncertainties in demand will use particular segments of the
secondary market, such as that represented in France by
temporary contracts ("interim"). On the other hand, workers
seeking a job with guarantees will always have to aim for
employment in the primary sector.

Nevertheless, for those who advance dualist theory the
primary cause of discontinuities in economic structure is
technological evolution. Thus Piore (Berger and Piore,
1980), discussing the control of uncertainty by firms,
writes:

> labour is treated as the residual variable in
> planning and engineering. These processes in
> modern industrial society are essentially
> sequential (rather than simultaneous or
> iterative). One aspect of a plan or
> engineering design is completed before an
> attempt is made to resolve the next. The labor
> component is generally the last factor to
> adjust to other aspects of the economic system
> rather than the other way around (p. 23).

The thesis thus put forward is quite clear: the segments of
the labour market are determined fundamentally by firms' own
plans and the way in which they translate their technological constraints into practices. As a consequence,
analysis of social roles and identities is concerned only
with the ways in which different groups are distributed
among these segments, that is, with the reasons why native
adult males are more likely to occupy the primary segments,
and women, young people, immigrants, etc. are more likely to
occupy the secondary segments. The practices of these groups
have no influence on the determination of the segments but
only adapt to them. At this point, any attempt to understand
the ways in which the segments are socially determined
breaks down [5]. This is perhaps a subtle extension of
Keynesian theory: to the constraints of the product or
financial market are added those arising out of technology
or the optimal utilization of capital assets, in short, out
of the supply side determination of employment practices,
with demand playing an active role only in the supply of the
different segments specifying those practices.

My own conclusion from this brief general survey is
that economic theory puts the structuring role of the demand
for labour at the centre of its analyses of the employment
"market". The most immediate effect of this for macro-
economic studies is the proposition that a law of wage
determination predominates [6], and for micro-economic
studies the almost exclusive emphasis is on firms'
strategies. Meriaux has shown convincingly that this was an
attitude common to most of the teams working in labour
economics, to the point that it was possible to conclude
that a sort of dominant "paradigm" existed in that
discipline [7].

Consequently it is difficult to understand Malinvaud's
classification of economists into two categories: "macro-
economists" who study "the major interdependent forces that
play the dominant role in determining the demand for
labour", and "labour economists" who "analyse in detail the

functioning of the labour market and the factors that
determine the supply of labour from the populace, in particular the demographic factors" (Malinvaud, 1980, p. 28).
The term "macro-economist", on the contrary, seems to me to
describe the essence of labour economics, to the extent that
this latter appears dominated by the problem of the
adaptation of the supply of labour to the productive matrix
determined by demand alone.

Economic theory is thus capable of conceiving a certain
number of dysfunctions linked in particular to poor
adaptability on the part of the labour supply or to a
structural imbalance between the supply of and demand for
labour that is created because supply and demand are
independently determined. This imbalance leads in turn to
unemployment.

But it has no means of conceiving of processes by which
supply and demand for labour might be determined inter-
dependently. The undeniable progress represented by
Keynesian theory concerns only the interdependence of macro-
economic variables, and in particular, of the different
"markets". What is needed, however, is to conceive of a
quite different type of interdependence which does not
assume that the supply of labour adapts to demand, but
which, by clarifying the reciprocal forces that determine
both processes, might cast doubt on the pertinence of the
analytical distinction between these two processes. Perhaps
there is no such thing as supply and demand. Perhaps there
is only one single process to be considered, the process
that determines the wage relationship, for which I have
suggested the term "mobilization" (de Gaudemar, 1979, 1981).
The current difficulties of economic theory seem to make it
necessary to develop a socio-economic theory of mobilization
that would analyse the reciprocal processes that determine
the behaviour of both categories of protagonists and which
would thus jointly take into account their social realities.

The main obstacle to such a procedure is that it comes
up against a much more complex problem, one that is usually
left to micro-sociology. This is the problem of the
relationships between the workings of the "labour market"
and those of social groups affected by these workings. It
may be thought that the abstraction, prevalent in economic
theory, that wage earners or those seeking employment
present themselves armed only with a qualification that
matches the productive criteria imposed by the demand for
labour, is an abstraction which, far from always facilitating analysis, sometimes detracts from its relevance. All
the detailed studies carried out in recent years clearly
show the importance of the ways in which the social

structure influences qualifications, a process that might be called the "territorialization" of the job markets. If we wish to progress beyond a macro-economic theory which ignores the influence of the social structure on employment patterns because of its assumptions of perfect mobility, and micro-sociology that concentrates only on the social influence at the expense of any general economic understanding, it is necessary to develop a theory capable of describing the relationships between the forms of social life in a given area of society and the "labour markets" that operate in that area. It is in this context that I have suggested introducing the notion of "mobilization network" (MN) [8].

II. AN ALTERNATIVE ANALYSIS OF THE LABOUR MARKET: MOBILIZATION NETWORKS

To give the simplest possible definition, the MN describes the set of social relationships which, when activated in a given area, supply the mediumn in which the forms of economic mobilization operate. The term mobilization refers to the concept, defined in earlier studies, of the processes that go to make up labour force structures. Thus the purpose of the notion of MN is to develop a theory of the ways in which employers' hiring policies and the behaviour of wage earners or of those seeking employment converge in the labour market, with regard to their respective places in the corresponding social networks.

This immediately raises some obvious questions. Is it possible to develop a typology of forms of MNs that are sufficiently general and consistent to be of relevance beyond mere local descriptions? What modifications is economic theory likely to undergo as a result of this concept? In what way does it help to illuminate the present situation and to diagnose unemployment? These questions indicate the three main areas of interest.

First, the morphology of labour markets would give way to the morphology of the mobilization network that would, for example, identify and distinguish the institutional and non-institutional forms (legal or otherwise) that are part of the social relationship specific to an urban environment, the collective forms that, in general, require an intermediary or more specific forms linked to adherence to particular territories or networks, or the specialized forms according to occupation, industry sector, etc., and the forms less influenced by social qualifications, but more linked to the mobility of the workforce. In general, the

purpose of this morphology would be to distinguish and thus
to specify the socially well-defined forms from the much
more diffuse or even clandestine forms of mobilization.
    Second, the possibility would arise of providing an
original explanation of employment and unemployment: they
would no longer be seen simply as the outcome of a process
by which the demand for labour determines the total number
of jobs and thus the level of residual unemployment relative
to the supply of labour, but as the outcome of social
situations defined in relationship to the existing forms of
mobilization. Unemployment would thus no longer be thought
of as the difference between the supply of and the demand
for jobs, but in terms of the access to employment, as
defined objectively by the mobilization networks, i.e. in
terms of the social opportunities for individuals to enter
these mobilization networks and to adapt to their dynamics.
Similarly, formal qualifications - to which labour
economists attach so much importance - would appear as only
one of the many factors (and sometimes of only minor
importance) in the determination of employment systems.
    Thirdly, a specific diagnosis of the current crisis and
unemployment would need to relate to the changes that the
mobilization networks are undergoing or have already
undergone. Has the current crisis modified the networks that
have functioned until now to the point that they have
disappeared to be replaced by new ones? On the other hand,
are those seeking work attempting further to activate their
friendship networks and are these networks still as
effective? What proportion of current unemployment, apart
from job losses, is due to the changes in the mobilization
networks? Is the increase checked or accelerated by the
network of social relationships specific to any localized
system and by the effects of this network on the working of
the labour markets?
    Is it possible to construct a rigorous account of
mobilization networks? The basis of my attempt to do so here
will be the notions of "habitus" and "sphere" developed by
Bourdieu (1979, 1980a, 1980b) and others.
    The need for economic theory to incorporate such
notions, or at least to examine their effects, will be
obvious to anyone who recalls that the market is first and
foremost a social sphere, a system of social relationships
that is all too often reduced to its objective, or
economically objectifiable effects, such as prices. There is
no economic system that does not have these "chains of
interdependence" between agents that are, quite rightly, at
the heart of Elias's macro-sociological analysis of social
change (1981). And if the above hypothesis that labour

markets are particular forms of the process by which social
networks are activated is accepted, our starting point must
be the methods used to analyse these systems of social
relationships.

It is certainly possible to define a mobilization
network as a "social sphere", that is, as the area of
relationships that is established when the wage relationship
is determined according to the forces at work in the
mobilization process. From the various definitions given by
Bourdieu (1979, 1980a) in his analysis of various specific
spheres, it can be concluded that the sphere is the social
space in which "some forces manifest themselves only in
their relationship with certain mechanisms" and which, as a
consequence, gives meaning to a social practice. The
"sphere" is an area with a specific purpose, "functioning in
and not for itself". It is thus organized according to
specific regular patterns, and all the actors who confront
each other within it have the same belief in the value of
what happens there.

These specific regular patterns necessary to the smooth
working of a sphere are exactly what Bourdieu calls
"habitus". He defined them as durable and transposable
systems of mechanism, structured entities able to function
also as structuring entities, that is, as the generators and
organizers of practices and representations that can be
objectively adapted to their purpose, but without specific
ends being envisaged and with no direct control over the
processes necessary to attain them, objectively regulated
and regular without in any way being the product of
obedience to rules, and collectively orchestrated without
being organized by a conductor.

The relationship with the habitus is thus likely to
provide the whole range of the ways in which power is
exercised. Conversely, the habitus enables the agents
positively to "occupy" the institutions by means of any
production that is free and compatible with the limits
inherent in any such acquired system of generative schemes.

From this we see that a central part of Bourdieu's
theory of practice is: the practical relationship that an
individual agent has with the future and by which his
present practice is controlled is defined by the
relationship between on the one hand, his habitus, in
particular the temporal structures and mechanisms for
dealing with the future that have been formed during a
particular relationship to a particular sphere of
probabilities, and, on the other hand, the specific state of
the opportunities objectively granted to him by the social
world.

These concepts can be of use in analysing the labour market. It is sufficient to point out the very specific kind of "exchange" described by the term "labour market": it is not goods that are being bought or sold, but a process of subordination presented as exchange of a commodity. Indeed, the wage relationship that is formed when that "exchange" takes place has a meaning solely by virtue of being a relationship of subordination, availability and mobilization, because it makes available to an employer the services of an employee.

The term "labour market" thus first of all described the expression, or, if it is preferred, the realization of a complex social relationship. Thus theories of the "labour market", even more than economic theories of other markets, run the risk of being trapped and locked into the imaginary effects of the social relationship that they are attempting to explain. This is the case, for example, with the theory of perfect mobility, even if it is accompanied by a statement of the policies aimed at overcoming "resistance" and removing the "imperfections" caused by real life behaviour: there is no doubt that it expresses nothing but the imaginary relationship of those who put themselves forward as potential employers with the reality of the methods of domination. To assume that the subordination of the employee to the employer is complete, or could be made so, is to ignore the real problems of how the social relationship in question is achieved.

An attempt might be made to indicate the possible link between the provisional definition that I have put forward for the mobilization networks and theory of the sphere and habitus.

In the context of the existing social networks, the MN is a specific form of economic activation that might at the same time have an influence on other economic behaviour patterns. In this sense, it should turn out to be a "structured entity" by virtue of the social relationships that make up its reference matrix; it would make it possible to conceive of the link between social living conditions and different behaviour patterns inherited from the collective history of the actors. It is undeniable that, behind the idea of the MN, lies the idea of the influence of a structural heritage, the heritage of a trade, for example, or even the determination of a "pool of labour".

But the term "mobilization network" refers also to a social dynamic: it should equally be a "structuring entity", or at the very least be able to function as such. The MN would be both a form of social network and a method of transforming that network, precisely because it is part of

the management not of an intangible social relationship, but
of the "market" of a social relationship. From this point of
view, it is impossible to conceive of the MN as socially
objectified sub-strata, as "rails" or "cables" guiding
individuals from one pigeonhole to another, from one job to
another according to their origin. Such rigid determinism
must be rejected, since what must be understood is the
"sphere" of mobilization, that is, the structure of the
configurations produced by the way in which the agents -
both employers and employees - adapt their patterns of
behaviour to an adverse structure of social relationships
revealed by the behaviour of others. This would be the case
for a firm that decided to move to an area where there was a
supply of labour, but took with it its existing managers. It
would also be the case for workers attempting to "convert" a
friendly relationship with the boss of a firm into a job.

For all that, would it be possible to consider the
mobilization networks as placing strategies in a social
context? In one sense this would be possible, since in this
labour market, each agent would be likely to express a
number of basic aims, such as finding a "good job" or
"competent staff", and to formulate what he would consider
to be the procedures necessary to attain those aims: go to
the job centre, or use the classified advertisements, in
short, activate the obvious social networks in order to
achieve his aim. But the most interesting part of the
hypothesis is that it might be possible to discover MNs,
i.e. regular patterns in the methods of gaining access to
jobs and in the processes that play a major role, even
though none of the actors might be aware that he is obeying
roles. This does not necessarily mean that the MN is the
ordered product of random behaviour patterns. The "habitus"
that would no doubt be functioning here would refer to a
partial randomness subject to the constraints of social
living conditions.

An attempt might finally be made to place this notion
of "mobilization networks" in relation to one of the
important characteristics of the "habitus" such as "the
means by which the institutions are occupied" and thus not
only the means by which the agents are able to behave freely
within institutional constraints but also the reasons why
subjection to constraint and control constitutes perhaps the
principle criterion in judging the efficiency of an
institution. It is immediately obvious that MNs might be
brought to light that are based on an apparently extremely
diffuse social network, or even on a social network far
removed from any immediate institutionalization of the
placement process, but tending, in fact, if not to replace

it at least to play a perfectly complementary role. It is
thus necessary, for example, to consider from a dual point
of view the way in which a firm bases its hiring policy on
the existence of family or immigration networks. When a high
level of family recruitment is observed in a sugar refinery
in the north of Marseilles, this indicates not only a method
of social control, but also means that recruiting procedures
are being made available to a whole district, as soon as the
family network in question expands to cover the district.
The district can then begin to "occupy" the factory in a
sort of consensus in which the factory owner will see a
guarantee of his control and the workers an image of their
community unconnected with their work. This dual perspective
may give rise either to real worker control or to an
alienation comparable to that of the company towns of the
nineteenth century. In a sense, the situation is simpler in
the case of an engineering firm in the east of Marseilles:
the frequent practice among the African workers of offering
their job to a relative while they return for a time to
their own country may indicate only the almost total
interchangeability of jobs that require no qualification. In
this case, the employer can leave control of the recruitment
virtually entirely to the African community, as long as the
work requires no qualification.

  With the aid of Fig.1, which derived from the one
suggested by Bourdieu to take account of lifestyles
(Bourdieu, 1979), it is possible to depict the ways in which
the supply of and the demand for jobs "come together" as a
"sphere" or as the point at which the effects of two
corresponding types of "habitus" intersect. The first of
these types arises out of the conditions in which the firm

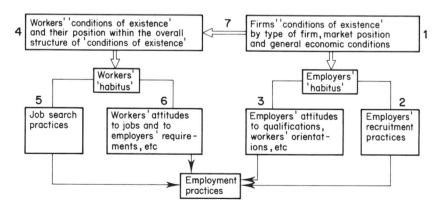

Fig.1   The sphere of mobilization

seeking workers exists. Let the following diagram represent
the "sphere" of mobilization.

Each of the numbers in Fig. 1 corresponds to one of the
elements that make up the "sphere". Broadly speaking, their
significance is as follows:

   i) The purpose here is to analyse the various
      characteristics of the type of firm, its
      sector and main activity, the production
      processes used, organizational structure,
      methods of work organization, productivity,
      profits and accounts, as well as the situation
      of the firm within its sphere, for example,
      its market position.
  ii) The firm's "conditions of existence" would
      thus define the main characteristics of the
      employer's hiring policy: a firm will adjust
      its recruiting policy to the general economic
      situation or the type of job vacancy. It
      might, for example, use permanent shift
      employment, "interim" or fixed-term
      contracts, with each of these different
      methods corresponding to a differet scheme.
 iii) Similarly, the "employer's habitus" would give
      rise to systems of recruitment, i.e. the
      criteria adopted by the firm to define the
      desired job profiles and to hire certain job
      applicants. These criteria would determine the
      employer's attitude towards qualifications
      (one employer might, for example, attach
      importance to formal qualifications whilst
      another would attach none at all) and the
      social area in which the firm would seek its
      potential employees.
  iv) The conditions of existence of the potential
      employees would have to be considered in the
      broadest sense (incomes, standard of living,
      cultural level) in order to cover the maximum
      number of instances in which the social
      network operates. Their position with the
      overall structure of existence affects the
      method of insertion into the social network
      under consideration, including relative social
      position, membership of associations, sports
      clubs, trade unions, political parties, local
      community work.
   v) The practices adopted in the search for
      employment would thus be a product of these

forms of social network. A high level of
social involvement in the local area, town or
profession would be likely to give rise to
considerable exploitation by the individual of
his membership of these networks including
friendship with influential people,
information from drinking companions, more
strictly professional connections, and family.
On the other hand, a lack of such social
involvement, or any form of isolation, might
lead to a greater use of institutional methods
such as job centres or temporary job agencies
and to the subjective feeling of a loss of
self-reliance.

vi) Similarly, the conditions of existence would
determine what is perceived as a "good job".
This perception might appear as explicit
criteria linked directly with the main
characteristics of the conditions of
existence. In a situation of high
unemployment, the criterion of stability would
certainly become very important; in a more
favourable situation, wages, promotion or even
"career" prospects, the appropriateness of the
job to the individual's training or job
satisfaction would play a greater part.
Bourdieu points out in this connection that
negative career potential (leading to
unemployment and underprivilege) is as
important in accounting for the measures taken
by skilled workers as are promotion prospects
in understanding the strategies of salaried
employees and middle managers (Bourdieu,
1979). It is at this level that job
applicants' perception of the requirements of
their potential employers would assume their
full importance since the "habitus" could not
be analysed independently of the effects of
domination, and of the standardization of
behaviour to which they give rise. Both the
perceptions that generate job seeking
strategies and the assessment of the chances
of obtaining a particular job would be largely
determined by the assumed knowledge of this
system of norms. As a result, a job applicant
will present himself to a prospective employer
and draw up his curriculum vitae in a
particular way. Popular perceptions would thus

be made up not only of lessons drawn from
known recruitment practices but also of the
applicant's own perception of employers'
strategies.

vii) This conditioning sequence thus acquires a
dominating effect. This effect would close up
the system for determining employment
practices by attributing the fundamental
leading role to the situation of firms and
their resultant policies. There would be
basically the same effect in the area of
employment that Bourdieu describes in the area
of cultural taste: "Everything points to the
conclusion that the most informed section of
the working class remains extremely
subservient in matters of culture and language
to the dominant norms and values, and thus
extremely sensitive to the effects of
authority imposed, even in the sphere of
politics, by anyone possessing cultural
authority over those in whom their education
system has instilled recognition without
cognition" (Bourdieu, 1979, p. 461).

There is no doubt about the determinist nature of this
conceptualization in terms of "sphere" of mobilization", but
it can be considered as a basically sound reaction to the
refusal by economists to take sociological factors into
account in their analysis of "labour markets".
     This determinism is apparent at several levels: class
position determines class "habitus" in so far as this
"habitus" is normally (i.e. with a high level of statistical
probability) associated with that position. The employers'
positions determine that of the wage earners as a result of
the effects of domination. Finally the schemes generated by
the "habitus" determine practices. It is significant that
Bourdieu often writes in terms of "a high degree of
probability": this is the expression in statistical terms of
this determinism. But as a consequence, it is the density
and interconnection of social relationships that are being
highlighted. The occupation of certain jobs is, for example,
the outcome of a process of entrenchment, of the
incorporation of various norms of behaviour, of the
internalization of inherited domination.
     Making a virtue out of necessity is the driving force
behind such a "sphere" and shows how the notions of "sphere"
and "habitat" can provide a framework, even a methodology,
for studying mobilization networks. It goes beyond

discussion of the exclusive structuring role of the demand
for labour, since it continually stresses the importance, in
the process of generating practices, of schemes that have
their origin as much in workers' objective conditions of
existence as in those of the firms. This is so because it
continually draws attention to neighbourhoods and the
difficulties, even the unlikelihood, of escaping from the
neighbourhoods in which we are raised.

This principle of the conservation of the neighbourhood
is at the centre of sociological interpretation, even when
this neighbourhood is composed of destructured
relationships, marginality and de-socialization. Even if it
becomes a virtue and a strategy for attacking over-
exploitation, the necessity born of the initial conditions
of existence does not determine outcomes. In other words,
necessity is a social destiny, a destiny that is either
loved or hated, improved upon or just tolerated. But it is a
destiny that the individual is very unlikely to escape. And
this is what can be termed a mobilization network: the
regular and specific ways in which the need for firms to
manage as best they can the uncertainties and risks of their
activity merge with the need of those seeking work to
control as best they can the uncertainties and risks
inherent in their conditions of existence [9].

III. MOBILIZATION NETWORKS IN PRACTICE

It was with certain of the above considerations in mind that
the CERS team carried out an initial enquiry with the aim of
testing the hypotheses put forward about mobilization
networks and thus of providing an empirical basis for the
notion. There follow a few remarks on this enquiry and on
the general conclusions that make it possible to suggest
that the theory outlined here is a relevant one [10].

In view of our theoretical preoccupations, it seemed to
us essential to interview both managers and wage earners.
Not only had we learnt to recognize the limits of enquiries
based on interviews with either managers or employees [11],
but our aim to reach some understanding of the functioning
of the "sphere" of mobilization made this approach
essential. It was fundamental to this point of view to be
able to interview the managers and employees of the same
firm. We did this every time that we were able to do so. In
one sense, therefore, we used the firm as the basis of our
enquiry, with the deliberate aim of questioning - through
the confrontation between the two parts of the enquiry - the
dominant paradigm in labour economics, according to which

only the strategies of firms are worthy of consideration in
an analysis of the structure of the "labour market".
Similarly, we also used individuals as our starting point,
if only because of the survey techniques used, but with a
very different point of view from that of methodological
individualism.

In fact, our aim was not to gain an understanding of
the network of relationships used by a particular individual
when seeking employment, but to locate that individual in
his own environment by attempting to understand the types of
behaviour and social relationships that might account for
his employment situation within the firm that was employing
him at the time of the enquiry, with reference to the
behaviour of the firm itself.

The important thing here is the relationship between
the strategies of the agents and their respective social
backgrounds. This made it necessary to introduce into our
questionnaires, in addition to strictly economic questions
on production and employment, questions on local social
networks, on the relationships between the firm and the
local area, on the circumstances that determine career paths
and recruitment policies, and on the different methods used
in contacts between employers and employees.

One important characteristic of our enquiry is that it
introduces a clear distinction between the initial meeting
between the employer and the person seeking work and the
subsequent selection process. This distinction, the need for
which is shown by the limits of a study like that of
Granovetter (1973, 1974), proved to be very fruitful from
the point of view of the typological analysis of recruitment
policies and mobilization policies.

The scope of our enquiry and our sample were
constructed with reference to the structure of activities in
Marseilles. We wanted to take into account the very wide
range of economic activity in that city, in particular the
importance of the tertiary sector in such a town. There is
already too strong a tendency in labour economics to focus
exclusively on industrial firms, with the result that little
attention has been paid to tertiary activities, particularly
in urban environments.

On the other hand, in order to limit ourselves to
consistent categories, in which relatively little was known
of their recruiting methods, we restricted ourselves
principally to manual and clerical workers.

Our sample divides into two basic parts. The first
contains only industrial firms and concentrates on an old
industrial quarter undergoing radical change. The bias of
our enquiry reveals our aim of attempting to understand the

possible future transformations of the mobilization networks
linked to this pronounced trend towards de-industrial-
ization. The second part focusses on tertiary activities in
the town centre: large stores, small specialist shops, banks
and local government.

The various patterns of behaviour revealed by our
enquiry can be related to two main types of "spheres" or
processes of mobilization, either in that they conform to
one or the other, or in that they borrow, according to more
complex processes, from both.

The first brings into play mobilization networks that
can be described as "closed" in the sense that the spheres
of the initial contact between firms and those seeking
employment are so circumscribed socially and geographically
- at the neighbourhood level, for example - that they
basically define the subsequent selection process. They are
thus the "habitus" specific to the social network of the
area which appear to regulate the "sphere" of mobilization.
The relationships between a firm or a group of firms and
their social environment thus become part of the history of
this social network, and help to define it. The behaviour
patterns of the various agents involved internalize, on the
one hand, the requirements of the production activity, and
on the other, those of the local conditions of existence and
social reproduction.

The second type brings into play mobilization networks
that can be described in contrast as "open", in the sense
that initial contacts and selection methods are clearly
distinct from each other, that the area of origin of job
applicants may be all the wider since the "sphere" is
basically structured around selection methods, and that
these latter tend towards optimal objectification of their
own criteria in relation to the economic aim of the firms
concerned, to the extent that they sometimes appear to be
totally independent of any given social environment. The
firm appears all the more socially isolated the more
recently it has been established or if it is located in
either a declining area or one which has been artificially
created.

Despite their very limited use of formal selection
criteria, the large stores in the Centre Bourse can be
located in this way, as can the chemical firms in the
industrial area, although in a different way, that attach
greater importance to formal qualifications. The importance
of the fact that our enquiry was carried out in an urban
environment now becomes clear: the city can, better than any
other area, act as the inexhaustible reservoir necessary to
the ideal functioning of these mobilization networks.

To take up again the language habitually used by
economists, it could be said that the first type corresponds
quite closely to the theory of "reserves of labour", whereas
the second corresponds to the "labour market" as postulated
by economic theory. And it may be, if my description were
widened slightly, that these two models of "spheres" would
reflect the major divisions – some of which are implicit –
in the dualist theories of segmentation.

But for most of the firms in our sample these two
models are only extremes. Most firms in practice use
mobilization processes that borrow from both models.
Analysis of the different "spheres" of mobilization and
their specific networks seems to be indispensable, even if
the only aim is an economic understanding of the urban
"labour market".

The enquiry also highlights an important aspect of the
evolution of employment in Marseilles, since it clearly
reveals a shift in its spatial organization. On the one hand
there is the old system, where there is a concept of
"territory" in which, according to the characteristics of
the first model, there is overall and local regulation of
the job market. If the economic situation is favourable in
the long term, there is full employment or recruitment of
external labour. On the other hand, in times of recession,
the relative occupational and social immobility of the
population will give rise to a certain level of employment.
A certain duality in the local market can thus be observed,
but the overall social regulation lessens the traumatizing
effects of this, since, with a few exceptions, those
temporarily excluded from employment continue to belong to
the social network that constitutes a sort of guarantee of
employment in the future. It may be easier to consider
unemployment as temporary and thus more bearable, because
of the social and local nature of the recognized
qualifications and because of the support, particularly
within the framework of the family, that this social network
can provide.

On the other hand, there is the new system. Here, there
is a process of de-territorialization at work, along the
lines of the second model. In this case the social
consequences of recession are quite different. A first
typical example would be the closure of local firms. In a
socially de-structured area, there can be no local
regulation similar to that outlined above. The only
solutions are mobility for the younger people, forced
retirement for the older ones on the basis of a reduced and
dehumanized social structure, and unemployment for the rest.
For the middle-aged, mobility would be socially painful and

uncertain, because of the characteristics of the
qualifications formerly required, which in any case would
probably not be recognized elsewhere. In general, the
consequence would be higher and more traumatizing
unemployment and an increased likelihood of emigration from
the area. A second, less well-documented, but doubtless
still valid example, would be for local firms not to close
but to make workers redundant, while at the same time
changing their recruitment strategies. They may do this for
various reasons, not all connected with recession. They may
be reorganized, taken over, or there may be a change of
management. The transition from a largely "closed" process
of mobilization to a mainly "open" process will have a
profound effect on all the local regulating mechanisms.
There will no longer be any structural correspondence
between the functioning of the local social network and the
firms' recruiting strategies. Firms might well begin to
recruit from other sources, or hire people with different
qualifications. A social equilibrium based on a long process
of mutual apprenticeship is undermined. In an extreme case,
the whole shape of the local area, or indeed the whole town,
may be transformed. The inevitable consequence is local
unemployment and enforced mobility, even if there are no
redundancies or closures.
        However, it is clear from the enquiry that a town like
Marseilles is subject to such changes. The examples of the
firms in the Centre Bourse, or of the chemical firms in the
industrial area seem to confirm the gradual dominance of the
second process of de-territorialization, unless the
development of some firms can be interpreted optimistically
as heralding the emergence of a third process of re-
territorialization. The town appears to be experiencing the
double effect of closures and of the re-definition of
recruitment strategies. While it is possible to be
reasonably optimistic for the young people who have the
opportunity of being trained to the standards of technical
skill and productivity that correspond to the increasing
demand for formal qualifications, or who accept that they
will have to leave the area, it is difficult to be
optimistic about the outlook for the other groups. At a
particular disadvantage are those young people whose only
qualifications are diplomas without any market value, either
as a consequence of the usual selective mechanisms of
compulsory education or as a result of a tradition that
assigned them, on leaving school, to a particular job (e.g.
the factory where one or other of the parents works), a
tradition in which the school is only of peripheral significance within a set of inherited arrangements. Also at risk

are adults, men and women, for whom the necessary re-
training seems almost inaccessible in that it requires not
only additional training, but also a complete change in
their behaviour, and even uprooting from their environment.
   In this sense, the enquiry reveals that what is at
stake in the economic crisis in Marseilles is the town
itself as it functions at the moment, or rather as it has
functioned until now, with the specific networks that are a
product of its history. If some of these networks at least
have had their day, is it not because the traditional
activities that still use them are now unable to provide
employment for a growing population?
   Clearly what is in question is not only the economic
recession, nor even the ability of such a town to attract
new industries, but the fact that the town and its people
are closing in on themselves and on the rigidities of their
inherited behaviour patterns, in the possibly unfounded
belief that they are still valid. It is by no means certain
that, faced with such a situation, increasing municipal aid
has any other effect than to put off the day of reckoning,
or even to strengthen the roots of the problem.
   What is at stake is perhaps the ability of the town to
come up with a real process of re-territorialization and to
become, without renouncing the essence of its cultural
heritage, an open area, inhabited by versatile people, who
are sometimes voluntarily mobile, able to adapt to the new
requirements of productive mobilization and to some degree
of flexibility of functions, and thus able to change the
corresponding "sphere" of forces in their favour.

NOTES

1. I shall use the term "labour market" from time to time;
    it is in common usage amongst economists, but I shall
    put it between quotation marks in order to indicate the
    problematical nature of such a concept.
2. E. Malinvaud (Malinvaud, 1980, p. 49 et seq.). A fixed
    price model is not a model in which prices are fixed
    and constant but one in which prices are autonomous in
    relation to supply and demand and to production and
    consumption. This is no doubt an acceptable hypothesis
    in the case of short-term equilibriums. "Rationing" is
    a view of general equilibrium seen from the point of
    view of the equilibrium of purchases and sales and not
    only of supply and demand.
3. See particularly the article by M. Piore in Revue
    Economique (1978).

4. This is pointed out by A. Azouvi in his paper "Theorie et pseudo-theorie: le dualisme du marche du travail", published in Critique de l'Economie Politique, 1980.
5. On this point I agree with the criticism of Berger and Piore's book made on several occasions by Azouvi, even if it seems to me to be put in a way that rather underestimates the real problem.
6. See particularly Aglietta in Revue Economique (1978).
7. See his article in Revue Economique (1978).
8. See the gradual development of this notion in de Gaudemar et al. (1981) and the various elements of the corresponding debate within the DGRST group.
9. The interesting article by Pialoux (1979) might be considered to be an illustration of this problem.
10. This is a brief summary of the more detailed analysis made by Centi in de Gaudemar et al. (1981) and de Gaudemar et al. (1982), in which the data referred to will be found; the interpretations suggested here are mine.
11. The particular importance of a study like de Gaudemar et al. (1980) is to show both the explanatory value and the limitations of these two types of surveys. In this sense, it is an important step in the research programme presented here.

REFERENCES

Berger, S. and Piore, M.J. (1980). "Dualism and Discontinuity in Industrial Societies". Cambridge University Press, Cambridge.
Bourdieu, P. (1979). "La Distinction - Critique Sociale du Jugement". Editions de Minuit.
Bourdieu, P. (1980). "Le Sens Pratique". Editions de Minuit.
Bourdieu, P. (1980) "Questions de Sociologie". Editions de Minuit.
Critique de l'Economie Politique (1980). Numéro Spécial, "Segmentation de l'emploi ou division du salariat?" No. 15-16, April-June.
L'Ecole de Chicago (1979). Naissance de l'écologie urbain. Ouvrage presenté par Grafmeyer, Y. and Joseph, I. La Champ Urbain.
Elias, N. (1981). "Qu'est-ce que la Sociologie?". Pandora Editions.
de Gaudemar, J.P. (1979). "La Mobilisation Générale". La Champ Urbain.
de Gaudemar, J.P. et al. (1980). "Usines et Ouvriers,

Figures du Nouvel Ordre Producti". Maspero, Coll.
    Luttes Sociales.
de Gaudemar, J.P. et al. (1981). Réseaux de mobilisation et
    marchés du travail en milieu urbain. Rapport DGRST No.
    80.7.0313 - CERS, October.
de Gaudemar, J.P. and Centi, C. et al. (1982). Réseaux de
    mobilisation et marchés du travail en milieu urbain.
    Rapport complémentaire DGRST No. 81.E.0236 - CERS,
    February.
Granovetter, M. (1973). The strength of weak ties. American
    Journal of Sociology, 78.
Granovetter, M. (1974). "Getting a Job". Harvard
    University Press, Boston.
Holland, P.W. and Leinhardt, S. (eds.) (1979). "Perspectives
    on Social Network Research". Academic Press, London and
    Orlando.
Lorrain, F. (1975). "Réseaux Sociaux et Classifications
    Sociales; Essai sur l'Algèbre et la Géométrie des
    Structures Sociales". Hermann.
Malinvaud, E. (1980). "Reexamen de la Théorie du Chômage".
    Calmann-Levy.
Pialoux, M. (1979). Jeunesse sans avenir et travail
    intérimaire. Actes de la Recherche en Sciences
    Sociales, 26-27, April-June.
Revue Economique. (1978). Numéro spéciale: Emploi et
    chômage, 1.
Vernieres, M. et al. (1979). "Les Marchés Locaux du
    Travail". La Documentation Française, Coll.
    Planification et Société.

Assignment of Women Workers to Jobs and Company Strategies in France

C. DUTOYA and A. GAUVIN

I. INTRODUCTION

The analysis of the structuring of the system of employment in French industry which this paper attempts to draw up hypotheses about the processes by which women workers are assigned to specific jobs. In addition, links between labour resources and job categories are examined. When economists specializing in labour problems deal with differences between men and women workers, they generally focus on qualifications and training, on concentration within specific sectors of the economy, or on wages and benefits; alternatively, they emphasize institutional or sociological factors such as union membership. These elements are held to interact and thereby in practice to explain each other.
    Without denying the importance of these factors, we hope to broaden the analysis of the conditions of working class women by taking into account the characteristics of work situations (job content, working environment, etc.) in industries where women are employed. The scarcity of relevant data (especially macroeconomic) largely explains the neglect of this area. In addition, the study of working conditions has been almost universally disregarded by economists and left to sociology and ergonomics. It is, however, essential to the understanding of the social and

economic basis of women's work.

After presenting information on the situation of women employees in France, and on the developments in the utilization and recruitment of "female labour", we describe the content of women workers' jobs with data from a 1978 survey carried out by the Ministry of Labour and National Institute of Statistics and Economic Studies (INSEE). Finally, this empirical analysis is then used to confront interpretations of labour market segmentation. We then advance hypotheses about the bases and nature of the sex segregation in employment and also about company strategies for personnel management in the recruiting and assigning of women to industrial jobs.

II. THE SITUATION OF WOMEN EMPLOYEES IN FRANCE

There has been a tremendous growth in the employment of women during the last 20 years in France as in all Western countries (Bouillaguet, Gauvin, Outin, 1961). It has been maintained that in spite of the generally worsening economic situation, women have not yet been forced out of the labour market. On the contrary, they have been taking up jobs in greater numbers (Table I). The proportion of working women in relation to all women has considerably increased, particularly for the age group between 25 and 40, from 40% in 1962 to 58% in 1980.

Table I. Working women as a percentage of all women above the age of 15

	Census Office %	Employment Survey (INSEE) %
1954	37.8	–
1962	36.2	–
1968	36.2	38.6
1970	–	38.9
1975	38.7	40.8
1980	–	43.4

Women have been integrated into the production process
as the latter has been restructured and as more and more
income earners have become employees with legally recognized
employment contracts, i.e. the proportion of self-employed
and family workers in the labour force has declined. In
1962, 69% of working women had this employment status, in
1975 85%. The expansion of female wage employment must be
related to changes in production itself (Bouillaguet, Germe,
1981), and to the sexual division of labour.

The usual explanations relating to physiological
differences between the sexes or changes in behaviour and
attitudes which purport to explain both the larger number of
women in the workforce and the types of jobs in which they
are found must be rejected. These explanations centre around
modifications on the supply side of the labour market, i.e.
the willingness or readiness of women to take jobs. The
explanation of women's activities and occupations must
instead come from an analysis that links the demand for
women workers with the necessity of using them for
productive purposes within a system of employment.

Jobs in the tertiary sector and office work particularly attract women. During the 1960s, however, as more
women were taking up wage employment, industry was hiring
more women, particularly in sectors such as mechanical
engineering, electronics and electrical appliances, which
had not taken on many women previously. Up until 1975, these
sectors, along with those producing durable and semi-
finished goods, led the growth in employment. Thereafter,
jobs declined in these sectors more rapidly than in others.

Table II. Percentage of women in worker categories

	1968 %	1980 %
Women among skilled workers	14	11
Women among semi-skilled workers	23	28
Women among un-skilled workers	37	47

Source: Enquête sur l'Emploi, INSEE

Nevertheless, this downturn has apparently had less effect
upon the number of working women than upon those of male co-
workers.

The position of women in employment indicates that
women have tended to acquire jobs in industry that have been
downgraded, for instance, operatives' jobs in highly
automated assembly lines. Statistics in Table II show
womens' structural role in industrial employment.

The limitations of aggregate data on female workers'
qualifications must be recognized (Cezard, 1979). In the
first place, each category covers jobs that differ widely
according to the production unit, industry, etc. Two workers
in the same job can be placed in different categories
depending, in particular, on the relative strength of the
workers and their representatives within their company or
industry. Also, a more general problem arises - recognizing
the qualifications or skills required for a given job and
applying the corresponding pay scale. The dexterity and pace
of work demanded of women workers are often neither
recognized nor paid as skills, even though they do serve as
necessary conditions for recruitment. In many cases, they
are learned during long periods of on-the-job experience and
in fact, the need for a lengthy apprenticeship of this type
may constitute a reason for selecting women. Sexual
differentiation is therefore probably directly related to
such under-recognition of qualifications or skills. As a
consequence, the contention that women workers are less
qualified or skilled than men, while still possibly valid,
needs to be handled carefully as a full explanation of
women's employment position (Craig, Garnsey, Rubery, 1985).

Going beyond aggregate national data, we need to pay
attention to the different patterns of recruitment of women
(both the quantity of women recruited, and the positions
into which they are recruited) which are linked to the
dynamic forces shaping economic activities and labour
markets at the local level. Local considerations intervene
along with factors related to the production process, such
as technology or the organization of work.

Three factors apparently affect the conditions for
recruiting and using women. They have to do with
geographical employment areas, technical and economic
aspects of production and characteristics of companies.
Studies of local labour markets can isolate further
criteria, such as regional traditions of women working. At
the level of the production unit with a given socio-economic
context, other key criteria can be adduced: technology and
the nature of the product; industry characteristics; size of
establishment; the latter's incorporation within an

industrial group; the position, dominant or otherwise, of
the firm within the local labour market; and the production
process itself.

III. DIFFERENCES IN JOBS AND WORKING CONDITIONS BETWEEN MEN
AND WOMEN WORKERS

In France in 1978, the Ministry of Labour and INSEE carried
out, for the first time, a national survey about the working
conditions of personnel with employment contracts. As a
result, totally new information is available about the
amount, division and control of time spent at work, job
content, the constraints on work rhythms, the repetitiveness
of movements, and also environmental factors such as noise,
lighting, heat, dust and dirt. The following comments are
based on this survey's general findings (Enquête, 1979 and
1980) and from a special processing (Dutoya, Germe, 1981) of
its data relative to branches of the economy where women
workers play a significant role: on the one hand, in
agriculture-related industries ("agro-industries") including
food processing firms and the fertilizer and pesticide
industries, and on the other hand, in electronics and
electrical appliances, hereafter referred to as "electrical
industries".

Sexual discrimination in types of work (Table III) is
quite strong even when workers apparently have equivalent
qualifications. Women are much more concentrated in
explicitly manufacturing jobs, which occupy 51% of skilled
women workers and 60% of the semi-skilled. Many also work in
processing and packaging, but few supervise or repair
machines.

Because Table III combines data on all sectors of the
economy, it must be interpreted carefully. For example,
since the law formally forbids putting women on nightshifts,
few hold jobs usually done at that time, such as repairing
equipment or overseeing machines in operation. Nor do many
women hold jobs in plants with robots or automatic machinery
that runs all day and night. Furthermore, job categories are
sometimes difficult to compare, especially because of
collective bargaining agreements in different industries.

Similar data for agro-industries and the electrical
industries refine the analysis, even though the afore-
mentioned criticisms are merely moderated but not eliminated. In these two sectors, certain jobs and levels of
activity are the almost exclusive prerogative of men,
namely; maintaining, repairing and adjusting machines;
supervisory work; and transporting goods inside and outside

Table III. Qualifications and principal types of work: percentages of men and women workers

Type of work	Skilled workers		Semi-skilled workers		Unskilled workers		All workers from apprentices to foremen	
	M	W	M	W	M	W	M	W
Mamufacturing	39.5	51.0	31.8	60.0	20.5	12.2	33.0	41.7
Stock & dispatch	2.8	4.7	7.0	6.2	41.7	11.0	8.8	7.5
Processing and packaging	0.6	3.8	1.6	9.4	3.1	7.7	1.3	7.6
Maintenance, repairs, adjustments	29.7	4.9	13.7	1.2	6.6	4.4	20.8	3.1
Machine minding	3.9	2.6	5.3	3.4	2.7	1.2	4.1	2.5
Taking care of buildings & grounds (janitors, watchmen etc.)	2.6	1.7	3.9	1.4	8.1	51.0	3.5	17.6
Misc. including transport	20.9	31.3	36.7	18.4	17.3	12.5	28.5	20.0
Total (%)	100	100	100	100	100	100	100	100
Total (in thousands)	2664	349	1746	768	662	555	5720	1703

Source: Enquête Nationale sur les Conditions de Travail, 1978.

Table IV. Qualifications and principal types of work in two industries: men and women as percentages of total numbers at given skill levels (i)

Type of work	Electronics and electrical appliance industries								Food processing, fertilizer and pesticide industries							
	Total workers		Skilled workers		Semi-skilled workers		Unskilled workers		Total workers		Skilled workers		Semi-skilled workers		Unskilled workers	
	M	W	M	W	M	W	M	W	M	W	M	W	M	W	M	W
Manufacturing	40.4	68.5	44.9	85.8	44.8	71.8	20.5	16.8	36.3	22.3	54.6	42.9	23.7	27.4		21.9
Stock and dispatch				10.9			49.4	30.4	12.2	15.7			11.2		49.9	29.7
Processing and packaging										46.2		33.3		53.3	17.6	42.5
Maintenance	20.4		22.6		23.1				13.9		24.4		10.9			
Machine minding													11.6			
Transportation									13.9				28.4			
Taking care of buildings and grounds								35.0								
Total numbers	178501	145913	94615	26871	46395	99369	13709	15933	3080951	95934	106078	15496	140879	44471	39397	33895

(i) Only the most significant percentages are given; therefore columns do not total 100%

Source: Enquête Nationale sur les Conditions de Travail, 1978.

plants. What Table IV does not show is that the few female shift-leaders or forewomen perform jobs similar to those of skilled male workers.

These male tasks are not generally physically arduous and are freer, more independent – less subject to temporal constraints. Moreover, they do not a priori imply high qualifications. Comparing Table V with the preceding tables can provide some interesting deductions.

Apart from areas exclusively reserved for men, differences between the sexes show up in various ways in the agro- and the electrical industries. To give an example, in the latter sector 58.1% of manufacturing jobs go to women, but 83.9% of manufacturing jobs in the former section go to men.

These differences in job assignments cannot be reduced to differences in qualifications. Skilled male workers are divided between manufacturing and maintenance jobs, whereas skilled women are mostly in manufacturing (and also in processing in the agro-industries). Moreover, men classified as unskilled in the agro-industries are distributed between the production line itself, maintenance services and transportation departments. Unskilled women in both sectors are more concentrated in manufacturing, processing and packaging.

Table V. Percentage of workers in given jobs under strict time constraints

Type of work	%
Manufacturing	29.0
Stock and dispatch departments	23.0
Processing and packaging	45.8
Maintaining, repairing and adjusting machines	3.7
Machine minding	54.8
Transportation within the firm	14.8
Transportation outside the firm	0.5
Staffing and organizing work	2.2
All jobs	17.6

Source: Enquête sur les conditions de travail. In Statistiques du Travail, Supplement 84, 1980.

The national survey brings to light distinct differences in working conditions between men and women workers,
even within categories with equivalent qualifications. In
terms of job-related constraints (Table VI), women are less
subject to physical strains such as remaining standing or
carrying heavy loads, but more liable to time pressures from
working on assembly lines or having to keep up predetermined
rates of work. With regard to the environment (Table VII),
women are somewhat less exposed to noise and heat, but more
often subjected to disciplinary controls which, for instance, keep them from talking or impose strict schedules
(Molinie, Volkoff, 1980).

These overall findings can be refined by reference to
our two sectors. Accordingly, Table VIII describes sexual
differences in working conditions for certain job classifications and personnel categories. Predominantly male
workers' manufacturing jobs in agro-industries are compared
with predominantly female workers' jobs, namely manufacturing in the electrical industries and food processing in
agro-industries. The conditions of skilled workers in both
branches – two-thirds male in the one and two-thirds female
in the other – are also compared.

Two criteria distinguish male and female job classifications and categories. The first is repetitiveness: the
more repetitive a job, the higher the probability that a
woman does it. The second is physical effort, particularly
the requirement to remain standing, which falls propor-
tionally less upon women.

Men and women definitely do not participate alike in
the production process. Men tend to take priority in
ancillary jobs characterized, independently of qualifications, by a degree of autonomy or a margin of manoeuvre.
Women tend to be concentrated in central jobs in
manufacturing and product processing that are "rationalized"
to the utmost and split up into short sequences of
repetitive movements.

These findings show that the apparent mixing of the
sexes within production units can cover elaborate discriminatory practices and even juxtapose exclusively male shops
with mainly female ones. Hence, we can hypothesize that
company strategies connect choices in the organization of
work and in production with choices and practices concerning
personnel management, particularly the utilization of
segments of the labour force. There is, in fact, a relative
homogeneity in the assignment of women workers to jobs.

Table VI. Job related constraints: percentage within each
skill level: men and women separately

Type of constraints	Skilled workers		Semi-skilled workers		Unskilled workers		All workers from apprentices to foremen	
	M	W	M	W	M	W	M	W
Work on assembly lines	2.2	15.1	7.7	26.5	8.1	9.1	4.5	18.3
Keep up with tempos set by moving products	3.6	6.3	7.1	16.5	7.9	5.2	5.0	10.6
Keep up with tempos set by machines	8.5	11.2	14.8	25.7	16.4	8.7	11.0	16.8
Have to fill production quotas	33.5	37.1	27.3	42.6	23.7	23.6		
Have to remain standing	73.7	44.4	57.8	49.8	77.8	81.7	68.6	59.5
Have to remain in other uncomfortable positions	32.6	31.1	23.2	29.7	19.6	18.7	26.4	26.1
Have to carry heavy loads	40.9	17.5	39.0	18.5	49.3	20.9	39.8	19.2

Source: Enquête Nationale sur les Conditions de Travail, 1978

Table VII. Environmental factors: percentage within each skill level: for men and women separately.

Environmental factors	Skilled workers		Semi skilled workers		Unskilled workers		All workers from apprentices to foremen	
	M	W	M	W	M	W	M	W
Cannot hear someone speaking to them	6.9	2.9	9.2	8.8	7.1	3.8	7.5	5.8
Work in constantly or frequently high temperatures	31.8	26.5	31.1	26.9	32.5	14.5	31.0	22.8
Work in constantly or frequently low temperatures	26.9	12.4	24.6	14.7	33.3	9.7	26.4	12.6
Cannot speak to workers for reasons other than noise e.g. disciplinary rules	1.7	11.2	3.3	11.1	2.2	5.9	2.2	9.4
quotas and tempos	5.5	12.4	6.8	13.4	6.9	5.0	5.8	10.3
Have schedules controlled by time-clocks	27.1	32.6	30.6	56.4	29.8	23.4	27.2	40.4

Source: Enquete Nationale sur les Conditions de Travail, 1978.

Table VIII. The sexual differentiation of work-related constraints in two industries

	Food processing, fertilizer and pesticide industries		Electronics and electrical appliances industries
Unskilled workers with:	Manufacturing (predominantly male) %	Processing and Packaging (predominantly female) %	Manufacturing (predominantly female) %
Repetitive jobs	55.6	74.0	86.3
Technical constraints on time	41.8	36.6	30.9
Production quotas	31.3	19.7	56.1
Under supervision	20.9	22.5	30.5
Assembly line	23.0	54.9	20.0
Standing position	90.6	79.5	48.1
Skilled workers with:	(two-thirds male) %		(two-thirds female) %
Repetitive jobs	52.6		69.0
Technical constraints on time	48.2		31.1
Production quotas	24.8		53.4
Under supervision	20.5		32.3
Assembly line	27.5		27.4
Standing position	62.9		37.8

IV. THE ASSIGNMENT OF WOMEN WORKERS TO JOBS IN INDUSTRY

Our study shows that the sexes are compartmentalized into different parts of the industrial job structure. Labour market segmentation theory offers a possible theoretical explanation of this segregation by sex. However, in our view, segmentation theory as traditionally formulated does not offer a satisfactory explanation. This is particularly true of those models that examine primarily the process of allocation of workers between different jobs in the labour market, without examining the nature of the labour process that these jobs entail (Blassel, Germe, Michon, 1979; Edwards, 1979). In this section we examine the factors that have been used in segmentation theory as the main bases for divisions in the employment structure against the experience of women in the French labour market, and suggest an alternative explanation of the main divide between male and female employment.

Whatever factor is said to cause segmentation, and however many segments or divisions in the labour force are proposed, there is a general expectation that women workers will be found mainly in the secondary or lowest segment. This hypothesis is put forward in Piore's 1980 theory of dualism.

Segmentation theory argues that economic, techno-logical, social and institutional factors combine and interact to structure the employment system. However, there are five main factors that are commonly put forward as the main explanation of a division between primary and secondary employment, or between male and female employment. These are skill levels, characteristics of establishments, trade unionism and employment stability. The usefulness of these criteria for explaining sex segregation in the French labour market is discussed below, and compared to the criterion of differences in working conditions which has formed the basis for this study of women's employment position.

A. Skill Levels

Skill levels or qualifications cannot be used as a basis for explaining segmentation or sex segregation. First, there are difficulties in comparing skills between different technologies and industrial contexts; secondly, there are differences in the extent to which skill levels are officially recognized, and here the existence of formal training or apprenticeship may be more important than job content; thirdly, sex segregation affects the recognition of

skills. However, it is also clear that women workers are
engaged on work requiring a wide range of skill levels, and
that this criterion cannot therefore explain sex segregation
alone.

B. Establishment Characteristics

Two frequently overlapping criteria for segmentation within
the industrial structure are commonly put forward: on the
one hand, large and small firms, and on the other, core and
peripheral firms. These criteria may be relevant for some
economies, including possibly the USA, but in France
secondary jobs and secondary workers are not only found
small and peripheral production units. Women in particular
are found employed in both large and small firms, and in
both core and peripheral sectors.

C. Trade Unionism

A criterion for segmentation such as unionized firms or
firms with closed shops sometimes suggested, for example,
for the US or the UK labour market, would have no relevance
in the French labour market with its different historical
traditions of industrial relations and union organization.
Union organization is less workplace centred in France.
Moreover, women are as likely to join unions as men in
certain industries, although their domestic roles may affect
their attitudes towards unions and their influence within
the union.

D. Employment Stability

Employment stability is commonly associated with labour
market segmentation but there is a general confusion between
stability of _jobs_ and stability of the _labour force_. This
confusion occurs at various different levels: companies may
provide both stable and unstable jobs for secondary workers
or women; low pay is not necessarily associated with
instability of the labour force as, in the case of women
workers, companies use strategies other than high pay to
secure stability, such as working-time arrangements to fit
family commitments or time off to look after sick children.
    However, although women workers are not inherently
unstable, companies do make use of the tendency for women to
quit the labour force in their employment strategies. Women
are therefore allocated to demanding and tightly controlled

jobs particularly at the start of their working life. By the
time they come to quit the labour force to have children
they no longer have the aptitude nor the physical stamina
for these jobs. The companies benefit from this labour turnover as it enables them to replace the older women with
younger, more suitable women. As Kergoat remarks (1978, p.80):

> If we observe typically feminine factories ...
> we notice that the type of work therein
> necessitates a young labour force whose
> physical soundness enables it to occupy jobs
> that require being meticulous (hence the need
> to have sharp eyesight) and being able to
> withstand a generally fast pace.

However, firms may be less able to pursue such strategies in
the future because of the increasing tendency for women to
remain in employment.

This employment strategy makes it clear that career
advancement, or internal labour market systems, are linked
to the question of worker instability. Women workers,
because of their tendency to quit the labour force are often
denied the chance for promotion and career advancement:

> Temporal discontinuity in the wage-earning
> life of women workers often goes along with
> discontinuity in skills, i.e. massive dequali-
> fication that worsens with age.
>   (Kergoat, 1978, p.81)

Moreover, many women may be forced into job mobility not
because of their own tendency to quit the labour force or to
change jobs, but because of the instability of the jobs in
which they are employed. firms can provide unstable jobs for
women because women are not included in a promotion chain or
career path.

E. Quality of Working Conditions

Our study shows that there do exist systematic differences
in the quality or type of working conditions between male
and female jobs. Working conditions typical of male jobs are
not necessarily uniformly good, but they are different from
those typical of female jobs. Male jobs have certain
specific requirements such as physical strength, and female
jobs have others such as time constraints and repetitiveness. Moreover, the latter type of jobs are found within

particular stages of the production process.

However, while not denying the heterogeneity of working conditions for women workers between industrial sectors and between firms, it does appear that women workers do form a homogeneous group in so far as they have the capacity to work on a permanent basis in jobs which require low or unrecognized qualifications, but which are repetitive, time-constrained and strictly controlled. It is this capacity, rather than their "supply side" characteristics (such as unstable workers) that provide the main basis for differentiation or segmentation between male and female employment.

This analysis contradicts interpretations which suggest that women are confined to particular industrial or labour market segments. Sex segregation, based on these differences in working conditions, is found in both secondary and lower tier primary markets, and is found with high-skilled and low-skilled employment areas. Sex segregation or discrimination therefore cuts across segments, and women's employment cannot be characterized by differences in qualifications or skill, pay, industrial segment or trade union organization. Employment strategies designed to use the capacity of women to tolerate constrained and repetitive working conditions, or designed to use women's tendency to quit the labour market to have children, are the prime cause of sex segregation of employment. This analysis provides a way of linking the employment position of, for example, female manual workers and female office workers, and indicates that the traditional criteria for describing segmented labour markets may obscure the main dividing lines within the employment structure.

V. CONCLUSIONS

At this point, an explanation must be proposed for the previously mentioned ways in which female labour is used. The origins of compartmentalization must be further analysed. We must look into the future.

A preliminary remark can be made: the compartmentalization of masculine/feminine jobs goes back to social stereotypes about the place of women (as "caring", as raising children, etc.) outside work and to their supposedly natural attributes (dexterity, attention to detail, etc.). Even when these stereotypes do not determine women workers' positions in industry, employers still make widespread use of them to justify discriminatory practices when making job assignments. Similarly, it is often said that a woman's

investment in the company is limited or that her job
commitment is slight. Companies accept these stereotypes and
put them into practice by the use of strategies which give
women inferior jobs.

Our findings raise the question of women's orientation
to work – reluctant acceptance, aversion or disinterest
(Linhart, 1981). Women's relationships to their jobs diverge
from men's, without their necessarily having less commitment
initially (Eymard-Duvernay, 1981). The image or conception
of women workers' jobs seems to differ. Two points
contribute to explain this. First of all, the tradion of
working women exists but differs from that of men. Being a
worker is a transitory situation for women. Career channels
are not as open for them as for men (Pohl, Soleilhavoup,
1981). Instead, there is considerable mobility between
women's occupations within and between the secondary and
tertiary sectors. Secondly, the awareness and demands of
women workers are not uniquely centred around the factory.
Their double lives have an inescapable impact on their
attitudes. In unions, discussions have a wider scope, taking
in home and the workplace, and in such cases, social factors
as well as employers' attitudes constrain union actions.

These two dimensions affect perceptions of women's paid
work. Present day developments such as the increasing number
of employed women, the general transformation of the
relationship to work, industrial and technological restructuring, and the fragmentation of the mass of employees will
undoubtedly modify this image. And companies will have to
re-adapt their strategies.

REFERENCES

Blassel, H., Germe, J.F. and Michon, F. (1979). Une autre
    approche des conditions de travail: Usage et
    reproduction des forces de travail. In "Emploi et
    système productif" pp. 233-250. Paris Documentation
    Française.
Bouillaguet, P. and Germe, J.F. (1981). Salarisation et
    travail féminin en France. Critique de l'Economie
    Politique, 17, 83-117.
Bouillaguet, P., Gauvin, A. and Outix, J.L. (1981). "Femmes
    au travail, prospérité et crise", p. 249. Economica,
    Paris.
Cezard, M. (1979). Les qualifications ouvrières en question.
    Economie et Statistique, 110, 15-36.
Craig, C., Garnsey, E. and Rubery, J. (1985). "Payment

Structures in Smaller Firms: Women's Employment in
Segmented Labour Markets. Department of Employment
Research Paper No. 48.

Dutoya, C. and Germe, J.F. (1981). Categories d'emploi et
catégories de conditions de travail. A paper presented
at the conference "Les Conditions de travail et
l'analyse économique" in July 1981 at Grenoble, France.

Edwards, R. (1976). "Contested Terrain, Transformation of
the Work Place in the 20th Century". Harper-Colophon,
New York.

Enquêtes sur les conditions de travail. In supplements to
the monthly edition of Statistiques du Travail (71,
1979 and 84, 1980).

Eymard-Duvernay, F. (1981). Les secteurs de l'industrie et
leurs ouvriers. Economie et Statistique, (December),
13, 49-68.

Kergoat, D. (1978). Ouvriers = ouvrières? Critique de
l'Economie Politique, 5, 75-97.

Labourie-Racape, A., Letablier, M.T. and Vasseur, A.M.
(1977). L'Activité féminine. Cahier du Centre des
Etudes de l'Emploi, 11.

Linhart, D. (1981). "L'Appel de la sirène ou l'accoutumance
au travail. Le Sycomore, Paris

Molinie, A.F. and Volkoff, S. (1980). Les conditions de
travail des ouvriers et ouvrières. Economie et
Statistique, 118, 25-40.

Piore, M. and Berger, S. (1980). "Dualism and Discontinuity
in Industrial Societies". Cambridge University Press,
Cambridge.

Pohl, R. and Soleilhavoup, J. (1981). Insertion des jeunes
et mobilité des moins jeunes. Economie et Statistique,
134, 85-108.

Part III

Case Studies of Labour Market
Processes

Industrial Structures, Employment Trends and the Economic Crisis: The Case of France and Japan in the 1970s*

H. NOHARA and J.-J. SILVESTRE

The first attempt at a comparison of the ways in which the labour markets are organized in France and Japan is based for the most part on two comparable enquiries into wage and employment structures carried out in 1972 and 1978 in these two countries. We have also collected some direct information on the mobility of wage-earners in industry, such as can be acquired from surveys like the INSEE employment survey carried out annually in France since 1968, and a similar one carried out in Japan every three years.

This kind of comparative research implies an ability to carry out successfully three widely differing types of analysis. The first is based on empirical observation and the construction of those indicators best able to reveal – on the basis of the phenomenon that they describe – the diversity of practices between two countries in several basic areas of wages and employment policy. The second uses these contrasting practices to infer the most significant differences at a more general level in the nature of the "spaces" in which these practices function. It is only an

*This article is based on a paper presented by H. Nohara and J.-J. Silvestre at the Nancy round-table on labour economics (4 and 5 February 1982).

this second level that the diversity of practices can be
seen to be something other than a consequence of the actors'
opportunist strategies or of the history of their struggles
with each other. The third form of analysis must enable
certain phenomena to be more fully described than hitherto.
Only through such a description can the general importance
of certain particular practices and the consequences of any
change that they might undergo in the future be fully
brought out. This last point is particularly important in
the present period of structural tensions on productivity,
employment, qualifications and the rules that govern their
interdependence.

The results presented in this article favour the
empirical approach and the contrasting of partial
indicators. The more comprehensive and general kinds of
comparative analysis will only be mentioned — by way of
provisional hypotheses — when the various statistical data
that we have collected are examined.

The results will be presented in two stages. In the
first, an attempt will be made to give an idea of the major
contrasting characteristics of the two labour markets at the
beginning of the 1970s as revealed in the data used. The
most recent available results show that these contrasts are
still apparent and thus form a good analytical basis for
comparing the two industrial labour markets at the end of
the long period of industrial growth that followed the
Second World War. However, more detailed observation reveals
that the two systems for organizing industrial wage-earners
did not undergo the same changes during the first years of
the economic crisis. On the one hand, these differences
reveal characteristics specific to the two systems that are
accentuated by the crisis. But they also enable changes in
the structuring of the industrial wage-earning class in both
countries to be pinpointed, and trends to be identified,
which, if analysed in detail, would be of particular
significance for the future of both France and Japan.

I. INDUSTRIAL STRUCTURES AND THE INTEGRATION OF THE LABOUR FORCE IN FRANCE AND JAPAN AT THE BEGINNING OF THE 1960S

The relationships between labour market and industrial
structures will firstly be discussed by contrasting
production units of different sizes. For the purposes of
simplification, greater weight will be given to contrasting
very small and very large firms (less than 50 or 100
employees and more than 1,000), and we shall be particularly
concerned with the specific characteristics of the behaviour

of large firms. This paper takes no account of sector and
all the results presented refer to the whole of industry
regardless of sector. It will, of course, be necessary to
verify, in the course of this study, to what extent the
results that seem to us the most interesting stand up when
the sectoral dimension is taken into account. It should
finally be made clear that our particular concern is with
manual workers. We shall refer to non-manual workers only
using the most simple indicators.

Firms grouped by employment size and the distribution
between manual and non-manual work have been further
disaggregated by the workers' sex and age. Our final data
source is a breakdown of wage-earners into seniority grades.
For each intersection thus defined , the average monthly
wage [5] and the total number of wage-earners are known. The
data used in the first section refer to 1972. The
developments outlined in the second section compare 1972 and
1978 in both countries.

A. Industrial Structures And Workforce Categories

There are two fundamental differences between the two
countries in the distribution of the workforce among large
and small firms:

i) The breakdown of the manual and non-manual
    workforce among firms of different size and
    their composition by sex.
ii) The interest shown by large and small firms in
    experienced and inexperienced workers.

The first point can be illustrated by Table I: "L" (large)
indicates firms with more than 1,000 employees and "S"
(small) here indicates firms with less than 100 employees in
Japan and 10 to 50 in France.

This table gives rise to two observations. There is a
clearer distinction between different sized Japanese firms
than between their French counterparts in numbers of non-
manual employees, and more particularly in numbers of male
non-manual employees. Thus, in Japan, those workers
generally considered to have the best technical or
organizational abilities are concentrated in large
production units. This tendency also exists in France, but
is less marked.

On the other hand, large French firms have relatively
more male workers than large Japanese firms, particularly
manual workers.

Table I. Comparative weight of non-manual workers and women according to size of firm

| | Structure of workforce according to size of firm | | | | | | Distribution of the male workforce | | | |
| | % Non-manual (i) | | % Women (ii) | | Non-manual males | | Manual | | Non-manual (iii) | |
	France	Japan	France	Japan	France	Japan	France	Japan	France	Japan
Large firms	34.5	40	17(15)	24(25)	33	41	31	38	35	50
Small firms	28.5	23.5	35(30)	38(39)	26	25.1	25	32	17	18
Total	31%	33%	30%	32%	30%	35%	100%	100%	100%	100%

(i) In large Japanese firms, for example, 40% of the employees are non-manual workers.
(ii) For example, 17% of the employees in large French firms are women (we have indicated in brackets the percentage of women among the manual workers).
(iii) Fifty per cent of non-manual workers in Japanese industry are in large firms.

Table II. Relative wage and employment share of labour by category (large firms)

	Wage relative to the average industrial wage for the category			Ratio of employment share in France to that in Japan (i)
	France 1	Japan 2	Ratio 0.5	
Women	0.75	0.52	1.44	0.71
Male manual	0.86	0.93	0.92	1.24
Male non-manual	1.43	1.16	1.23	0.87

(i) % of male manual workers in the wage earning population: France. For example, 1.24: % of male manual workers in the wage earning population: Japan.

These differences in the relative employment levels for different categories of worker can be compared with differences in the relative wages of these categories.
    Relative to their French counterparts, large Japanese firms employ more men and women in non-manual jobs, which enables them to take advantage of the lower wages of these categories of workers in the Japanese labour market. Similarly, the tendency of large French firms to employ relatively greater numbers of male manual workers is not inconsistent with the relative costs of this type of labour in the two industrial labour markets (Table II).
    Such a directly economic "explication" is certainly not the only one possible, and it has in any case to be relocated within a series of determining factors of which the economic "explanation" is only one. We shall see later that the female workforce in large Japanese firms (particularly the manual workforce) is subject to a particular type of institutional control that may explain both its lower wage and its greater employment, at least in a period of growing employment. As far as the high proportion of male supervisory and training personnel is concerned, this can be seen as indicative of the greater role played by large firms in Japan in the systematic

organization of subcontracting, which encourages a tendency to concentrate production tasks in small units and co-ordination and management tasks in large units.

Thus, relative to France, the manual workforce in large Japanese firms is predominantly female and in a minority compared with the large numbers of supervisory staff in the middle and upper categories. It is also significantly younger. Here, there is a considerable difference between the two countries, as can be seen from Table III.

The relative position of large and small units is totally reversed here. In large Japanese firms, the manual work is done for the most part by a young workforce, whereas in their French counterpart the manual workers are mostly workers already past the age of 30. There is not a very clear distinction in France between large and small firms, although the latter do tend to make more frequent use of young manual workers. On the other hand, there is a very clear distinction in Japan, where almost 70% of the production in small firms is carried out by workers well into the second half of their working lives (and who are even − as we shall see later − more likely to be over 50 years of age).

This situation can be seen to correspond to systematic differences in hiring policies, by comparing the distribution by age of workers recruited in the year preceding the surveys that we have used [6]. In Japan, 67% of the workers recruited by large firms were under 20 years of age. This proportion was only 15% in small units, where 56% of those recruited were over 30 [7]. There is no very

Table III. Percentage of manual workers under 30 years of age

	France			Japan		
	Large	Small	Total	Large	Small	Total
Manual workers aged under 30	36%	42%	41%	55%	31%	44%
Women among manual workers	15%	30%		25%	39%	

significant difference in France, where the percentage of
very young workers recruited is fairly similar at around
32%. The most that can be said is that large firms tend to
favour recruitment of workers between 20 and 30, whereas
small firms tend to recruit workers over 30.

Seniority is usually advanced as the main factor in the
structuring of the Japanese labour market and of firms'
manpower policies, particularly those of the larger firms,
which have an active role only in the recruitment of
inexperienced workers. But the evidence suggests that a
worker's age may be just as important, or even more
important than seniority. This characteristic does not
appear to be a fundamental one in the case of France, where
the distribution of workers recruited according to the stage
of their working life seems to be more random, with the
possibility of competition in recruitment - particularly of
the larger firms - among all categories of the labour force.
However, this does not mean that the Japanese labour market
is more clearly divided into large firms, constituting
perfect internal markets, and small firms, whereas the
French labour market is more open and more favourable to
opportunities for mobility with a wider area. The basic
difference seems to us to lie rather in the processes
according to which workers become mobile. An explanation of
this basic point implies consideration of the way in which
mobility or immobility of workers in firms depends on the
different stages of a working life, i.e. on the
relationships between the age and seniority of workers.

B. Stabilization and Destabilization of the Workforce and
Labour Mobility in the Two Countries

We shall bring into play here an indicator which gives a
rough but sufficiently significant measure of the extent to
which firms take responsibility for the career of each
employee [8]. If they took complete responsibility (the
perfect image of employment for life for all), the
probability for an employee of a given age of having maximum
seniority, taking account of the time at which he began his
working life, would be one (for example, all workers aged 30
would have between ten and twelve years seniority). The
available statistics do not allow a precise measure of the
relationship between age and seniority. At best, indicators
can be constructed for the proportion of workers in each age
group with a certain level of seniority.

Examination of these indicators may focus on two points:

i) The difference between their observed value
   and unity [9].
ii) The homogeneity between these indicators
    (which indicates a tendency for seniority to
    progress with age), or the disparities which
    may result from a history during which the
    workforce is less mobile for some periods and
    more mobile in others.

If these indicators are applied to female manual workers,
several significant results are obtained.

Table IV. Rate of integration of female manual workers
(1972)

Age groups	France 1	Japan 2	Ratio: 0.5
Under 20	16%	24%	0.67
20-30	27%	36%	0.75
30-50	27%	16%	1.69
50-60	21.3%	5.9%	3.61
Over 60	27.2%	7.9%	3.44

The differences observed between the two countries are wide
enough to be of significance despite the approximate nature
of the indicators used. Firstly, there are differences for
women under 30, who seem more frequently able in Japan to
have a stable career. This should not be seen simply as
differences in the behaviour patterns of young women in the
two countries, since it can be observed, by refining the
data in Table III, that there is a direct link between this
"propensity to stability" and the fact that 77% of female
workers in large firms are young women (as against only 47%
in France) [10]. This institutional stability linked to a
specific characteristic of the employment and recruitment
policies of large Japanese firms seems to have a limit,
since the trend is suddenly reversed from the age of 30
onwards, leaving only a very small proportion of women at

the end of their working lives who have benefitted from total institutional stabilization [11]. We shall see later that this greater mobility undoubtedly corresponds often to a break in working life, with those women who do return going back for the most part to small production units, in which almost 75% of the female manual workforce is over 30 [12].

There is a much clearer trend towards integration for female workers in France, even if the proportion integrated over long periods in particular firms remains relatively low. The proportion of women who have less than two years seniority is 59% for those aged under 30 but has fallen to 27% for those aged over 30. In France, therefore, young women seem to make relatively better progress from the precariousness of seeking employment in the labour market to a position of relative integration, at least for those who do not interrupt their working life. In Japan, such "strategic" progress on the part of the individual does not seem to be of much significance, since both the early stabilization of young women and their predictable mobility seem to be highly institutional and collective in nature.

This contrast, put forward here as a hypothesis, between more strategic and individual mobility in France and more collectivized and institutionalized movements in the Japanese workforce, is also found to be true, although it takes rather different forms, for male manual workers. This is shown by the results presented in Table V.

Table V. Rate of integration of male manual workers (1972)

Age groups	France 1	Japan 2	Ratio: 0.5
Under 20	12%	16%	0.75
20–30	24%	45%	0.53
30–50	49%	50%	0.98
50–60	37%	31%	1.19
Over 60	37%	12%	3.08

Two trends emerge from Table V. Firstly, there is a considerable disparity, more marked than for female workers, between the rates of integration for workers aged between 20 and 30 in the two countries. In Japan, the first part of working life seems characterized by the acceptance of responsibility for workers by firms, whereas in France there is a strong tendency towards external mobility. This was no doubt encouraged - as will be seen when the situation six years later is examined - by the continuous growth in industrial employment at the end of the 1960s and the beginning of the 1970s. This greater propensity towards external mobility in France can be confirmed by the widely differing numbers of recently recruited workers (less than two years seniority) in this phase of their working life: 48% in France compared with only 32% in Japan.

It should be noted in passing that there is an inversion of the relationships between men and women in both countries, which no doubt indicates - over and above quantitative disparities - differences of a more qualitative nature. The higher rate of integration for men in Japan is more indicative of their more established position in the process by which firms take responsibility both socially and professionally for their workforce and around which the labour market in that country is organized. In France, on the other hand, the position of individuals in the social and professional hierarchy goes through a more complex process of integration, precariousness and strategies for obtaining employment that arise out of actions of both firms and employees. It might be concluded that male manual workers in this context are on average more mobile, more encouraged to be so by the competition among firms, and thus less well integrated at this stage of their career. There is thus a real disparity between men and women in both labour markets. However, it is formed by very different processes and in very different social and institutional frameworks [13].

Indicators similar to those in Table V and calculated according to size of firm show that the difference in the rate of integration between the two countries is even more marked for small firms than for large ones. There is a very low level of stabilization for young workers in small French firms. This difference can be explained by characteristics already mentioned above. In particular, it has been stressed that large Japanese firms favour the recruitment of young, inexperienced workers, which leaves little room for manual workers over 20 or 25 to move from small firms to large ones. Large firms are much less "closed" in France, where young men between 20 and 30 seem to account for most of

their recruiting [14]. It cannot be confirmed whether this
recruiting is among workers moving from small firms to large
ones, where the opportunities for long-term integration and
promotion are higher. Thus there is a contrast between two
types of mobilization and selection. In France, the first
third of the working life is characterized by external
mobility, part of which at least is "strategic" in nature
and creates competition for access to the best jobs. In
Japan, there is a marked trend towards integration resulting
from earlier selection processes and takes place at school
leaving age. Thus this trend is partly active (the
stabilization offered by the system of employment for life –
the Nenko system – in large firms) and partly passive, for
those who remain in small firms, since access to the most
structured and attractive internal markets is closed to them
by the method of very early selection characteristic of
these markets.

In the 20-50 age group, there is at least an arithmetic
convergence in the two systems of integration and, contrary
to what is true in the case of women, it is only above the
age of 50 that there is an inversion of the relationships
between the two countries. The number of male manual workers
over 50 who are well integrated into their firms (having
more than 20 years seniority) is 37% in France and is no
more than 28% in Japan. Although the system of employment
for life seems, a priori, to be adhered to in large Japanese
firms, where 63% of workers over 50 have more than 20 years
seniority compared with only 55% in France, those
benefitting from the system are fewer in number; 15% of
workers in large French firms are over 50, compared with
only 7% in Japan. The corollary of the system of stabilization in large Japanese firms is a process of selection, on
the basis of which an external market develops for older
workers that is significantly brisker than in France. (Thus,
55% of workers over 50 have less than ten years seniority in
Japanese industry compared with only 35% in France). Once
again, we must stress the inadequacy of a statistical
approach that does not reveal the social and occupational
mechanisms that divide older externalized workers in Japan
from others, and that in France maintains in employment
workers whose qualifications may be characterized by a high
degree of obsolescence.

These differences, that relate to both men and women,
enable a contrast to be made – even if the indicators used
are imperfect and indirect – between two systems of mobility
and stability arising out of very different individual and
collective mechanisms in the two countries. In Japan, a
system of stabilization has been developed that applies to

young workers who have already been differentiated from each
other at the time of entry into the labour market. The
duration of this period of stabilization depends to a large
extent on external categorizations established and
controlled by the firms [15]. Collective forms of mobility
of a quasi-institutional nature have also been developed, in
which the organization of the various stages of working life
of very different categories of workers plays a role that
may turn out to be more important than the division of jobs
within the industrial structure or the aggregation of
individual strategies. In France, a labour market has grown
up in which competition for access to jobs is more open, or
at least less bound by rules governing its operation.
Individual strategies of mobility or stability, within the
employment systems, are thus linked in a more balanced way
with the policies or practices that may contribute towards
their institutionalization [16].

     Do the qualitative differences that have apparently
been revealed in the organization of labour flows go hand in
hand with the quantitative differences in the intensity of
these same flows, and if so, in what direction do these
differences make themselves felt? Comparison of the direct
data available, based on the French employment survey and
its Japanese counterpart, reveals a greater intensity of
inter-firm flows in France than in Japan [17].

     The annual rate of inter-firm flows within the same
industry is twice as high in France as in Japan (5.7% of
industrial jobs are affected by such mobility in France,
compared with only 2.5% in Japan) [18]. This disparity is
comparable for men and women, although it is a little higher
for men, who show the greatest difference between the two
countries in the rate of inter-firm flows from which the
industry "benefits". These results are not incompatible with
our previous conclusions to the extent that it has been
observed that the mobility in Japan seems to be concentrated
within minority categories in industry (middle-aged women
and male workers at the end of their working lives), while
the other categories are better integrated than in France in
a system of stabilization which, although less strong in
small production units, is not restricted to large firms.
The use of surveys that give a direct measure of mobility
also enables this result to be qualified by taking account
of two other basic differences between the industrial labour
markets in the two countries [19]. The first of these is
that the small numbers of workers changing firm in mid-
career in Japan means that previously unemployed workers
play a significantly larger part in industrial recruitment
(job take-ups). Their share in the recruitment of new

workers from one year to the next is 55% in Japan, compared
with only 40% in France. A large part of this difference is
due to the relatively greater numbers of women returning to
work in Japan [20]. It would be necessary to clarify the
mechanisms responsible for the probable link between this
flexibility caused by exit and re-entry of women into the
industrial labour market and the existence of two female
labour markets – one for women under 30, the other for women
over 30 – to which attention has already been drawn above.
    The relatively greater weight of entries into
employment in the adjustments that take place in the
external market in Japanese industry does not invalidate the
main conclusion that can be drawn from a comparison of
mobility rates in the two industrial systems: there are many
more external flows to firms in French than in Japanese
industry [21]. This difference [22] might lead to
"mechanical" explanations related to the uneven levels of
instability in the productive system (appearance and
disappearance of firms; inequalities in the growth rate
between sectors) that cannot be checked, at least for the
moment. It might also lead to an examination of data
relating to the different ways in which the flexibility of
firms' internal workforces is organized in the two
countries. This latter explanation is undoubtedly a
fundamental one since, according to the scanty indications
we have been able to gather together, labour flows between
factories belonging to the same company are much higher in
Japanese than in French industry, being of the order of of
7% of the male industrial workforce in Japan, compared with
only 2% in France. This internal flexibility within firms is
not restricted, as has been shown in more specific analyses
carried out by Japanese researchers, to movements between
factories, but relates also to movements between departments
or jobs [23]. Thus from one point of view, this flexibility
would appear to offset a low level of external mobility or
to be, more precisely, another way of controlling the
integration of the workforce. Moreover, this goes hand in
hand with significant differences between the two countries
in the methods of determining rewards. This will be the
final point in this part of the paper.

C. Two Contrasting Types of Internalization of the Manual
Workforce

The main difference in this respect between the two
countries that is immediately obvious relates to the extent
to which seniority is rewarded, particularly in large firms.

Table VI. Restrictive wages of very experienced manual
workers and non-manual staff

	France	Japan
Average wage of very experienced workers as a % of the wage of male non-manual workers	0.63	1.08
Wage of newly recruited manual workers as a % of the wage of male non-manual workers	0.51	0.54
Wage of very experienced manual workers as a % of the wage of female non-manual workers	1.07	2.19
Non-manual wages as a % of the manual wages	1.58 (1.65) (a)	1.25 (1.26) (a)

(a) The figures in brackets are for male workers.

It is true in both countries that the average manual wage
increases with seniority, and it is possible to construct a
simple indicator of the rate of increase by relating the
average wage of workers with more than 20 years seniority to
that of newly recruited workers. The ratio is 2.00 in large
Japanese firms compared with only 1.25 in their French
counterparts. It is also true that the percentage of very
senior workers (more than 20 years seniority) is a little
higher in France (23% compared with 14% in Japan), in view
of the selectivity that has already been stressed among
older workers in large Japanese firms [24]. There are
nevertheless two systems for rewarding experience. Moreover,
this unequal rewarding of experience has a decisive
influence on the very different relationships in the two
countries between manual and non-manual wages [25]. For
example, the following situation exists in large firms.
    The situation is very similar in the case of newly
recruited male manual workers, whose wage represents

approximately half that of non-manual workers [26]. The
situation is very different for experienced workers whose
wage is higher than that of non-manual workers in Japan,
whereas in France experienced manual workers receive only
two-thirds of the wage of non-manual workers. Two indicators
have been added: one of these (line 4) reveals a difference
in the wage hierarchy (manual and non-manual) that is
comparable to the difference between France and Germany
[27]; the other (line 3) stresses the importance of the
reward attached to holding a non-manual job, which puts all
salaried employees in large firms in French industry at a
level of remuneration comparable to that of the most
experienced manual workers in the same firms.

    Not enough is known of the relationships between
mobility, qualification and reward for it to be easy to put
forward "explanations" for these differences in the
evaluation of manual workers' qualifications. However, on
the basis of other studies already mentioned, it can be said
that one factor common to both Japan and Germany − although
there are considerable differences − is the existence of
very efficient systems for constructing and legitimizing a
versatile qualification for industrial workers. In Germany,
qualifications are gained within a system of occupational
training, which means that there is a high degree of
disassociation between the system of mobility and worker
qualification and the systems of technical division of
labour [28]. It should be noted that this system of
qualification for manual workers has the double characteristic of being based on the firm (apprenticeship), while
being independent of the categories of employment systems
(jobs, productive functions, economic sectors, etc.).
Industrial workers in Germany (the men at least) thus
possess a form of intrinsic qualification that is both
professional and social, and of which the collective and the
individual, the specific and general components are closely
interwoven.

    In the case of Japan, the professional diploma system
is of negligible importance, and a manual worker acquires a
qualification that is independent of the employment system
by systematic use of the mobility between categories of
tasks. The acquisition of the versatility that defines the
industrial worker's qualification both professionally and
socially is based on this mobility. The mechanism is thus
very different from the re-training of skilled workers in
Germany. This versatility goes hand in hand with the
relatively high position of industrial workers, at least on
the scale of professional capabilities and the economic
reward for these skills. This would appear to be further

example of the apparent paradox of the coexistence of two
characteristics already discovered in the case of Germany:

i) The qualification of an industrial worker
   appears to be relatively general and
   autonomous in comparison with the specific
   nature of the actual job held or with their
   divergence within the system of the division
   of labour.

ii) There is a close link between acquisition of
   this qualification and, on the one hand, the
   firm, seen as a place for the collective
   organization of individual apprenticeships and,
   on the other, the actual carrying out of tasks,
   used specifically to further the development of
   general capabilities.

In both cases, rigid rules for recognition of qualifications
(experienced workers or those holding a diploma) coexist
with organizational flexibility that is apparently used
within the area defined by these rules and with strictest
regard for their legitimacy [29]. This rigidity seems to go
beyond the internal rules of the working class. It indicates
the fairly strict limits that develop between manual and
non-manual workers in industry and between employees in
industry and other employees in these countries.

    One difference between the two countries that must be
pointed out is the nature of the more general framework
within which these systems of reward are located. In the
case of Japan, the acquisition of a qualification through
work experience is not distinct from the use of age as the
criterion around which a hierarchy, the principles of which
go beyond the social relationships within the productive
sphere, is organized and finds its legitimacy. Age may seem,
even through the differences in the role that it plays for
each sex [30], to be the expression of a form of recognition
of needs — both economic and non-economic — as they are
reflected in the relationships of the family structure to
society [31]. In the case of Germany, the system of
occupational training in its widest definition is the more
general framework for the link between the relationship
within the productive system and society as a whole.

    The French system for acquiring and recognizing manual
workers' qualifications seems to be characterized by a more
complex interaction between the job held, and, more
generally, the position within the system of tasks,
seniority and occupational or general training. The
hypothesis that we favour in our attempts to analyse the

industrial labour market in France is that there is a
correspondence between the complexity of the terms in this
process or the more strategic nature of the conditions under
which worker mobility occurs (within firms and from firm to
firm) and the more specific nature of the various forms of
qualification to which the industrial manual worker may have
access [32]. This hypothesis can then be extended by
assuming that the more strategic, and thus conflicting,
nature of the "rules" governing access to jobs and the
recognition of qualifications - and thus the wages linked to
them - goes hand in hand with a lower degree of
organizational flexiblity that is reflected in the rigidity
of hierarchical practices, in the difficulty of finding
widely accepted forms of versatility and in the bitterness
of conflicts about internal or external "redeployment" of
the workforce at a time of crisis.

This stress on the more strategic and more complex
nature of the rules in France does not imply any deliberate
simplification of the behaviour patterns of the actors in
Germany and Japan. We know that such a contrast is
unacceptable. Nevertheless, we do feel that such complex
interactions between specific actors contribute to the
formulation of the rules in France, whereas in Germany and
Japan they form part of more collective and wider social
regulations (the occupational diploma system and the Nenko
system).

Finally, it should be noted that one important result
of the main criteria around which the hierarchy,
qualifications and social relationships are organized in
Germany and Japan is to make a clearer distinction than in
France between the male and female labour markets. This is
very obvious for manual workers, for whom the wage
relationships of men to women are 1.96 in Japan, 1.55 in
Germany and 1.32 in France, and is still true, though less
marked for all industrial employees, for whom the
relationships are respectively 2.03, 1.55 and 1.45.

These brief remarks of a more qualitative nature do not
claim to be a summary, much less an integration of the
results of the comparative analysis put forward in the first
part of the paper. They merely indicate the general
direction that might be taken by a more systematic or even
more theoretical exploitation of comparative analyses and of
the often considerable differences that they reveal between
the ways in which industrial labour markets function.

II. INDUSTRIAL EMPLOYMENT TRENDS IN TIMES OF CRISIS: A
COMPARISON OF SOME RECENT TRENDS IN JAPAN AND FRANCE
 - 1972-78

A. Substitution Between Labour Categories and Employment
Policies in Times of Crisis

The first thing to note is the unevenness of the fall in
industrial employment in the two countries. As measured in
the two surveys used, industrial employment fell over six
years by 8% in Japan and by only 4% in France. However, it
must be stressed that the main significance of these surveys
is that they compare employment structures, according to
various criteria, and in that respect, the developments
observed indicate a similarity in the indicators measured in
the two countries.
    The fall in employment in France is accompanied by a
greater relative loss of manual jobs, particularly of those
held by men, greater resistance by the female workforce and
a sharp increase in non-manual jobs held by men. The
dominant characteristic of the evolution of the industrial
labour force in Japan is that the fall in employment is more
highly concentrated among the female workforce (-12% in all
categories compared with -4% in France). In addition, the
employment of male manual workers has held up relatively
well, and there has been a slower growth in the numbers of
male non-manual workers. These differences between the two
countries seem to be greater in large firms. For example,
the fall in the number of female manual workers amounts to
50% of total manual employment lost in large Japanese firms,
compared with only 6% in France. Moreover, the percentage of
non-manual workers in the total labour force has increased
almost twice as fast in French firms (+15%) as in large
Japanese firms (+8%). This difference is of the order of
three to one - +15% compared with +5% - if the total
increase over six years in the share of non-manual workers
of all industrial employees is taken into account [34].
    If this analysis is extended by a more detailed
structural examination - by age or seniority - of manual
workers (particularly in large firms), quite different
trends are revealed, both in a comparison of the countries
with each other and in the structural evolution of the
manual and non-manual population in each country taken
separately. In the case of Japan, the relative resistance of
manual employment, particularly among men, went hand in hand
with a marked trend towards an older workforce, due for the
most part to the fact that those in employment remained in
their jobs and that new recruiting came to an abrupt halt

[35]. In large firms, the percentage of workers under 30 decreased in six years from 49% to 37% of the total labour force. There was an even more spectacular fall in the number of male workers with less than two years seniority, which fell from 23% of the total in 1972 to 6.5% in 1978. The ageing of the labour force is not linked to a change in policy on the structure of recruitment, since the great majority of workers recruited continue to be under 20 (65% in 1978 compared with 60% in 1972). However, certain indices reveal an increased trend for large firms to select their workforce by raising the general level of training of the young people recruited for manual jobs.

The main factor preventing the fall in the employment of manual workers from being too rapid must therefore be the fact that the system for stabilizing the existing labour force was maintained and even strengthened during the early years of the economic crisis. Thus the share of workers with more than ten years seniority increased from 40% to 56% in large Japanese firms in just a few years. These trends are in sharp contrast with what happened in their French counterparts, at least during the period of our study. The trend in France was for the labour force to become younger (the share of workers under 30 increased by 2%, whereas it fell by 11% in Japan) and for the fall in recruitment to be much less rapid than in Japan (23% of the labour force in large firms in both countries had less than two years seniority in 1972, whereas in 1978 the equivalent figure was 15% in France and 6.5% in Japan [36]. This continuing high level of recruitment seems to go hand in hand with a trend – new to large French firms – towards a lowering of the age of men recruited for manual jobs. Thirty eight per cent of workers recuited in 1978 were under 20, compared with 30% in 1972, and the proportion of recruitments over the age of 30 was becoming insignificant.

The relative vulnerability of manual jobs in large French firms in the crisis thus seems to be associated with a questioning of the value of the system of stabilization, particularly for workers already benefitting from a high level of integration within the system of internal qualification – in-house training – at the beginning of the 1970s. In contrast to Japan, where the percentage of workers with more than 10 years seniority increased in six years by 15%, the proportion of these workers fell by 1% in France (47% compared with 48%) during the same period. The fall in manual employment thus appears to go hand in hand with a trend towards a renewal of its structure. The question then arises of the role played by the level of training (general or vocational), in the criteria governing this (assumed) policy of renewal and of the importance attached to the possibility of changing not the "quality" of the workforce, but the form of the contracts – in the widest sense of the word – that define its link with the firm. From this point of view, the first reaction to the crisis observed in France between 1976 and 1980 (institutional forms of precariousness, productive decentralization, individualization of wage negotiations) is only one stage in a process of greater change in organization, in the nature of social relationships and in the demographic balance within the industrial workforce.

This difference in stabilization policies becomes even more complex, and gives rise to more conjecture, if we compare what happened to male manual and non-manual workers in large production units in the two countries. In Japan, the number of highly integrated manual workers (with more than ten years seniority) increased in absolute terms by 15% between 1972 and 1978, whereas the same figure for non-manual workers increased by only 3%; in France, the corresponding figures are -9% and -16%. The contrasting trends in the structure of qualifications, to which attention has already been drawn [37], obviously correspond to decisions based on the general principles guiding the short-term and subsequent structural reaction of internal markets to the crisis. It would be of interest to seek a better understanding of the "arithmetic", the demographic and sociological processes (particularly as reflected in the number of promotions from manual to non-manual jobs [38], as revealed by the selective use of collective dismissals or "organized departures" in France and the nature of the consensus that was established on the basis of the high degree of stabilization of the manual work force in large Japanese firms.

Of particular importance is the extent to which the trend towards renewal of the labour force in France is one of the strategies used by firms to counteract the organizational rigidities that could only be associated – all things being equal – with a sharp increase in the average seniority of workers [39]. Conversely, the strengthening of the Nenko system in Japan would only have been made possible by the existence prior to the crisis of practices on which there was a high degree of consensus or that were already well integrated into the concepts underlying the qualifications of industrial workers, i.e. internal flexibility in the widest sense of the word; movement between jobs, workshops, functions, factories, types of production, etc. This does not of course exclude the hypothesis that this stabilization was an important

concession by the employers, made as part of more wide-
ranging decisions, the purposes of which was to reduce other
constraints (real wages, for example, or at least the
average wage cost).

   The figures obtained for the female labour force
(manual workers in particular) will not be examined in
detail here. It should, however, be pointed out that the
trends towards an ageing workforce and stabilization were
observed in all areas, most particularly in large Japanese
firms. These trends are fairly consistent with the relative
rigidity of female manual employment in France, which seems
to correspond to extensive use by women of the opportunities
offered to them - when this is the case - for keeping the
job they had before the crisis. These trends pose several
problems if an attempt is made to understand how massive
numbers of women left work in Japan, unless it is assumed
that a net reduction in recruitment (although less marked
than for male workers) has more immediate consequences for a
population whose average seniority within the firm is
reduced by the practices of "institutionalized mobility"
already described in the first part of this paper.

B. The Probability of Integration and a Reduction in the Number of Jobs

The general trend is towards an increase in the rates of
integration for industrial wage earners in employment [40].
Table VII shows the trends for the six year period in both
countries.

   The most significant differences are for men. Japan is
characterized by similar increases for all groups, which
could be seen as an index of the healthy state of the Nenko
system [41], particularly for populations who traditionally
benefit from it (manual workers over 50 years old). On the
other hand, there is a fairly clear difference in France
between the "rigidification of employment" for manual
workers at the beginning of their working life (20-30 years
old) and the erosion of the relative trend towards
integration at the beginning of the period for older
workers, particularly for those over 50. There is undeniably
an element of convergence, statistically at least, between
the two systems of integration and mobility. This
statistical convergence is accompanied by divergence of the
form of social relationships (the concept of qualification;
the principles that govern worker mobility; the main issues
around which employer-employee relationships are structured)
associated with these two systems. Analyses of a more

H. Nohara and J.-J. Silvestre

qualitative nature would be necessary in order to take
account of the conditions and consequences of this trend:
the apparent rigidification of the mobility – previously
described as "strategic" – of workers aged between 20 and 30
in France.

In the case of France, these figures raise an important
question about the mobility of young workers. It is well
known that recent developments in the education system have
emphasized the difference between young people with fairly
high levels of vocational training and others who fail
miserably at school. The question is what category is
affected by the trend towards rigidification of the labour
market for young people under 30 and what are the
consequences for the more dynamic firms who traditionally
recruited the most active and best qualified workers.

The differences are less marked for female manual
workers, for whom there is a contrast in both countries
between greater vulnerability for older workers and
increased integration for the other categories. However, it
should be pointed out that the disparity in the evolution of
the rates of integration is very favourable to French female

Table VII. Index of the rate of integration in 1978 (base
100 in 1972) (a)

Age Group	Male manual		Female manual	
	France	Japan	France	Japan
20–30	1.54	1.29	1.50	1.25
30–50	1.08	1.18	1.36	1.32
Over 50	0.83	1.23	0.90	0.90

(a) For example, the indicator 1.5 represents the following
ratio:
% of male manual workers from 20–30 with more than six years
seniority in France in 1978: % of male manual workers from
20–30 with more than six years seniority in France in 1972.
The indicators in lines 2 and 3 are constructed on the same
principle, with the respective limits being ten and twenty
years seniority.

workers between 20 and 30, which is consistent with our
observations for male workers in this age group.

The direct data available on changes of firm or annual
job take-ups in industry are still too aggregated (covering
the total number of industrial workers) for these
observations to be confirmed or elaborated. The trend in
both countries is towards fewer changes of firm and job
take-ups. The rate of mobility between industrial jobs fell
by about 35% in both countries, with a slightly more
pronounced decline for men in Japan (-40% compared with -30%
in France). However, it must be borne in mind that the
period over which this took place is six years for France
(1972-78), whereas the data available for Japan covers only
three years (1974-77). It must therefore be assumed that
Japanese industry has in fact adapted to a greater reduction
in external mobility, particularly among men, than in French
industry [42]. On the other hand, we should consider whether
the changes in France in the organization of mobility have
not been more profound, at least at the beginning of the
1980s, because of the transition from predominantly
strategic mobility to essentially insitutionalized or
enforced mobility [43] arising out of the mechanisms already
described and commented on in other studies: "interim"
contracts; fixed term contracts; collective dismissals.

C. The Relationships Between Wages and Seniority and the Relative Rewarding of Qualifications

Only male manual workers will be considered here. The trend
is towards stabilization of the indicators in Japan and
towards an increase in France. There is still a considerable
gap between the two countries, since in large firms the
ratio went from 2.00 to 1.97 in Japan and from 1.25 to 1.35
in France.

There are three additional remarks to be made about
these trends. First, it seems that the reduction in the pay
of workers of long standing in France was less (at least for
those who managed to keep their job!); their relative wage -
in comparison with the average pay of male non-manual
workers - rose from 0.63 to 0.68, whereas there was a fall
in Japan (1.04 compared with 1.08). The difference between
manual and non-manual workers is thus decreasing in France,
although in large firms the average pay of a recently
recruited non-manual worker is still 10% higher than that of
a manual worker with 20 years experience. However, this
difference was previously 20%, and in large Japanese firms

was −45%, the difference in favour of the manual workers for
the whole period.

The second significant trend is less striking, but
might profitably be studied in greater detail at the level
of the firm. It was observed in both countries that the
already significant influence of seniority was maintained or
increased, and that this was associated with a slight trend
towards a fall in relative earnings during the first years
in a firm. The percentage difference between the average
wage of workers with between four and six years seniority
and that of recently recruited workers fell from 14% to 12%
in France and from 25% to 20% in Japan while the
differential between new recruits and workers with over 20
years service increased in France (from 25% to 35%) and
decreased in Japan from 100% to 97%. These contradictory
results need to be examined in more detail in order to
determine whether there is really a move towards new
conditions for rewarding seniority for workers recruited and
stabilized since the beginning of the economic crisis. The
change might indicate that new forms of assessing workers'
qualifications are gradually being introduced, with more
importance attached to diplomas, particularly in France.

Our final observation is that in Japan the resistance
of the relationship between seniority and wages seems to be
supported by the strengthening of the relationship that we
consider to be more fundamental in Japan: the rewarding of
age. The gap between the average wages of workers aged
between 20 and 30 and those of workers aged between 50 and
60 is growing significantly in large firms and even more so
in small firms, where the influence of seniority is
traditionally much less marked. The same trend exists in
France, but it is much less pronounced in absolute terms
and, in particular, in relation to our observations for
seniority.

NOTES

1. This is only the most fleeting reference to the
    methodological and, in the last instance, theoretical
    decisions that have been the basis of the international
    comparisons carried out at LEST in recent years. For
    more detailed discussion, see the following works:
    Maurice et al., 1979; Nohara, 1981; Eyraud, 1981;
    Maurice et al., 1982.
2. The period for which we have attempted to pinpoint
    these trends is the same as that separating the two
    surveys of the employment and wages structure available

in France: the end of 1972 to the end of 1978.

3.	For both countries, we have data available for firms of
	more than 1,000 employees. Data on small firms directly
	available for Japan refer to firms with ten to 100 employees
	employees and for France to firms with ten to 50
	employees. To obtain comparable estimates, French data have
	have been adjusted using data on the next available
	size group (50 to 200 employees). In making these
	adjustments, we have checked the homogeneity of the
	behaviour of firms of between 50 and 200 employees
	against those with less than 50. It should be added that
	that in certain cases all industrial populations are
	being compared irrespective of size.

4.	Excluding in both cases the building and public works
	sector.

5.	The Japanese wages referred to take no account of the
	not insignificant share (25%) of bonuses. Nevertheless,
	we have checked that their introduction does not alter
	the structural relationships put forward in this art
	article.

6.	A comparison was made of the structure by age (under
	20; 20-30; over 30) of workers with less than one year'
	year's seniority. It is obvious that this indicator is no
	not a direct measure of the recruitment structure in
	the year preceding the enquiry. We do have direct data
	from another source on the recruitment structure for
	Japan (cf. Nohara, op. cit.) which agree completely
	with the results that will be presented later, based on
	measurement in terms of stocks and not in terms of flow.
	In France, the use of recent data on labour flows
	ought to produce results close to those of a direct
	survey. In general, we are well aware of the fact that
	use of data on the supply of labour - particularly
	expressed in terms of age and seniority - is very
	unsatisfactory as a way of describing the actual
	movement of workers. This is, however, what we shall
	do several times in this article, while accepting the
	criticisms that might be made.

7.	It is possible to speak of a systematic policy on the
	part of large firms active in the youth labour market,
	in which they operate a rigorous selection policy. On
	the other hand, the behaviour of small firms is
	determined more by the constraints imposed by their
	poor competitiveness, in the same labour market, in
	which the relationship between the supply of jobs and
	the available workforce is very favourable to young
	workers, particularly in a period of expansion.

8.	This notion of responsibility is not necessarily linked

just to the behaviour patterns of firms and their
ability to "organize" the labour market. It is a <u>de
facto</u> responsibility, which must be analysed on the
basis of the relationships established (which may later
become constraints for firms) between their patterns of
behaviour (both individual and collective) and those
(again both individual and collective) of the employees.

9.   This reference to unity is perhaps not absolutely
     rigorous for the first two classes. It is certainly so
     for the final three.

10. The same data presented differently reveal that 42% of
     young female workers in Japanese industry are in large
     firms, compared with only 13% in France.

11. It would obviously be important to trace more closely
     this exodus from large firms by Japanese women between
     25 and 35 years of age. However, we have no further
     details at present.

12. Thus 46% of female workers over 30 are in small firms.

13. The inversion of the relationship between the rates of
     integration for the sexes in France for age groups over
     30 confirms our interpretation of the mechanisms that
     form the differences between the two sexes.

14. Forty five per cent of recruitment in France compared
     to only 20% in Japan.

15. In the results presented here, the essential difference
     is that between men and women or between workers
     distinguished according to age. It could no doubt be
     shown that the "quality" of secondary education or
     access to or exclusion from higher education plays a
     very important role.

16. This does not mean that this strategic mobility does
     not occur within a system of rules to which both firms
     and employees adhere. The Parodi categories, the basic
     institution of the French system of classification,
     form the framework for such an institutionalization of
     the movements of workers and assessment of their
     abilities.

17. The relative mobility of industrial jobs has been
     broken down into three constituent parts: A) the number
     of workers having changed firms in the period from one
     survey to the next, while remaining in the same
     industry; B) the number of workers recruited for an
     industrial job from a non-industrial job; C) the number
     of workers unemployed in the previous year holding an
     industrial job in the year of the survey. The sum of
     A+B+C represents the total number of industrial wage
     earners in the survey with less than one years
     seniority. This will be designated the number of job

take-ups in the period under consideration. A or A+B
are indicators of the mobility from one job to
another which ends up in the industrial sector.
Comparison between the two countries are made up using
these mobility flows as a proportion of the industrial
workforce.

18. The periods in question are from 1971-72 in France and
from 1973-74 in Japan. These different periods of time
make it even more essential to take into account only
particularly marked disparities between the two
countries.

19. A third difference must be mentioned, although without
any comment. The relative mobility flows between
employees and the self-employed (which are included in
the statistics used) seem to be higher in France. It is
unlikely that this difference would call into question
the identification made implicitly here between the
disparities in the mobility rates for the working
population as a whole and the disparities relating to
employees alone.

20. This phenomenon seems to be widespread throughout the
labour market, as is suggested by comparison of the
participation rates for women in the two countries in
1972: 15-25 years - Japan 51%, France 44%; 25-35 years
- Japan 43%, France 55%; over 40 - Japan 47%, France
41%. Participation rates for the 35-40 age group are
roughly the same in both countries.

21. The annual level of all "new job take-ups" for workers
already in employment - whether in industry or not - or
who were unemployed in the previous year, represented,
in the first half of the 1960s, 18% of total industrial
employment in France, compared with 10% in Japan.

22. Data is available on changes of firm relating to longer
periods and thus less subject to the influence of the
economic situation. In France, between 1965 and 1970,
27.7% of men in employment at both dates had changed
firms at least once; in Japan, in the ten years from
1960 to 1970, the comparable figure is 31.5%. This is
only slightly higher, although the period in question
is twice as long. The differences are also very
revealing if the rates of change of firms are broken
down by age group. The relative rates (base = 100 for
the 20-30 age group) are as follows: 20-50 - France 53,
Japan 64; over 50 - France 32, Japan 62. These figures
confirm - in an area wider than just industry - that
there is a trend towards greater relative mobility for
young workers in France and older workers in Japan.23.
On this point see the thesis by Nohara already cited,

particularly Ch. 4. These studies clearly highlight the
end in large firms to "organize" the abolition of the
restrictions on the movements of workers represented in
France by trades, functions, jobs or even workplaces.

24. This refers only to male manual workers.

25. Already implicit in Table II.

26. All categories added together, including management.

27. Cf. the comparative studies in France and Germany
    already mentioned, which reveal a ratio of the order of
    1.28 for male industrial employees and 1.30 for all
    industrial employees. The two industrial countries with
    which the French situation is being compared thus turn
    out to be fairly similar from the point of view of the
    disparity between the wages of manual and non-manual
    workers in industry.

28. The qualification system for manual workers is thus
    organized around a diploma acquired at the end of an
    apprenticeship. In this case, the influence of
    seniority is practically neutralized.

29. This respect is both a precondition for and a
    reflection of the apparently greater co-operation in
    these two countries between employers and employees in
    the case of conflicts over jobs or qualifications and
    between supervisory staff and those employed in
    execution tasks.

30. If the relationship between pay and age for all
    industrial employees (all qualifications mixed
    together) are compared, a hierarchy of countries for
    men emerges: +100% in Japan; +67% in France; +34% in
    Germany (for those under 21 to those over 50). For
    women this influence is virtually nil in Japan and 22%
    for Germany and 33% for France.

31. A reference of this type can obviously not be
    disassociated from the characteristics of the Japanese
    system of social security and the acceptance - or non-
    acceptance - by the state of the cost of dependents,
    including the cost of educating children.

32. It might be possible to assume that there is a link
    between the differences in acquisition of industrial
    qualifications in the broadest sense and the
    differences in the institutionalization of the
    relationships between employers and employees,
    particularly where wages are concerned. In Japan, this
    procedure is relatively "concentrated" on the Spring
    negotiations, but much more diffuse in France.

33. The fact that it is impossible for the moment
    to take into account the years 1978-81 may have a
    considerable influence on the results obtained. It

would be necessary to check in any follow-up to this article to what extent these years show a continuation of the trends that we are going to describe, or new developments, the nature and scope of which would then have to be examined.

34. In neither of the two countries does there seem to be a trend towards a relative reduction in the categories of the labour force (according to the distinction already used - male manual workers; male non-manual workers; women) in which relative costs are highest.

35. The data used take into account temporary workers with more than one month's seniority. It cannot thus be assumed a priori that this cessation of recruitment concerns only full-time workers. Moreover, it does not seem that the rate of part-time workers has increased significantly during the years under consideration. Data on changes within industry is not yet available, but for all non-agricultural employees, this rate decreased from 5.9% to 5% between 1972 and 1978 for men, and increased from 17% to 20% for women. It should be added, by way of a point of reference, that in 1977 this rate in industry was 3.2% for men and 14.8% for women (all qualifications together). All these rates include temporary workers and day labourers and relate to all firms, including those with less than ten employees, where large numbers of part-time female workers are concentrated.

36. Data available for France of labour turnover show that it has remained at a high level since 1976 (of the order of 12% in industrial firms with more than 200 employees (Source: Ministry of Labour), with recruitment rates of the order of 11%); in Japan, where figures are available for longer periods, the rate of recruitment seems to have been 7.5% on average for the period 1971-74, and 2.5% for 1976-78. However, it must be made clear that these figures are for the recruitment of full-time male workers in firms with more than 1,000 employees (this figure is not available for France).

37. In France, there was more substitution of non-manual workers for manual workers, particularly in large firms.

38. It would appear, for example, that the crisis, at least not in its early years has not significantly changed manual-non-manual mobility flows (technicians, foremen). Cf. Pohl and Soleilhavoup, 1981.

39. This strategy is linked with the procedures already described in other research on fragmentation of

companies' creation of subsidiaries, etc., the use of
sub-contracting and various new forms of contract. Cf.
in particular Germe and Michon, 1979-80.

40.   It is obvious that the situation could be reversed, at
      least in France, if industrial wage earners seeking
      work were taken into account, which from one point of
      view would not be unreasonable.

41.   Both as we have seen in large firms, and in the area of
      mobility that they form with smaller firms.

42.   This difference in trend was significantly reduced by
      the increase in Japan in the weight of new recruits in
      industrial job take-ups, which was greater even before
      the crisis.

43.   These mechanisms already existed in Japan before the
      crisis and have not become more widespread since.

REFERENCES

Eyraud, F. (1981). "Action Syndicale et Salarié: Comparison
      France - Grande-Bretagne". Doctoral thesis, Faculty of
      Economics.

Germe, J.F. and Michon, F. (1979-80). Stratégies des
      entreprises et formes particulières d'emplois.
      Seminaire d'Economie du Travail, 1 and 2, December 1979
      and June 1980.

Maurice, M., Sellier, F. and Sylvestre, J.-J. (1979). La
      production de la hiérarchie dans l'enterprise:
      recherche d'un effect societal, comparison France-
      Allemagne. Revue Française de Sociologie, June.

Maurice, M., Sellier, F. and Sylvestre, J.-J. (1982).
      "Politique d'Education et Organisation Industrielle".
      Presses Universitaires de France and MIT Press.

Nohara, H. (1981). "Espaces Professionelles et Dualisme du
      Marché du Travail au Japon". Doctoral thesis, LEST.

Pohl, A. and Soleilhavoup, J. (1981). Entrées des jeunes et
      mobilité des moins jeunes. Economie et Statistique,
      June.

The Institutional System, Labour Market and Segmentation in Hungary

G. KERTESI and G. SZIRACZKI

In the past fifteen years there has been a continuing discussion on labour market segmentation in Western Europe and in the United States. But how far can we talk about segmented labour markets in Eastern Europe, and more specifically, in Hungary, and is a similar analysis of forms and causes appropriate? This paper considers the labour market in Hungary first in terms of how the institutional system of the socialist economy relates to the labour market; second, the phases and characteristics of labour market transformation; and third, how divisions in the labour market have arisen in the 1970s. The analysis represents our first attempt to bring together evidence and findings which are currently available.

I. THE INSTITUTIONAL SYSTEM OF THE SOCIALIST ECONOMY - FROM A LABOUR MARKET ASPECT

After the Second World War, between 1947 and 1948, the political power structure in all of the Eastern European countries underwent major changes, and the rationalizations which occurred then or later led to a new, socialist institutional system which - despite modifications it has seen during the past 30 years - has remained basically

unchanged. The economy's organizational system is a
hierarchical, strongly centralized one: on the lower levels
of the hierarchy there are the enterprises; in the middle of
this hierarchy there are the regional organs of economic
control, trusts and branch ministries which in some cases
control a whole branch of industry; at the top of the
hierarchy is the state and the main economic decision-making
institutions.

For a better understanding of the socialist economy one
should look at the role of the state. The state's role is to
integrate the majority of the economic organizations into
the socialist sector, which comprises state-owned
enterprises and co-operatives. On the one hand it creates
direct dependence between the organs of economic control and
the economic units and, on the other, it sets the "rules of
the game" by force of law.

The state establishes the enterprises, determines their
field of production, regulates their markets, nominates and
dismisses the directors, etc. At the same time the state
sets the targets of economic development and the means to
achieve them, that is, the given system of regulation and
control: it determines the price system, the aggregate wage
bill, the system of taxes, etc. As Galasi (1982a) puts it,
under the socialist system the "invisible hand" of the
market is replaced by the "visible hand" of the state. The
enterprises are under obligation to produce and work within
an economy which is integrated and regulated by the state.

The enterprise-state relation is paternalistic. State
and enterprises are mutually interdependent. Through
regulation, the state may make enterprises unprofitable or
too profitable. If enterprises are unprofitable the state
"helps them out", while if they are too profitable the state
siphons off the "unjustified" profits. Because of this
paternalism, the enterprises' demand constraints are "soft"
and are not cost-sensitive [1], so that their demand for
almost all resources is relatively unrestricted. But the
actors in a socialist system are in every field motivated by
an inner expansion drive, which is most typically reflected
in the unlimited "investment hunger" (Bauer, 1978), and in
excess demand for labour (Gabor, 1979). Thus the expansion
of the enterprises and of the whole economy is determined
not by effective demand, but by the constraints of the
available resources. In this way, the socialist economy is
resource constrained and differs from the capitalist economy
which is often demand constrained.

Although the enterprises' structural position under
socialism is totally different from that of capitalist
enterprises, they are still independent units. The extent of

their autonomy under the different economic regulation
differs, but, even in the strictest system of centralized
control, they cannot be regarded as mere executives of
central plans. The state-enterprise relations can be
characterized not only be subordinate-superordinate
relations but by bargaining situations as well.

The basic characteristics of the labour market are
rooted in the institutional structure of the socialist
economy, and differ in a number of ways from those in a
capitalist system. First of all, the state's far-reaching
control of the labour market covers the employees on the one
hand and the economic units on the other. The main fields of
direct state control over employees are the choice of
occupation (through the educational system), the allocation
of labour to enterprises and the possibilities for
supplementary sources of income. The state also exercises
control over the enterprises. Its control covers the
enterprises' labour management, (number of workers, hirings
and layoffs), the determination of wage relations, the
enterprises' wage level and wage bill, those enterprise
activities that influence the workers' alternative
employment and income possibilities, and last but not least,
the state has an active role in the nomination of managers.

The second characteristic of the socialist economy's
labour market is the particular role of the socialist trade
unions concentrating mainly on socio-political issues at the
enterprise level and not permitting unionization to promote
the collective interests of employees through public
political pressure as it does in the West. One of the major
consequences of this is that, on the supply side, the labour
market is atomized, strengthening the employers' position on
the labour market. There are no institutionalized ways of
regional, branch or national workers' representation based
on the solidarity of employees. The assertion of individual
or group interests depends mainly on the <u>individual</u>
bargaining power of the workers.

The third characteristic of the labour market is that
enterprise behaviour is only partly regulated by the
economics of its own operation. The behaviour of enterprises
is affected more by the continuous bargaining process
between the state and the enterprise concerning the expected
output and the necessary resources. Generally the larger the
enterprise, the stronger position it has in the bargaining,
which is one of the reasons for the expansion drive.

Since enterprises have soft budget constraints, there
are no natural limits either to the labour demand or to the
size of the wage-bill in each enterprise. Up to the level of
full employment the state had no reason to restrain the

demand for labour since under socialism this is not only an
economic but also a political end. After full employment was
achieved, the state could not effectively restrain the
enterprises' demand for labour, leading in the early 1970s
to an overall labour shortage. The strict regulation of the
growth of the wage bill has been more successful. Its
control was a more urgent matter since a sudden rise in
purchasing power could lead to inflation, forced savings or
a combination of the two, and would upset the state's living
standard policy, bringing about social tension.

These characteristics of the socialist labour market
are reflected in its dynamics and particular tendencies of
development. In the long term, the development of flexible
and rigid structures are determined partly by the extent of
state paternalism, and with it, by the form and extent of
state regulation, and partly by the level of employment and
the size of labour reserves. In the short term, however, the
cyclical development of the economy also plays an important
role in the changes of flexible and rigid structures.

The extent of paternalism and the permanent element of
state control characteristic of a longer period have had an
impact on the given power relations of the labour market,
and set the limits of the possible strategies of employers
and employees. Whenever there is a change in state control,
the strategies of the parties also change, the labour market
becomes restructured, and new flexible and rigid structures
come into being. The level of employment and size of labour
reserves also affect power relations in the labour market.
During times when the employment level is low and there are
large labour reserves, the labour market favours the
employers, while in the opposite case it favours the
employees.

II. THE PHASES OF LABOUR MARKET TRANSFORMATION

In the history of the Hungarian socialist economy two main
periods can be distinguished. the period between 1949 and
1967 is characterized by strict state control which allowed
market relations only in consumer goods industries. The
centre's far-reaching intervention greatly limited both the
enterprises' independence and the movement of employees.
But, in spite of the rapidly increasing level of employment,
there were labour reserves available for the system to
expand.

Since the economic reform was introduced in 1968,
enterprise independence has increased, the labour market has
become more liberal, full employment has been basically

achieved and labour shortage has emerged. The extent and
scope of the state's paternalism diminished somewhat and
state control took more the form of monetary regulation.

A. Strictly Controlled State Labour Market 1949–1967

After 1949, the abolition of the private sector,
industrialization and the increase in the labour force
participation rate were accompanied by a rapid and major
restructuring of society and the labour market. More
precisely, the labour market and the labour force became
homogeneous.

From the aspect of long-term processes, an unstructured
and potentially fluid labour market characterized the first
period. But this unstructured labour market was also rigid,
since the state strictly limited the flexibility of both
employees and employers and thus the state's own flexibility
as well. The system of economic regulation and the
institutionalized relations between state and enterprise
limited the rational labour management at the micro level.

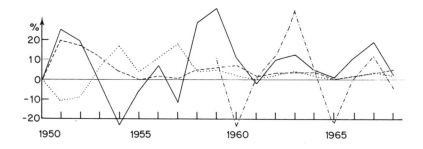

Fig. 1 Investment cycles and the
development of employment, overtime hours and real wages

_____ Yearly growth rate of investment

---------- Yearly growth rate of employment (socialist
            industry excluding food manufacturing)

—··—··—··— Rate of change in the ratio of overtime hours to
            total working hours performed.

·········· Growth rate of real wages per worker (socialist sector)

Source; Statistical Yearbooks, 1950–1968.

At the same time, the monopoly position of the state-owned
sector and the elimination of all alternative income sources
put great masses of workers into a dependent position. For
the employees this meant fewer possibilities to make
rational use of their labour power; their only possibility
was to restrain work performance [2].

The overall rigidity of labour market structures,
however, did not prevent various forms of flexible
adaptation to short-term economic cycles. The best known
form of the socialist economy's cyclical development is the
periodic fluctuation of investment [3].

At the bottom of the investment cycle, when investments
are kept back, enterprises have the better position in the
labour market. There is a slow-down in the growth rate of
real wages, the flow of employees towards industry
diminishes and there is an overall decline in overtime
hours, although there are no layoffs. At the top of the
cycle, however, employees have the better position: there
is a growing demand in enterprises, the flow of labour
towards industry increases, and the growth rate of real
wages and the number of overtime hours also increase
(Szekffy, 1978) [4].

B. Economic Reform, Liberalized Labour Market (1968)

The second period in the history of the Hungarian labour
market began in the late 1960s when the available labour
resources were exhausted and full employment was
established. The economic reform in 1968 liberalized the
system of economic control and the labour market. There was
a decrease in the extent and scope of state paternalism and
an increase in the freedom of decision of labour market
actors, with the removal of the earlier restrictions on
labour turnover leaving a practically free choice of jobs.
One of the important consequences of the reform was that it
enabled the expansion of the second economy, which had begun
to emerge in the mid 1960s but was restricted and of little
importance at that time. The second economy is defined here
to cover all activities and income redistribution outside
the centrally organized system of production and
distribution. The most important fields of the second
economy are small-scale agricultural production on household
plots and auxiliary farms [5], private dwellings building
activity, legal private small-scale industry and small
shopkeeping, and illegal service and repair activities.

The second economy came into being because the totally
nationalized socialist economy was unable to continuously

satisfy public demand. Some of the needs (such as repair
services and part of food production) could be satisfied
only by way of expensive state investment, if at all. Thus,
the transfer of these activities into the second economy
freed resources (in the socialist sector) that could be used
for other purposes to improve public supply.

The rapid spread of the second economy, since it made
employment possible outside the socialist sector, changed
the labour market position of workers considerably, by
increasing their opportunities for employment and income.
This brought an end to the labour market monopoly position
of the enterprises. It also led to new behaviour patterns.
The period of the rapid improvement in the living standards
(from the late 1960s to the mid 1970s) brought about great
changes in the economic attitude and behaviour of households. Consumption was an end in itself for most of the
families and resulted in the predominance of employee
behaviour characterized by wage earner strategies to maximize family incomes [6]. Workers began to attempt to

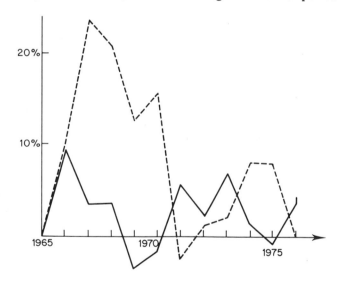

Fig.2 Yearly growth of incomes from agricultural
cooperatives and small scale farms

_____ Total income from household, auxiliary and private
           farms
- - - - - Wage-income in agricultural cooperatives

maximize incomes by making use of both their good bargaining
positions in the socialist sector and the alternative
possibilities in the second economy. The combination of both
sectors' advantages is, for many workers, much more
advantageous than working only in the socialist sector or in
the second economy, combining the security of the socialist
sector with income maximization through a second job.

The liberalization of the labour market, the rapid
expansion of the second economy, more independence of
enterprises, full employment and a permanent labour shortage
together created, in contrast to the earlier period, a
structured labour market offering more opportunities for
employees. However, there can also be found some new short-
term flexible adaptation mechanisms. For example, some
groups of employees, by short-term re-allocation of their
labour power between the socialist sector and the second
economy, are able to adapt flexibly to the income fluctuations in the socialist sector caused by the economy cycles.
When the growth rate of wages is high, the workers concentrate their activity mostly in the socialist sector, but
when wages fall, they compensate by working more in the
second economy, as can be seen in the case of agricultural
workers in Fig. 2.

III. THE EMERGENCE OF SEGMENTS IN THE LABOUR MARKET

Having discussed the general tendencies, we will go on to
outline the most important interests and strategies that
divide the national labour market into differently
functioning segments. We will concentrate mainly on the
developments of the 1970s, and on the labour market of
manual workers in the state sector, explaining the formation
of labour market structures by the joint effect of the strategies of all three labour market actors: the state, the
enterprises and the employees.

Our starting point is that in the socialist system
there is a continuous expansion drive resulting from the
organizational system of economy. In the labour market,
enterprises have an unlimited demand for labour and the
general labour shortage in the 1970s forced the enterprises
to devise particular strategies. But conflicts emerge
between state regulation and the growing aspirations of the
enterprises.

The best known conflict from the labour market aspect
is caused by central wage regulation. A self-regulating
mechanism to keep the balance between incomes and the supply
of consumer goods at a fairly stable price level is

impossible because of the soft budget constraint of the
enterprises. This function is taken over by the state. One
of its means is the central wage regulation. The enterprises
find themselves in a paradoxical situation. The state's
restrictive wage regulation is continually depriving them of
the financial means by which the jobs they offer could be
made attractive; at the same time the enterprise is always
interested in hiring new workers even when the marginal
return from a newly employed worker is zero or negative.

The competition for labour between enterprises leads
them to adapt in two extreme ways: either by emphasizing
their own importance to the national economy as an argument
to get wage preferences from the state, or by altering their
internal structure to increase their flexibility concerning
enterprise wage and employment relations. As a rule the
first strategy is followed by the big enterprises, the
second by the middle-sized and small ones. But the most
common behaviour of the enterprise is the combination of the
two strategies. However, we will deal here with the second
solution since it is the key to segmentation within the
enterprise, the most common form in Hungary [7].

Enterprises have conflicts with state regulation in
this respect. The state strives from time to time towards a
uniform regulation of wage relations: it introduces
administrative regulations with which the proportions of
wages in the individual occupations or industrial branches
can be compared at national level. The state aims at
eliminating disparities in wages across regions, between
branches of industry and between enterprises in order to
follow the ideological principle of "equal pay for equal
work". To achieve this end the state attempts to introduce
the uniform system of wage tariffs, based on a complicated
system of scores for measured quantitative indicators. In
the case of manual workers, skills and working conditions
have special weight.

Two groups of workers are able to make use of the above
described opportunities for flexibility. The first group
includes those workers who are picked by the enterprise in
order to fill the key jobs permanently. For these so called
"elite workers" wages are determined in a way that makes
leaving the enterprise particularly "expensive" for them.
The second group have a weaker position in the enterprise.

To understand the nature of these key positions we must
take into account the fact that an enterprise's work
organization does not function like a precision instrument.
There are always problems on the shop floor that need to be
solved quickly in the interests of continuous production.
In a socialist economy, the problems are greater and more

common because the resource-constrained character of the
enterprises manifests itself not only in attempts to
maximize production beyond every limit (and, because of
their soft budget constraint, quite regardless of costs),
but also in the fact that since every enterprise behaves
alike in this respect, they all have a permanent shortage of
inputs. Shortages crop up in inputs of raw materials, semi-
finished goods, spare parts, labour etc., and a frequent
form of adjustment is that the enterprise, being short of
certain inputs, changes its output mix and forces it on its
customers. But the enterprise can also cope with the
uncertainties and variations in input supply by the ad hoc
changing of its own input mix. These ad hoc adjustments,
such as substituting "home-made" spare parts for standard
ones in short supply, and making up for a shortage of labour
by having one worker work on several machines, etc., give
ample scope for informal bargaining processes within the
enterprise between workers and management. As much as the
workers depend on the uninterrupted supply of materials,
parts, etc., so does the management depend on the ability of
the workers to cope with the above disruption in supply [8].

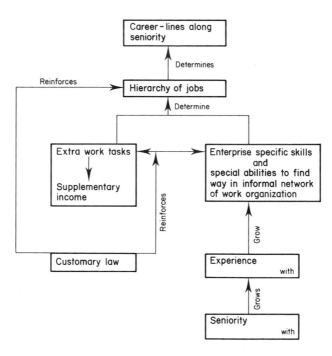

Fig. 3. Career lines
characterising the cluster of elite jobs.

The more enterprise-specific skills a worker has, the better
he finds his way in the network of intra-enterprise informal
relations, the likelier it is that he gets a job where he
has to undertake the above ad hoc adjustments with some
frequency. It is such jobs that we define as the key positions in an enterprise. Since the management is interested
in the smooth working of these recurring ad hoc adjustments,
it rewards the special work tasks connected with these
adjustments with extra income through regular overtime and
other means. The incumbents of these key jobs, on the the
other hand, tend to regard these extra work tasks and the
possibilities for overtime earnings that go with their jobs
as their possessions under a sort of customary law.

Since enterprise-specific skills and the ability to
find one's way in the complex of intra-enterprise informal
relations tend to vary with the length of employment with
the given enterprise, there will be a hierarchy of jobs
according to the length of employment and the incumbents of
these jobs, set up on the basis of skill content and
customs. This is also the case even if these jobs with
different pay and prestige belong formally to one and the
same occupational category. The hierarchy of jobs formed
according to seniority means that, for workers loyal to the
enterprise, career lines open up, at a rate dependent on the
pace of demographic change, towards jobs with higher pay and
prestige. The logic of the career lines characterizing the
cluster of elite jobs is shown by Fig. 3.

Enterprises have other means of increasing the pay of
their elite workers. Workers in key positions often happen
to be classified as working under specially hard conditions,
so that they can be paid wages higher than designated for
them by the tariff system. There is no mechanism of central
regulation fixing the number of such workers, but the number
does not vary very much. Yet when the uniform tariff system
was introduced, there was a jump in the number of workers
working under hard conditions.

By applying these internal allocation and wage
determination mechanisms, the enterprise is able to pay them
much more than is "prescribed" by the tariff. As a result
there is an inclusion [9] procedure in the internal labour
market for this group. If a privileged worker leaves the
enterprise, he gets in his new job the wage prescribed by
the tariff system which is much lower, along with other
disadvantages placing him in an unfavourable bargaining
position and making it difficult for him to change jobs.
Thus, the enterprise increases the opportunity cost of
leaving the company for these workers.

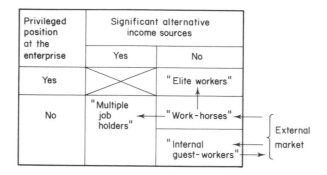

Fig. 4. Demarcation lines between
elite workers and other groups.

The advantageous opportunities for the workers to earn extra
pay within the enterprise are, of course, limited. The elite
workers are therefore interested in excluding the other
groups within the enterprise from these opportunities [10].
That is why this segment of the internal labour market is
closed not only from the inside, but from the outside as
well. There is a strong demarcation line between the elite
workers and the other groups in the internal labour market
(see Fig. 4).

Let us now look into the position of a second group of
workers who are needed by the enterprise but do not obtain
all the above mentioned privileges. Their structure differs
because of state wage regulation, the intensive labour
demand of the enterprise and its efforts to form an internal
labour market.

The enterprises are interested in hiring as many low-
paid workers as possible, for because state regulation
determines the per capita wage level or wage bill of
enterprises as the basis of the allowed yearly rise in
wages, other workers' wages can then be increased. One group
of workers are willing to adopt a strategy which results in
them being low paid. Within the enterprise they mostly
restrain work performance and effort as well as working
hours. They supplement their low incomes in the state
regulated labour market with incomes from legal or illegal
activities in the second economy. Their strategy can be
interpreted in terms of employment security and income
maximization. Employment security explains why this group
does not want to live solely on income from the second
economy. Alternative income sources are not always available

outside the enterprise because of major variations in demand
in the second economy, and because some of these activities
are not legally guaranteed, the state's attitude towards the
second economy is quite ambiguous. So workers interested in
having a stable, reliable monthly income want jobs in the
state-owned enterprises. At the same time, they either have
no monopoly skills that would place them in the elite
group's position within the enterprise, or even if they have
such skills, they decide upon the combination of the two
types of activities for reasons of higher incomes.

In the case of these multiple job holders the
enterprise puts up with their strategy of restraining work
performance, so these employees neither want nor can get
elite jobs. The separation of the two groups can be best
described by the notion of demarcation: the border line is
kept from both sides [11].

However, inside the enterprise, there is a further
segment which is different from both the elite workers and
the above mentioned multiple job holders. They are workers
who are not in key positions within the enterprise, and who
are also excluded from income opportunities outside the
enterprise. Workers in this segment are different as regards
their social status. There are young, urban skilled and
semi-skilled workers, who because of their youth, have not
yet organized their activities in the second economy. There
are also young rural workers who are detached from their
traditional surroundings (they do not have household plots)
but are not yet accustomed to industrial or urban
conditions, or semi-skilled workers who do not have skills
to make use of in the second economy.

Their efforts to improve their underprivileged position
are constrained, on the one hand, by the strategy of
exclusion followed by elite workers and, on the other hand,
by the lack of opportunities for extra income in the second
economy which prevents them from achieving a favourable
compromise with the enterprise. The only way for them to
obtain higher incomes is to increase work performance and
work intensity. Some of these workers increase work
performance in order to get into "overtime jobs"; the
enterprise often takes advantage of it by pressing for
higher work performance while saying that it is the closed
group of workers and not the enterprise that excludes them
from the privileged positions. It appears as if these young,
skilled workers who keep up a stiff pace of work are in jobs
in the lower tier of the career lines which lead to the
elite jobs. The problem is, however, that to get into the
elite jobs is much more difficult than to get into higher
income brackets inside the cluster of the elite jobs. This

group of workers is characterized by employment stability,
more effort and limited possibilities, and so can be
described as "workhorses".

For a better understanding of worker behaviour in this
segment, we note that in Hungary work intensity and work
performance in the various occupations is not regulated
either by the state or by trade unions. Western trade unions
place special emphasis on equalizing work intensity among
enterprises, industrial branches or regions for the same
occupation, but in Hungary the division between work
performance and wages are a matter of "free bargaining"
between employers and employees. This "free" - not
institutionalized - bargaining mechanism is favourable to
workers who have monopoly skills or supplementary income
sources within the enterprise (elite workers) or who have
some alternative income sources outside the enterprise
(multiple job holders).

In these two dominant segments, although workers do not
have formal union-like representation of interests, they
are sometimes able to promote their interests collectively
because of their strong bargaining position. But the workers
in the third segment can be made to keep a stiff pace of
work because they are motivated by the desire to get into
elite jobs. So their bargaining strength is weak and is
further weakened by competition inside this group to get
into the key positions which prevents them from adopting a
collective strategy on the division between work intensity
and wages. Therefore, it is usually the enterprise that is
stronger and increases in work performance are followed by
lower increases in wages. Workers in this group leave the
enterprise only when it presses for work performance beyond
that which the workers will tolerate.

The fourth group of workers have jobs where training is
usually not needed, employment is unstable and jobs require
hard physical work under poor conditions. Demand and supply
mechanisms and state regulation have an impact on the
formation of this segment. The segment itself can be
described by the socio-economic characteristics of a social
stratum. Its social traits are low educational and skill
levels, workers usually coming from underdeveloped parts of
the country where there are few jobs and the wage level is
low. Since it is hard to make a living under such
circumstances, these people are more or less forced to
migrate. They could be called the segment of the "internal
guest workers".

There is permanent demand for this type of worker.
Since in the allocation of investment funds new investment
projects are preferred to modernizing ones, the limited

amount of money the enterprises have for modernization is used for modernizing the main work process. So the gap between jobs is further widened by the type of technology, and jobs where modern technology is introduced become isolated from other jobs where the modernization process is slow (material handler, loader, packer, etc.) [12]. This type of technical division of labour considerably increases the demand for unskilled workers. These workers can be found in every enterprise, but there are certain enterprises that employ them in large numbers. Such jobs are in the building industry, road construction, railways and agriculture (mostly for seasonal work). The result is a group of workers whose number is more or less constant, who can be found wherever there is a large investment project and who are constantly moving from one job to the next.

Work organization itself creates a similar division. Good jobs – in the main stream of technological development – require trained workers. The organization of work in marginal industries does not require many such jobs and so a primary labour force is used to a limited extent. But there are a great number of jobs in this segment without any restriction on entry, that is, with no requirements for training, so that almost all jobs are ports of both entry and exit. Marginal industries may offer higher wages but this will only come through longer working hours [13].

Consequently there is great instability of employment for these workers. It is obvious, however, that the instability is not itself a social trait of the workers, but results from the interaction of the social traits of the workers with the labour demand of enterprises employing them and the organization of work.

IV. CONCLUSION

In this paper we have tried to explain the pattern of segmentation in the Hungarian labour market with reference to the institutional features of the socialist economy. We have shown that the institutional pattern (the role of the state in economic integration, the hierarchical links and paternalism) explain soft budget constraints, relatively unlimited demand for resources (including labour), and a shortage economy. These in turn induced certain behaviour patterns for enterprises and workers. On the labour market, this means that:

i) Since the state pursues an extensive economic regulating activity, the wages paid by the

enterprises are not determined by profitability but rather by the central regulation
of wages or, more precisely, by the bargaining processes between the state and the
enterprises.
ii) Because of the limited role of trade unions,
the supply side of the labour market is
fragmented.
iii) Because of the absence of market composition
in the economy, the enterprises' labour
demand is nearly unlimited.

We distinguish two major periods: the first between 1949-67
and the second from 1968 to the present. The first period
was characterized by an unstructured and, in the long run,
rigid labour market whose rigidity was somewhat mitigated by
flexible adjustment processes to the short-term economic
cycles. More flexible labour market structures emerged in
the liberalized labour market since 1968, mainly due to the
expansion of the second economy and the permitting of a free
choice of jobs, which accelerated the spread of consumerism
that accompanied higher standards of living. New types of
workers' strategies appeared that combined income sources in
the first and second economy, and the enterprises were
forced into developing internal labour markets.

The social and labour market processes of the 1970s led
to marked stratification among the workers. With the
emergence and strengthening of the internal labour market,
the segments within the enterprise became more and more
sharply demarcated. These inequalities can be best
demonstrated in the distribution of privileged intra-
enterprise positions and the availability of alternative
income sources in the second economy. The outcome was four
distinctly delineated segments in the state labour market of
the 1970s.

NOTES

1. See Kornai (1980). Kornai's book is the first
    theoretical attempt to give an overall explanation for
    the functioning of the socialist economy. In the
    following we also use Kornai's conceptual apparatus
    when treating the Hungarian labour market.
2. This widespread worker behaviour was reflected in the
    press from time to time and described as "destructive
    to national property", "waster", "negligent",
    "prodigal", "wage and norm defrauder", "arbitrary

learner", "skulking", "notorious absentee", "defrauder
of sickness benefit", "simulator". the propaganda made
them responsible for the lack of labour discipline
and for low productivity.

3. The peculiarity of socialist investment cycles – as
    against capitalist cycles – is that the enterprises
    with soft budget constraints have an excess demand for
    investment goods and from time to time they are able to
    break the efforts made by the state to establish macro-
    level equilibrium. There is a continued demand for
    investment goods and an increase in investment up to
    the point when the chronic disequilibrium prompts the
    state to restrain investment activity in the whole of
    the economy. Thus tension is temporarily reduced and at
    the same time the state becomes less sensitive to the
    need to maintain equilibrium. Enterprise investment
    activity is given a green light again and the whole
    process is repeated. A description of the investment
    cycles in socialist economies, and an overall
    explanation of their causes was given by Bauer (1978,
    1981) in his comprehensive theoretical and economic
    historical work.

4. The above described relations are valid for real
    wages only from 1957–58 onwards. During the period of
    forced industrialization (1950–55) investment and real
    wages were moving in opposite directions. The reason
    for this was that investment increased at the expense
    of consumption (consumption-symmetrical cycle), while
    from 1958 it was at the expense of foreign trade
    balance (foreign trade-symmetrical cycle). (Bauer,
    1978, 1981).

5. The land associated with household plots (small-scale
    family farms) is given to the co-operative members and
    employees by the employer (generally 1–2 cad. yokes).
    The auxiliary farms comprise the cultivated land around
    the houses of village people, and form the larger share
    of the land in the second economy.

6. Consumer behaviour which became widespread in the 1970s
    in Hungary is similar to what Goldthorpe and Lockwood
    called "instrumental orientation" of Western affluent
    workers. At the same time there are major differences.
    The Western new workers' behaviour can be described
    by "instrumental collectivism", instrumental in the
    sense that work is subordinated to familial income
    maximization, and workers' participation in economic
    organizations is a means of achieving this aim. It is
    collective in that they get involved in union activity
    in order to achieve higher wages. In contrast to this,

the consumption-oriented Hungarian worker who also
works in the second economy can be described by
"instrumental individualism". What is involvement in
the the union's economic actions in the case of Western
workers are individual, scattered actions in the case
of the Hungarian employees, which leads to highly
differentiated bargaining positions. C.f. Goldthorpe
and Lockwood (1963) and Goldthorpe et al. (1968).

7.   In the following paragraphs we again relied heavily on
     Kornai's (1980) concept.
8.   It was Kemeny (1978) who - in a case study on an
     enterprise in engineering - first called attention to
     the fact that even in the case of a seemingly extremely
     fixed technology (assembly line), the workers are able
     to significantly transform the work process and actual
     work organization - exactly because there is a shortage
     economy. Laki (1981) points to similar phenomena when
     designating the forms of forced adjustments to
     shortages as the typical terrain of innovative activity
     in the socialist economy.
9.   The social closure is a particularly important factor
     in understanding the nature of cleavages in the social
     structure and the social mechanisms that bring about
     cleavages, since such closures occur at times when,
     because of the scarcity of jobs or goods, there is
     increased competition. It was Max Weber (1921) who
     first called attention to this, stressing potential for
     its labour market interpretation (pp. 23 and 201-203).
     Fifty years on, Parking (1974) discussed this problem.
     Since then it has been mostly German research workers
     who have used this conceptual apparatus to describe
     labour market processes. See Bieler et al. (1979);
     Kreckel (1980); Sengenberger (1981).
10. Haraszti (1977) in his case study gave an overall
     picture of the mechanisms by which elite workers
     exclude others from the opportunities to earn extra
     income.
11. This process is clearly shown by the respective case
     studies of two enterprises. Sziraczki's (1982) case
     study of a motor transport enterprise shows that due to
     the emergence of the internal labour market two large
     groups of workers get progressively differentiated. On
     the basis of seniority the elite workers move
     continuously forward along career lines made up of a
     sequence of jobs with ever higher pay and prestige
     (from the intra-city lorry transport up to
     international transport). The other large group of
     workers get stuck on the lower steps of the career

ladder and they compensate for their relatively low
wages in the enterprise with income from work on the
household plot. This kind of demarcation takes on even
more extreme forms when there is a split in the
internal labour market not only between the different
jobs of an occupation, but between different plants of
the same enterprise as well. See Kollo's (1982) case
study on the textile industry.

12. In the mid 1970s in Hungary about one million workers
were employed in jobs where they had no mechanical
handling equipment.

13. There is a similar situation among secondary workers in
the US according to Osterman (1975).

REFERENCES

Bauer, T. (1978). Investments cycles in planned economy.
Acta Oeconomica, XXI (3).

Bauer, T. (1981). "Tervgsazdasag, beruhazas, ciklusok"
("Planned Economy, Investment, Cycles"). Kozgazdasagi
es Jogi Konyvkiado, Budapest.

Bieler, H. et al (1979). Interne und externe Arbeitsmarkte –
Theorie und Empirie zur Kritik eines neoklassischen
Paradigmas. In "Arbeitsmarkt-segmentation – Theorie und
Therapie im Lichte der empirischen Befunde" (C.
Brinkmann, ed.). Beitrab 33, Nurnberg.

Gabor, R.I. (1979). Munka erohiany a mai szocialista
gazdasagban (Labour shortage in today's socialist
economy). Kozgasdasagi Szemle, 2.

Galasi, P. (1982a). "A munkaeropiac mukodese a mai
szocialista rendszerben" ("The functioning of the
labour market in today's socialist system"). Budapest,
manuscript.

Galasi, P. (ed.) (1982b). "A munkaeropiac, szerkezete es
mukodese Magyarorszagon ("The structure and functioning of
the labour market in Hungary"). Kozgasdasagi es Jogi
Konyvkiado, Budapest.

Goldthorpe, J. H. and Lockwood, D. (1963). Affluence and the
British class structure. Sociological Review, II (2).

Goldthorpe, J.H. et al (1968). "The Affluent Worker:
Industrial Attitudes and Behaviour". Cambridge
University Press, Cambridge.

Haraszti, M. (1977). "A Worker in a Worker's State".
Penguin, London.

Kemeny, I. (1978). La chaine dans une usine hongroise. Actes
de la Recherche en Sciences Sociales, November.

Kornai, J. (1980). "The Economics of Shortage". North-
    Holland, Amsterdam.
Kreckel, R. (1980). Unequal opportunity structure and labour
    market segmentation. Sociology, 4.
Kollo, J. (1982). A kulso es belso munkaeropiac kapcsolata
    egy pamutszovodeben (Connections between external and
    internal labour market in a cotton-mill). In "A
    munkaeropiac szerkezete es mukodese Magyarorszagon"
    ("The Structure and Functioning of the Labour Market in
    Hungary") (P. Galasi, ed.). Kozgazdasagi es Jogi
    Konyvkiado, Budapest.
Laki, M. (1981). "A kenyszeritett innovacio - Muszaki
    fejlesztes az eladok piacan" (Forced innovation -
    Technological development on the sellers' market").
    Budapest, manuscript.
Osterman, P. (1975). An empirical study of labour market
    segmentation. Industrial and Labour Relations Review,
    4.
Parkin, F. (1974). Strategies of social closure in class
    formation. In "The Social Analysis of Class Structure
    (F. Parkin, ed.). Tavistock, London.
Sengenberger, W. (1981). Labour market segementation and the
    business cycle. In "The Dynamics of Labour Market
    Segmentation" (F. Wilkinson, ed.). Academic Press,
    London and Orlando.
Szekffy, K. (1978). A berek es a termelekenyseg kapcsolata
    az iparban 1950-1974 kozott (Wages - productivity
    relations in the industry between 1950 and 1974).
    Kozgazdasagi Szemle. 7-8.
Sziraczki, Gy. (1982). Egy belso munkaeropiac kialakulasa es
    mukodese (The formation and functioning of an internal
    labour market). In "A munkaeropiac szerkezete es
    mukodese Magyarorszagon" ("The Structure and
    Functioning of the Labour Market in Hungary") (P.
    Galasi, ed.). Kozgazdasagi es Jogi Konyvkiado,
    Budapest.
Weber, M. (1921). "Wirtschaft und Gesellschaft". J.C.B.
    Mohr, Tubingen, 1976.

The Impact of Privatization on the United Kingdom Local Government Labour Market

J. WALKER and R. MOORE

I. INTRODUCTION

The fastest growing areas of state expenditure and employment in the post-war period have been those areas covered by the "local state" with expenditure almost doubling as a proportion of GDP since the late 1940s. There has been debate about the theoretical specificity of the local state, whether it can be defined in terms of <u>class</u> relations, as Marxists see it (Cockburn, 1977), or in terms of the <u>community</u> using a Weberian analysis (Saunders, 1980). The functions of the local state may then be described as reproduction of labour power (housing, education, social services) and of the relations of production (education, police) by Marxists, or as social consumption by Weberians. In either case they are seen as gains to the working class, but the gain is always limited by the restrictive nature of the social relations involved in gaining access to the state (London Edinburgh Weekend Return Group, 1980).

These gains are under attack as part of the Tory New Right's strategy for restructuring British capitalism and the State. Incorporation and concession are being replaced by exclusion and repression. In terms of the state, it involves a rolling back of state activity and a restruc-

turing of what remains, increasing law and order services
and reducing welfare services. This is being achieved with
much popular support, based on a strong ideological campaign
which builds on peoples' "anti-state" feelings arising from
their experience of relations within the state.
Privatization is also a part of this restructuring. Given
the crisis of profitability in British capitalism, the Tory
right is seeking to move the boundary between direct state
production and production for private profit, expanding the
area of the latter. The central state has strongly
encouraged sub-contracting of local government services to
private industry, introducing restrictive legislation on the
operation of direct labour organizations (DLOs) and
commissioning reports on the possibilities of privatization
(Coopers and Lybrand, 1981). Many Tory local authorities
have been keen to take up the calls for privatization. The
main areas affected so far have been refuse collection,
cleaning and maintenance and repair, but the possibilities
are numerous.

Workers in the local state lose out as both consumers
and workers. As workers they are under pressure of job
losses and encroachments on working practices to increase
the rate of exploitation. Privatization is one means of
evading union controls and increasing exploitation. It
enables the local authority to evade national collective
bargaining agreements on pay and conditions. Where
contractors have been used, they employ non-union labour and
avoid restrictions on working practices. This is the source
of the gains in "efficiency" which accrue from the sub-
contracting of services to the private sector.

The paper proceeds by examining the arguments for
privatization in orthodox economic theory. We then place the
pressures for privatization in the context of the crisis of
Keynesianism and the Tory New Right as an alternative for
managing British capitalism. The main section of the paper
examines privatization in terms of its impact on the labour
force. The various arguments are brought together in the
conclusion.

II. ORTHODOX THEORY AND THE PUBLIC SECTOR

There are two different issues at stake for neo-classical
theory with regard to public provision of goods and
services. First, there is an issue of finance: should goods
be paid for from tax revenue with output politically
determined, or should it be financed by user charges with
output determined by the market? Second, there is an issue

of production: should the goods or services be produced by
directly employed state workers or by private companies?
These two sets of alternatives give four different possible
combinations of production and finance (Prest, 1982; Coopers
and Lybrand, 1981).

According to neo-classical welfare theory, the market
system should produce pricing at marginal cost, and hence a
Pareto optimal allocation of resources. In the cases of
market failure there is a role for the government to
supplement the price system. In the case of public goods,
characterized by non-rivalry in consumption and generally by
non-excludability, an optimal allocation of resources is
achieved when the sum of individual prices equals the
marginal cost. Since it is generally impossible to get
people to reveal correctly their preferences and hence
charge appropriately, due to the "free rider" problem, the
state may use tax finance to provide the service. In the
case of externalities, there is a divergence beween private
and social costs and benefits. The government can compensate
for externalities by a combination of taxes and subsidies,
although again there is a problem of getting preferences
correctly revealed. In the case of falling costs, marginal
cost pricing will not cover average costs, and the
government must provide subsidies, as in the case of public
transport. These are all issues of relevance to local
authority services. Garbage collection and disposal both
involve externalities in terms of health hazards to others
and to future generations if they are not adequately carried
out. Foster et al (1980) concluded that the standard public
goods characteristics applied to less than 10% of gross
expenditure (excluding roads) and hence that the majority of
services should be financed by user charges, a conclusion
supported by others (Coopers and Lybrand, 1981; Committee of
Enquiry, 1976). But all these cases are issues of public
finance, not production. If goods and services are to be
financed out of taxation, to correct for market failure,
they may be produced either directly or by sub-contracting
to a private company.

The argument for private versus public production
involves a completely different set of arguments. The
arguments in favour of sub-contracting to the private sector
are those put forward by the Adam Smith Institute and
others, that the profit motive and the need to maintain
custom leads to greater "efficiency" in the private sector:

> It is the need for profit which keeps the
> private sector alert to consumer requirements,
> and the competition which keeps it both

efficient and innovative. The public service,
having no need to attract custom, no
profitability requirements to pare its costs,
and no competition to fear usurping its
position, tends to operate in the interests of
those who administer it (Forsyth, 1981, p. 1).

Indeed, Forsyth has discovered "...an amazing thing called
'Savas's Law'":

'Savas's Law' says that if you take the cost
of any service when provided by direct labour,
and divide it by the cost as provided by the
private contractor, it always comes out the
same: 5/2 (Butler and Pirie, 1981, p. 35).

The notion that private industry is in some sense more
"efficient", to the universal benefit of all, stems from the
failure of neo-classical economics to distinguish between
labour and labour power. They see the firm as a "black box"
combining inputs in a technically defined way to produce
outputs. Supporters of private contractors continually point
to the lower manning levels, longer hours and more flexible
working practices in the private sector as major sources of
greater "efficiency" which is to the benefit of the
ratepayers. Such gains in "efficiency" are achieved by a
higher rate of exploitation at the expense of the workers in
the service.
      The disadvantages of using contractors – from the
perspective of orthodox theory – are twofold. First, there
is the cost of regulating private contracts, ensuring that
services are carried out to the required standard. Second,
in the case of building work, there are future costs of
repairs and maintenance, which will be higher if work is
skimped in the interests of the contractors' profits.
      Forsyth apparently has not grasped the distinction
between arguments concerning the financing of a service, and
arguments about production. Introduction of user charges is
seen as a method of introducing market discipline on local
authorities:

Making a direct charge for services to the
public is another route to economy. Again, it
is a method which brings some of the
disciplines of the private sector to local
government. The charge not only raises offsetting revenue and acts to ration the
service, it also demands a useful indicator of

how much the service is demanded and
appreciated (p.2).

Charging will only produce the optimal output and indicate
how much the service is appreciated if the goods or service
in question are private ones or if preferences are correctly
revealed for public goods.

III. CONSENSUS KEYNESIANISM AND THE LOCAL STATE

Until the mid-1970s, all post-war governments tended to
implement policies in line with the historic compromise
between capital and organized labour. The working class
gained access to the Welfare State and a rising standard of
living, but in return limited its demands within narrow
economic and political boundaries, posing no fundamental
challenge to the rights of capital.

At the national state level this led to an extension of
government economic intervention through defensive
nationalization of key industries and utilities and the use
of fiscal and monetary regulation, combined with attempts at
both command and indicative planning. Politically, it led to
the deployment of institutional arrangements aimed at
integrating and incorporating organized labour.

Although subject to what have been deemed to be
different political pressures, the local state performs
functions similar to those of the state in general, securing
conditions favourable to capital accumulation by
contributing to the production and reproduction of the
forces and relations of production (Cockburn, 1980;
Saunders, 1977). Specifically, the local state is
responsible for many functions of the Welfare State which
are concerned with the reproduction of labour power, which
formerly fell almost solely to the family and therefore on
women.

Keynesianism was a balancing act, with the aim of
maintaining growth - ensuring that capital accumulation was
maintained, while at the same time offering the working
class gains through rising real wages, a more equitable
distribution of income and universal social welfare
provision.

Notwithstanding the desire to ensure the best possible
conditions for the extension and stabilization of
capitalism, local state provision constituted real gains for
the working class - gains which in the recent period certain
sectors of organized labour have fought to defend. But those
gains, along with the very stability and continuity of the

social, economic and political system, have been steadily
undermined both by a host of internal contradictions
particular to the local state, and the irrevocable slide
towards collapse of the British economy, the conjunctural
crisis of the 1970s and 1980s representing the culmination
of de-stabilizing factors and circumstances which emerged in
the late 1950s.

A whole range of factors have contributed to the
undermining of the original Keynesian social welfare model
of the local state, and some of the more crucial areas which
can be identified are

  i) The rising burden of wages in a sector of low
    productivity growth.

 ii) The disjuncture between the professed social
    welfare aims of the local state and its
    actual dominance by interest groups rep-
    resenting capital.

iii) The failure to provide any alternative
    organization of services which might provide
    workers with some control over services, but
    rather the creation of a burdensome and
    undemocratic structure, particularly where
    the power of the executive officers has
    usurped that of the elected representative.

 iv) The allocation of Rate Support Grant as a
    residual out of a falling national surplus,
    accompanied by a general belief that such
    expenditure is non-productive.

  v) The self-financing nature of the Welfare
    State which places a rising tax burden on the
    working class, creating resistance to tax
    increases and government spending per se,
    reinforced by their experiences of the state
    as inegalitarian and alienating [1].

 vi) The resistance of capital to any extension of
    the local state and to its financial costs,
    especially as the crisis deepened. They
    pushed the burden even more heavily onto
    workers not only in terms of general fiscal
    pressure, but also specific pressures on
    workers in the local state.

Fundamentally, it is within this latter area that many of
the greatest problems arose. It is not only workers as a
class who have paid dearly for their access to state welfare
provision, it is public sector workers in particular who
have been in the position of consumers, tax payers and wage
labour in their relations with the state.

The persistent refusal of workers in the local state to passively accept onerous terms and conditions of employment has prevented them from paying fully for the adjustments needed to overcome respective state crises. The local state has become a major arena of conflict, which spilled over into the political sphere, negating the very objective which the Welfare State sought to achieve — class harmony.

The refusal of capital to absorb the costs of adjustment which are needed to keep the local state viable put pressure on the state workers to absorb it by low wages and high rates of exploitation. Both Conservative paternalism and Labour corporatism have foundered upon the unwillingness of these state workers to endure the hardships demanded of them. The former approach depended on a relatively compliant workforce, prepared to offer labour services "beyond the call of duty", based on an appeal to civic pride, for little increased pecuniary reward. Such a system depends on a minimizing of antagonisms and a high trust relationship between workers and the state. With the post-war expansion of the local state into an area of mass proletarian employment with poor pay and conditions, such an anachronistic system could not survive.

The system of managerial corporatism which gradually replaced paternalism has its origins in the reorganization of local government after the war and that part of the settlement with labour which allowed for full trade union recognition in much of the public sector. Institutional arrangements were created, based upon the Whitley Industrial Relations model (see Appendix 2), through which conflict could be channelled and contained (Somerton, 1977; Fairbrother, 1982). This highly centralized form of constitutional bargaining depended for its success on the trade union leadership being fully integrated into the bargaining structure and the membership being willing to accept the authority of their leaders. Workers had left the world of municipal subservience only to find themselves ensnared within the constraints of corporate bargaining [2].

In many respects the system worked reasonably well up to the period of crisis in the 1960s. However, the idea that industrial relations problems would easily be controlled simply by pulling the appropriate institutional lever and deploying the correct managerial tactic took quite a knock with the upsurge of rank and file militancy in the 1960s.

While the union leaderships were perfectly prepared to accept the continuation of bargaining compromises between parties of goodwill, the membership were not, because the compromises demanded of them were in fact sacrifices they were unable or unwilling to bear. Incorporation, like the

system which preceded it, depends upon legitimacy and failed
to contain the conflict which emerged in the 1960s because
it was essentially a system dependent on economic growth and
an expanding local state sector. As the post-war Keynesian
system of macro-economic regulation crumbled it took the
local state with it. The former willingness of local state
controllers to negotiate compromises was abandoned in favour
of confrontation and repression.

As the crisis within the local state deepened in the
1970s workers were subjected to wide-ranging attacks on
their living standards and terms and conditions of service.
On the wages front both official and unofficial incomes
policies were used in an attempt to reduce wage costs: the
impact on public sector workers of incomes policy in the
1960s was indeed a fundamental cause of the breakdown of the
Whitley system of collective bargaining (Tarling and
Wilkinson, 1977). Moreover, redundancy and the substitution
of part-time for full-time jobs were also used to both
reduce the wages bill and to intimidate those workers who
reamined in employment. Taylorist scientific management
techniques became widely used as local state employers
sought to increase efficiency through the intensification of
work. However, these attempts at trying to overcome the
crisis in the local state at the expense of it workers only
succeeded in exacerbating the existing level of conflict.

The refusal of state sector workers to accept falling
real incomes and work intensification was central to the
demise of the local state. The Whitley system of centralized
national collective bargaining failed to contain industrial
conflict. This led to the development of a system of
collective bargaining based more on the workplace. The
development of rank and file based unionism made public
sector industrial relations more uncertain and less
predictable. This instability was matched by a tendency for
public sector industrial relations conflicts to overflow
into the political arena, as during the strikes of 1972 and
1974 and especially during the 1979 "winter of discontent".
Capital in turn became disenchanted with the whole social
welfare enterprise, especially as the costs of this low
productivity growth sector began to rise. Combined with the
failure of Keynesian macro-economic policies and the crisis
of profitability facing British capital, the virtue of free
market theory began to fall upon receptive ears.
Privatization fits neatly into such a scheme for rolling
back the state and extending the discipline of the market.

IV. THE POLITICAL ECONOMY OF THE TORY NEW RIGHT

The 1979 Tory Government came into power with a political, social and economic package of "radical reform" clearly based on the ideas of Hayek, Friedman and Edmund Burke. In their programme they emphasized the importance of nation, liberty and freedom through law and the market: they also emphasized the importance of the family and traditional British virtues. They laid greater emphasis, in terms of policy aims, on the need to reduce the state sector; taking government out of peoples' lives, and moreover proposing to liberate the market and individual workers from trade union tyranny.

They sought to undermine the strength of organized labour through the use of monetary policy and controls of public expenditure (cash ceilings at both central and local government levels), which increased the impact of the world crisis, thereby forcing up unemployment. The real value of unemployment relief and supplementary benfit was reduced, with the aim of making labour lean and keen to seek work at whatever levels of wages. Meanwhile, the extension of part-time working and casualization provided another way of atomizing the working class, setting the non-unionized against the unionized, the unemployed against the employed. It is this sort of predatory system which the Tories view as the engine of growth, the driving force behind the virtuous spiral of enterprise, helping to launch Britain on its take-off into a universe of freedom, property, liberty and private market dominated economic growth. But for this to succeed it is seen as crucial that the State should be drastically reduced in size and that labour laws should be reconstituted to take government out of the labour market and force labour to become legally subservient to capital.

The Tories see the state as bureaucratically inefficient, and responsible for a misallocation of resources, which in turn stifles enterprise. Tory anti-state policies involve a break with the post-war consensus of a bargained corporatist compromise and social welfare capitalism. Their view of social welfare is that it is better handled by a mixture of family support, altruism, voluntarism and free enterprise insurance (i.e. sickness relief, pensions and medical care). The state should only underpin the system by providing a minimal social welfare net, whether in terms of social benefits, community welfare services or health care.

Not only do the Tories reject the social welfare aspects of welfare capitalism, but they also believe that there should be minimal state involvement in production, non—welfare services, transport and energy utilities. Soon after entering office they started to decentralize parts of the state industrial sector (aerospace, gas, oil); to "hive off" parts of the nationalized transport system; where possible they attempted to cajole public sector purchasing departments to use private sector suppliers rather than other public corporations or utilities. Another important feature of this policy was their intention to privatize as much as they could of the local government sector.

However, success in marketizing the economy is seen to be crucially dependent on the Tories' ability to reduce the power of the unions. At one level they consider that the rolling back of the state will expose the sheltered internal labour markets of the state sector to the realities of competition through the market. Indeed, many Tory ideologies put special emphasis on the need to root out trade union power in the state sector, if the policy of attempting to restore the balance of industrial power in capital's overall favour is to stand a chance (see Dimbleby, 1981; Congdon, 1982). However, their labour policies don't stop there. Their central proposition is based on the premise that industrial relations should be a matter for capital, labour and the law: like their classical progenitors they believe that the importance of the market is that it takes politics out of economics. Hence the importance they place on introducing a framework of labour law (dealing with strikes, dismissal, picketing, the closed agency shop and union membership) which leaves the unions fully exposed to civil litigation triggered by the employer, and the common law interpretations (of the lawfulness of trade disputes) of the judiciary. This is the objective of restricting the unions' immunities from civil torts.

Another key aspect of policy involves the abandonment of pay comparability systems (with the abolition of the Clegg Commission and Civil Service Pay Research Unit). The Tories maintain that pay rates in central and local government should be determined by market worth. The abolition of fair wage provisions is a step in the same direction.

The importance of the Tory attacks on trade union regulation of internal and external labour markets is that it has the objective of destroying the consolidation of pay and terms and conditions of employment, with the aim of encouraging greater wage competition. They seek to foster the exploitation of the unregulated small firm sector of private capitalism, and in turn promote the sort of casualized labour market to be found in the construction sector (Moore, 1981).

V. PRIVATIZATION AND THE LABOUR FORCE

Privatization of services simultaneously fulfils two
objectives for the state. In the first place, it extends the
boundary of private capitalist production for profit. It is
part of the general restructuring of the British economy and
the state, which also includes selling off the profitable
parts of the nationalized industries. The most popular area
for privatization has been refuse collection and cleaning,
where there is an existing contract industry. In 1982, local
authorities employed 46,000 employees in refuse collection
and cleaning, 36,000 cleaners in offices and 134,000 school
cleaners. The estimated value of this work for the contract
cleaning industry was £5-6 million per annum, while the
turnover of the entire contract cleaning industry was only
£400 million per annum (Labour Party, 1982). Clearly,
privatization is highly desirable for private profit.

Second, it achieves changes in the internal
organization of the state. With the financial squeeze
imposed on local authorities through the Rate Support Grant
system (see Appendix 1), if local authorities are to avoid
either increasing rates or reducing services, they have only
two alternatives: either reorganize their own labour force
to raise the rate of exploitation or get the private sector
to do it by contracting out services, which may be an easier
option. Lord Bellwin, as Environment Undersecretary, spelt
it out:

> a reduction in the range or quality of
> services, or an increase in the rates, are not
> the only courses available. It is also
> possible for local government to become more
> efficient.

> This requires an objective examination of all
> the variables which affect performance,
> including staff costs, manning levels,
> organization management practice, accumulated
> restrictive practices and inefficient
> incentive bonus schemes.

> In addition, it is important to examine the
> scope for the increased involvement of the
> private sector in the provision of local
> services (Local Government Chronicle, 6
> February, 1981).

Local authorities' direct labour force has always been
characterized by permanent employment relationships, strong
trades union organization (77.5% of the labour force in
local government and education in 1979 were unionized (Price
and Bain, 1983)), and a national negotiation of pay and
conditions through the Whitley Councils (see Appendix 2).
The 1970s have seen growing militancy among local authority
workers, with the development of shop floor organization
around shop stewards and an outburst of strike activity. The
1978-9 "winter of discontent" involved many local authority
manual workers and directly prompted many local authorities
to consider privatizing services, as in the case of
Southend:

> In addition to the previous attempts to remove
> task and finish, another important influence
> on members was the refuse collection strike of
> 1979, when Southend manual workers stayed out
> until the wage settlement was agreed, contrary
> to the general union approach (Coopers and
> Lybrand, 1981).

Privatization involves an evasion of trade union
organization and an increase in the rate of exploitation.
The contract cleaning industry generally employs non-union
labour and private firms who sub-contract to the local
authorities and are not subject to the national Whitley
agreements. The contract cleaning industry has been reported
on by both ACAS and the Low Pay Unit for its poor pay and
conditions of employment (ACAS, 1980; Sullivan, 1977). The
labour force is 85% female working less than 16 hours a
week, and therefore exempt from the Employment Protection
Act. Their income is generally less than the threshold for
National Insurance Payments and so they have no rights to
sick pay or unemployment benefit (ACAS, 1980). The 1982
Employment Act made it illegal for contracts to require
union labour only, and the Fair Wages Resolution, which
applied to contracts with the public sector since 1891 and
obliged the contractors to pay the "going" wage, has been
abolished.

The so-called greater "efficiency" of the private
sector has two aspects. First, the technical aspect of
efficiency embodied in more modern capital equipment, and
second, a higher rate of exploitation. The second aspect
involves workers working longer hours and more intensively.
In particular, for refuse collection, private contractors do
not operate a "task and finish" system, common to most local
authorities.

Private industry has responded to unemployment and uncertainty with an increased casualization of the labour force. Local authorities also face a situation of uncertainty and restriction in their finance, and seek to evade the rigid institutionalization of the direct labour force. Privatization shifts all the uncertainty and responsibility for labour management onto the private sector:

> Through contracting out, a locality not only
> divests itself of the responsibility of
> managing a workforce, it also places
> responsibility for labour relations directly on
> the shoulders of the private sector (Brettler-
> Berenyi, Governmental Finance, March 1980).

Where the private contractor employs non-union labour with little or no employment protection, labour relations are a much easier matter than for the local authority dealing with its own direct labour force. The local authority is paying for a specified service when contracting out, rather than purchasing labour power and then having to extract the service.

The most important areas for privatization so far have been construction and maintenance of houses, schools and roads, refuse collection and cleaning services.

In October 1979, 532 of the 549 local authorities in Britain had a Direct Labour Organization (DLO) of some kind, employed on construction and/or maintenance work, employing 158,757 operatives and 89,086 associated clerical workers (Labour Party, 1982). DLOs have existed since the 1890s to provide local authorities with a high standard of work for a reasonable price rather than being subject to the vagaries of the construction industry, and to ensure fair wages and trade union rights, while the private construction industry is characterized by casual employment and unsafe working conditions. Whenever there is a downturn in the building industry, DLOs come under attack from the private building companies, since local authorities represent a substantial share of the market and DLOs are a centre of trade union organization.

After the collapse of the construction boom in the early 1970s a major campaign was launched by the National Federation of Building Trades Employers and by Aims of Industry to discredit DLOs. The 1980 Local Government Act Part III, which came into operation in April 1981, introduced a new set of regulations on the operation of DLOs, essentially requiring them to operate as private

companies competing for work. They are required to keep
commercial revenue accounts for each of four categories of
work, which are all required to show a surplus: general
highway works; other new construction works over £50,000;
other new construction works under £50,000; and all other
maintenance work, unless in the previous financial year no
more than 30 people were employed in a category. The
Secretary of State has the power to prescribe categories of
work for which at least three tenders must be invited and
made known to those interested. In the first year of
operation these categories were: general highway works - all
work over £100,000; sewerage works - all work over £50,000;
other new works - all work over £10,000. As a result of
strong pressure from the building industry, from October
1982, the threshold for highway work was reduced to £50,000
and 30% of maintenance work below £10,000 also had to be put
out to tender. From October 1983, the partial tendering
requirements for both new work and maintenance were
increased to 60%. During the first year of operation, the
definition of a "job" was sufficiently loose that many local
authorities could evade the tendering requirements. This has
now been tightened up. Each of the four accounts is required
to show a prescribed rate of return on capital employed on a
current cost accounting basis. This is currently set at 5%,
which is much higher than the private construction industry
can earn in the present recession. Each DLO must produce an
annual report on its operations, which from 1982 must
identify contracts awarded to the DLO where it was not the
lowest bid. The Secretary of State may also ask for a
special report at any time and subsequently close it down if
they are not satisfied with its performance, for example,
because it is not earning the required rate of return.
Another reason identified as a possible ground for closure
is "unfair conditions of contract":

> The Secretaries of State have noted with
> concern and regret evidence submitted that ...
> authorities have imposed requirements which
> must, in their view, deter contractors from
> responding to invitations to tender for these
> authorities' work, reduce competition and
> unecessarily inflate the price of such tenders
> as contractors submit. They have noted and
> deplore in particular union labour only
> requirements and contract conditions ...

> The attention of authorities is therefore
> drawn to the provision that has been included

> in the current Employment Bill ... Authorities
> are also reminded of the powers of the
> Secretary of State to call for a special
> report from them on their DLO operations, at
> any time under the provisions of Section 17 of
> the Act (DOE circular 6/82, pp. 4-5).

So DLOs are being squeezed from both sides; they have to
competitively tender for work with the private sector firms
employing non-union labour and operating in unsafe
conditions, and it is "unfair" of the local authority to
require similar employment conditions from the private
contractor as are standard in the DLO.

Cleaning and refuse collection have been the other main
areas promoted for privatization. There is an existing
contract cleaning industry, enjoying the advantages of a
cheap part-time female labour force, ready to take up the
lucrative field of local authority work, and to branch out
from office and window cleaning into refuse collection.
Until the 1950s, most household refuse collection was done
by direct labour, and during the 1950s all major councils
discarded remaining private contractors in favour of direct
labour. In 1967 a government committee on refuse collection
stated that "Local authorities should not employ contractors
to collect household refuse." (DoE, 1967). In 1978-79 only
15 local authorities employed contractors for any household
refuse collection and generally only for a small percentage.
Maldon was the most significant with 95% contracted out
(Hansard, 1980). The 1979 "dirty jobs" strike was a
significant turning point. Many local authorities brought in
private contractors and began to think about doing it on a
permanent basis. This was the case in Southend, which was
the first major council to contract out its entire cleaning
service in April 1981.

Southend council had been trying for several years to
end the "task and finish" system for refuse workers and
introduce new working practices for street cleaning. The
failure of this, and the militancy of Southend workers in
the 1979 strike, led the council to put the whole cleaning
service up for tender in 1980. The contract was awarded to
the Exclusive Cleaning Group on the basis of £492,920
"savings" - 20% of the previous cost. Such savings were
achieved in three ways: by subsidies from the council in the
form of cheap access to the depot and workshops; by
increased charges for collection of trade and garden waste;
and at the cost of the workforce (LRO, 1981, 1982; New
Statesman, 1982). All staff (except five who became
inspectors) and manual workers were made redundant and

Exclusive employed 180 manual workers to do the same job as
the 232 previously employed by the council (Labour Party,
1982). Significantly, the nine union stewards were not taken
on by Exclusive. Pay and conditions of employment have
deteriorated for the workers, who have no trade union
protection. While average basic <u>wages</u> have increased by 25%,
there is no bonus scheme and no overtime pay for emergency
services. Differentials have increased, so that <u>earnings</u>
have only increased for HGV drivers and some refuse
collectors, while the majority of workers earn less. Holiday
and sickness pay and pensions are all significantly worse:
holidays from five to four weeks, paid sick leave from the
maximum of 26 weeks on full pay and 26 weeks on half pay
down to four weeks on full pay and four weeks on half pay.
Hours and intensity of work have both increased. Task and
finish has been replaced by a standard 40-45 hour week. Each
refuse collection gang has four rather than five loaders,
and loads are three tons over the legal limits (for which
they are finally being prosecuted) (TGWU, 1981).

Following success at Southend, Exclusive paid for a
quarter of a million pound newspaper campaign, advertising
the "success" of Southend and the enormous benefits which
could accrue from contracting out. In October 1981, they
sent a letter to every councillor in the country
guaranteeing at least 10% savings. Their campaign was backed
up by the Adam Smith Institute, who produced two pamphlets
and a manual explaining how to deal with private
contractors. They held a one day seminar, and sent out a
"privatization pack" in March 1981 to 22,000 councillors.
The Government has strongly supported the privatization
drive and commissioned a report from Coopers and Lybrand on
pricing and service delivery in local authorities.

Other councils have followed the lead established by
Southend. Wandsworth, for example, contracted out its street
cleaning to Pritchards. Again, "savings" are achieved at the
expense of the workforce. The job previously done by 138
workers is now done by 63. Only one of the old labour force
was taken on and all labour is non-union. Task and finish
has ended and workers must work five days out of Monday to
Saturday with no overtime pay. Workers have no national
agreement on grievance procedure, and hence have
significantly worse conditions than under direct labour.
Sick pay has been reduced from six months full pay and six
months half pay to four weeks full pay; holidays are three
weeks instead of five; and there is <u>no</u> pension scheme. With
no trade union protection or grievance procedure, workers
can be dismissed at a moment's notice, so it is hardly
surprising that absenteeism is so low!

When Wirral council decided to privatize refuse
collection, council officers did an analysis of the work
rates involved in the tenders. The Direct Labour Force bid
expected workers to walk 14 miles per day, at an average of
2.72 mph, shifting 2.3 tonnes of rubbish in 210 bins. But
Waste Management — who won the contract — expect each worker
to walk 17 miles per day, at 3.67 mph, shifting 3.0 tonnes
of rubbish in 275 bins (Labour Research, April 1983).

While privatization has so far concentrated on DLOs and
cleaning, the possibilities go much wider. Catering, with an
existing contract industry, would be an obvious example, and
has already been used in other parts of the public sector,
e.g. Ministry of Defence. Again, it is an industry which
benefits from exploiting a particular segment of the labour
force — cheap, unskilled married women rather than qualified
cooks (Craig et al., 1980). The Local Authorities Management
Services and Computer Committee (LAMSAC) "Value for Money"
studies quoted an example of a local authority bringing in
contract caterers. A stated constraint in the pre-existing
situation was:

> The conditions and rates of pay of staff were
> tied to nationally negotiated awards that took
> no account of local conditions in the catering
> trade (LAMSAC, Example 9).

Again, the use of contractors provides a means of evading
national agreements and shifts the burden of uncertainty and
labour management onto the contractors. The contractor has
to deal with any adjustment of employment and providing they
offer some alternative will probably not have to pay
redundancy.

The alternative to privatization, in terms of a
strategy towards labour, is to increase the rate of
exploitation of the direct labour force. The threat of
privatization has been used as a stick to beat the unions
with in this respect, and private contractors have
complained that they bear the cost of preparing tenders in
this process (Coopers and Lybrand, 1981). In Rochford, for
example, following the manual workers' strike in 1979, the
council approached both the unions and private contractors
for schemes to "improve" the refuse collection service. They
decided to retain the in-house service, but with new methods
of collection and a revised bonus scheme. Manning levels
were reduced from 42 to 34, and task and finish ended, the
number of rounds was reduced from ten to seven, and the
number of vehicles from 13 to ten. The new arrangements are
estimated to have saved £123,940 in 1981-82.

VI. CONCLUSIONS

The Tories base their economic policies on a free market
philosophy which extends beyond monetarism. Accordingly they
see privatization as a means to achieve both a reduction in
the size of the local state and a radical shift in power
away from organized labour. If privatization succeeds, the
role of the State in local government will consist of simply
transferring the preferences of the electorate into market
transactions: local authorities would have the task of
co-ordinating, specifying prices and standards and would
cease to be a significant employer in their own right. This,
in conjunction with changes in industrial relations
legislation, would help in the creation of a labour market
unfettered by trade union interference and consolidation.
      In practice, however, the universal privatization of
the local state is fraught with problems - for neither the
politics, economics nor practice of privatization is
particularly well founded. Furthermore, if the Tories are to
succeed in their privatization strategy they need to break
not only the resistance of the trade unions and certain
sectors of capital, but also that of some local state
officials and councillors, many of whom are Tory Party
members. However, it is at the theoretical level that the
problems begin. Proponents of privatization confuse issues
of public finance with issues of public production, and
argue in favour of the latter on spurious grounds of
"efficiency" , while ignoring the future social costs of
their policies and the fact that in practice they ensure
that much of the working population is made worse off.
      There are also failings in applying these theories.
Despite the fact that the Treasury is harassing local
authorities to get rid of their directly employed workers,
as part of cost cutting, and despite a minority of local
authorities being prepared to accept almost any contract for
privatization so long as it limits rate rises and reduces
short-term costs, the general trend has not been that
desired by the Government. Resistance has led the Treasury
minister Leon Brittan to threaten to take draconian measures
against local government including the takeover of central
government spending functions (Guardian, 1982), which has
exacerbated the political tensions between the central and
local state. The threat of imposed central financial
controls has raised the hostility of local councillors and
officials, who already display doubts as to the potential
long-term savings of privatization. Despite a massive
propaganda campaign by the private contracting firms only a
few local authorities have actually gone in for extensive

privatization, while some have shown that privatization is
actually more expensive. A survey published by the Local
Government Chronicle found that during the 12 months up to
April 1983, of councils considering privatization of refuse
collection, 79 had rejected it and only eight had carried it
through (Local Government Chronicle, June 1983). Many firms
with existing contracts with the local state are also
unhappy about privatization. It upsets parochial forms of
clientalism and patronage, while introducing market
uncertainty. It is also not always the case that capital
willingly seeks the deregulation of the workplace and the
labour market: since the last century capital has
reluctantly come to accept the regulatory role played by
trade unions, minimum wage legislation, health and safety
laws, and other forms of legal protection for labour,
because they prevent unfair competition.

Nonetheless, it is the trade unions who most fully
appreciate the dangers of flexibility through privatization.
The unions only have to look at the construction and
building industry to understand what the Government is
trying to achieve, and why privatization features so
predominantly in the rhetoric of free market economists. The
idea is not to use market discipline as a threat, but as an
actuality [3]. Free market theory depends crucially on the
reduction of trade unions to the status of friendly
societies. If this is to succeed then there is no better
place to begin a drive against unions than in the highly
unionized sector. It is with this fear in mind that trade
unions have set out to oppose privatization. If they are
successful in preventing deregulation of the labour market,
the success of free market policies is problematic. If they
fail, the large number of workers who at present are
protected by collective agreements will find themselves set
free into the predatory jungle of an unregulated private
sector labour market. There workers will find themselves
exploited as often casual, part-time, non-unionized
employees with no recognized negotiating or grievance
procedures to protect them and with no consolidation of
wages. The full costs of capital restructuring through
market competition will fall squarely on the working class.

APPENDIX 1

A. Local Government Finance in the United Kingdom

Local authorities receive their incomes from five main
sources as shown in the pie chart below. Rates are a tax on

the notional rental value of property and are the local
authorities' main independent source of finance. They also
raise some money by charging for services such as swimming
pools and laundries. But the main source of finance for
current expenditure is grants from central government. The
last ten years have seen many changes in the way that
central government grants are determined, as they have
increasingly tried to resrict the level of local government
spending. Capital spending is mainly financed by borrowing,
and since 1980 has been strictly determined by central
government.

     There are two stages to determining the level of Rate
Support Grant (RSG) going to each local authority. First,
the total amount of grant for all local authorities is fixed
as a percentage of approved "relevant expenditure". This has
been cut by: first, reducing the level of approved spending;
second, by reducing the percentage support for that
spending; and third, by the introduction, since 1976, of
"cash limits" – upper limits on the level of inflation in
costs that will be supported, determined prior to the
financial year.

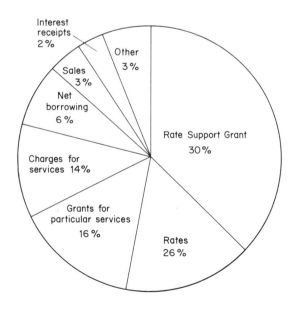

Fig.1 Local government finance in the United Kingdom. All
   incomes are by sources. Source: Local Government Financial
        Statistics, England and Wales, 1980–81, HMSO.

    Second, the distribution of total RSG between indi-
vidual local authorities is determined. Prior to the 1980
Local Government Act, this was determined in two parts, the
"needs" element, which gave more grant to authorities which
had characteristics associated with high spending, and the
"resources" element which made up the differences between
an authority's rateable value and a national standard rateable value, on the basis of the actual rate poundage levied
by an authority. Both elements led to an increasing proportion of grant going to the high spending authorities (mainly
urban, helping to ease the fiscal gap created by inner city
decline).
    The 1980 Act brought in more stringent controls over
the spending levels and grant contribution for each local
authority. The needs and resource elements were combined
into a single "block grant". Central government determines a
Grant Related Expenditure (GRE) for each local authority
based on service by service assessment of client groups and
average costs. Block grants are the difference between
actual expenditure for block grant purposes and a notional
rate income, the product of a prescribed "grant related
poundage" (GRP) and the authority's rateable value. The prescribed poundage increases with the local authority's level
of expenditure. When expenditure goes above a threshold
level GRP increases more rapidly, so that a higher proportion of any additional expenditure must be financed from
rate income, and for some authorities there will be an
actual reduction in the total level of the grant. Determination of a published GRE and GRP schedule for each local
authority involves much tighter control over spending levels.
But in addition, a second set of controls were added by the
1982 Local Government Finance Act. This involves a system of
"targets" for reductions in the volume of expenditure for
each authority and increasing levels of grant abatement when
spending rises above these targets. Since 1983-84, these
targets have essentially replaced GRE, since councils
spending below GRE but above target are still penalized.
    The 1982 Act also introduced a ban on supplementary
rates (which some councils had used to compensate for
clawback of grant) and established an Audit Commission with
considerable powers to investigate "Economy, Efficiency and
Effectiveness" in local authorities.
    When these measures still did not produce the required
reduction in spending levels, the Government brought in new
powers to limit the rates which "high spending" councils
could levy. These powers are covered by the 1984 Rates Act,
which also introduced a requirement on councils to consult
"local business interests" before setting the rate.

APPENDIX 2

A. Whitleyism and Public Sector Employment

1. Origins of Whitleyism

Whitleyism as a collective bargaining system emerged in
specific historical circumstances at the end of the First
World War. It takes its name from the recommendations of a
Committee set up in 1917 under the Chairpersonship of the
Speaker of the House of Commons, J.H. Whitley, whose brief
was to:

> 1. Make and consider suggestions for securing
>   a permanent improvement in the relations
>   between employers and workmen.
>
> 2. To recommend means for securing that
>   industrial conditions affecting the
>   relations between employers and workmen
>   shall be systematically reviewed by those
>   concerned, with a view to improving
>   conditions in the future.

The impetus behind the setting up of the Whitley Committee
came from the militant trade unionism and industrial unrest
which had characterized the period during the war. It was
hoped that the Whitley Committee would come up with
proposals capable of leading to the orderly resolution of
industrial conflict.

The Committee produced a total of five reports up to
1918, although it was the first which was the one of
practical significance. The main recommendation was that
each industry should have an organization which represented
the interests of capital and labour, with the objective of
securing the progress and well being of that industry, and,
importantly, being capable of achieving industrial relations
harmony. These national bodies were to consider the
establishment of local and works organizations to supplement
and make more effective the work of the central bodies. The
report also concluded that an effective national framework
of industrial relations could only succeed if there were
strong trade unions, integrated into that framework. It was
also clear from the recommendations of the original report
that the idea was to take conflict out of the workplace by
resolving as many contentious issues as possible at national
level.

The recommendations were taken up with a varying degree

of enthusiasm in different industries. However, the most
significant tendency was that the recommendations were
almost totally rejected in those industries which were well
organized along traditional trade union/employer association
lines, and where, in many cases, conflict remained endemic.
Whitleyism as a system of industry level or centralized
bargaining, with its strong consensus orientation, was only
effectively introduced in industries which lacked effective
shop floor organization.

2. Collective bargaining in local government

A system of national collective bargaining in local
government goes back to the creation of a national joint
council, following the Whitley format, which was created in
1919. The success of this NJIC for local authorities' non-
trading services (manual workers) was limited during the
inter-war period by a combination of weak trade unionism and
local authorities' obsession with autonomy, which made them
reluctant to tie themselves too closely into national
collective bargaining machinery.

It was after the Second World War that Whitley
bargaining expanded throughout local government. In 1944
white collar workers were brought into the structure with
the creation of the permanent national joint council for
local authority administrative, professional and technical
staff (APTCS). Importantly, the success of these national
joint councils depended upon growth in trade unionism, which
was to some degree both facilitated and promoted by statute
in all fields of state employment; from the nationalized
industries (gas, coal, docks, electricity, steel) across to
public sector workers within local authority employment.
However, the emphasis was on a particular form of sanitized
and passive trade unionism which fitted in with the
character of this form of collective bargaining. The real
weakness of collective bargaining in the state sector was
its inherent tendency to overcentralize and over-
bureaucratize industrial relations, which as the paper has
argued, more often than not created conflict which the
system could then not contain - hence the perceived need for
outside arbitration and conciliation.

As far as the mechanisms of the negotiation machinery
are concerned, all the national bodies follow a fairly
general format. There is negotiating machinery covering
wages disputes and grievances at national, provincial and
local levels. The national bodies agree on the overall terms
and conditions for all employees in the appropriate local

government categories. The local authorities tend to follow
the terms of those agreements, while there remains some
flexibility in the scheme, with space for more localized
bargaining at the provincial and local levels. The
introduction of various forms of corporate planning,
scientific management, strategic planning and performance-
linked payment systems encouraged further growth in local
collective bargaining.

The employers' side within this system is made up of
the following associations of employing authorities: the
Association of County Councils (ACC); the Association of
Metropolitan Authorities (AMA); the Association of District
Councils (ADC); and the Convention of Scottish Local
Authorities (COSLA). The Local Authorities Conditions of
Service Advisory Board (LACSAB) provides industrial
relations and manpower advisory services, acting as the
employers' side secretariat on national negotiating
committees.

Employees are represented by some 60 trade unions with
very high levels of union density in almost all sectors. On
the NJIC for Local Authorities Administrative, Professional,
Technical and Clerical Staff, for example, some half a
million employees are represented mainly by three unions:
National and Local Government Officers Association (NALGO),
GMWU's Managerial, Administrative, Technical and Supervisory
Section (MATSA), and the National Union of Public Employees
(NUPE). Likewise on the NJIC, covering some one million
manual workers, the trade union side consists of the General
and Municipal Workers Union (GMWU), NUPE and the Transport
and General Workers Union.

This structure of employer/employee representation is
replicated at provincial council level, which is where
matters referred by the main NJCs are interpreted, and
recommendations to the NJCs in respect of issues arising
within the provincial area are put forward. As well as
handling disciplinary and grievance issues, which have come
from the local joint consultative committees (JCCs)
provincial councils also deal with such matters as local
working practices, standby arrangements, plus pay rates and
training schemes: their importance is amplified by the fact
that provincial councils deal with issues upon which there
exists no national agreement.

Finally, there is the lowest tier within the structure,
the local JCCs. It is at this level that much of the
conflict has occurred in recent years, over such issues as
productivity and bonus schemes, job evaluation, demarcation,
special leave and sickness, redundancy redeployment, health,
safety and employee welfare.

NOTES

1. A description of the system of local government finance
    in the United Kingdom is given in Appendix I.
2. The transformation from paternalism to corporatism in
    managing local state workers is parallel to the
    transformation from simple to bureaucratic control in
    private industry, described by Edwards (Edwards, 1979).
3. "... the lump properly managed, it is a very effective
    institution", Norman Tebbit, quoted in New Socialist,
    May/June, 1982.

REFERENCES

Advisory, Conciliation and Arbitration Service (ACAS)
    (1980). "The Contract Cleaning Industry", Report No.
    20. Report of an inquiry referred to ACAS by the
    Secretary of State for Employment on the question
    whether a Wages Council should be established for the
    contract cleaning industry. 13 November.
A.S.I., (1982). "Working with Contractors". Adam Smith
    Institute, London.
Bain, G.S. and Price, R. (1980). "Profiles of Union Growth -
    A Comparative Statistical Portrait of Eight Countries".
    Warwick Studies in Industrial Relations. Blackwell,
    Oxford.
Bellwin, Lord (1981). Why Lord Bellwin says contracting-out
    is a great opportunity. Local Government Chronicle.
Boddy, M., Saunders, P. and Bassett, K. (1980). Chapters in
    "The Local State: Theory and Practice" (M. Boddy and C.
    Fudge, eds.). School for Advanced Urban Studies (SUAS)
    Working Paper 20. Papers from a Conference held on 6
    December.
Brettler-Berenyl, E. (1980). Public and private sector
    interaction patterns in the delivery of local public
    services". Government Finance, March.
Brown, C.V. and Jackson, P.M. (1980). "Public Sector
    Economics". Robertson.
Butler, E. and Pirie, M. (1981). "Economy and Local
    Government". Adam Smith Institute, London.
Cockburn, C. (1977). "The Local State - Management of Cities
    and People". Pluto Press, London.
Committee of Enquiry (Layfield) Local Government Finance
    (1976). Report Comnd. 6453. HMSO, London.
Congdon, T. (1982). Why has monetarism failed so far? 2. The
    public sector problem. The Banker, April.

Coopers & Lybrand Associates Limited (1981). Service
    provision and pricing in local government. Studies in
    Local Environmental Services, September, HMSO, London.
Dimbleby, D. (1981). The monetarist experiment: A half-term
    report on Mrs Thatcher's progress by Hayek and
    Friedman. The Listener. 12th March.
Department of the Environment (1982). "Local Government,
    Planning and Land Act 1980: Direct Labour
    Organisations: Year 2" (1982/3). Circular 6/82. 15
    March.
Department of the Environment (1967). "Refuse Storage and
    Collection".
Edwards, R. (1979). "Contested Terrain". Basic Books, New
    York.
Fairbrother, T. (1982). "Working for the State". W.E.A.,
    London.
Forsyth, M. (1981). "Re-servicing Britain". Adam Smith
    Institute, London.
Foster, C.D., Jackman, R. and Perlman, M. (1980). "Local
    Government Finance in a Unitary State". Allen & Unwin,
    London.
Gamble, A. (1981). "Britain in Decline". Macmillan, London.
The Guardian, 1982, July 17th, London.
Halford, R. & Wheen, F. (1982). Our muck – their brass –
    privatization. New Statesman, 5th February.
HANSARD (1980), 28th February, col. 726.
The Labour Party (1982). Municipal Services vs.
    Privatisation. (Background paper for Working Group).
    26th Local Government Conference, Sheffield, 12–14
    February 1982.
Labour Research Department (1982). "Public or Private – The
    Case Against Privatisation". June. LRD Publications
    Ltd., London, June.
Labour Research (1981). "Public Health or Private Wealth".
    December.
Labour Research (1983). "Running Off With the Spoils".
    April.
LAMSAC (1980). "Value for Money Studies in Local
    Government". September.
Local Government Chronicle (1983), 17th June.
London Edinburgh Weekend Return Group – a Working Group of
    CSE (1980). "In and Against the State". (Expanded
    Edition, November). Pluto Press, London.
Moore, R. (1981). Aspects of segmentation in the United
    Kingdom building industry labour market. In "The
    Dynamics of Labour Market Segmentation" (F. Wilkinson,
    ed.). Academic Press, London and Orlando.
Prest, A.R. (1982). On charging for local government

services. Three Banks Review, 133, March.
Price, R. and Bain, G.S. (1983). Union growth in Britain:
    Retrospect and prospect. British Journal of Industrial
    Relations, XXI (1), March.
Saunders, P. (1980). Local government and the State. New
    Society, March 13.
Somerton, M. (1977). Trade unions and industrial relations
    in local government. Studies for Trade Unionists, 3
    (11), September.
Sullivan, J. (1977). "The Brush Off: A Study of the Contract
    Cleaning Industry". Low Pay Unit Pamphlet,5, February.
Tarling, R. Wilkinson, F., Rubery, J. and Craig, C. (1981).
    Industrial and staff canteens. EEC Project 1980-81.
    Case studies in L.M.S.
Transport and General Workers Union (1981). Report "Southend
    Privatisation - Facts". Branch Secretary (Arthur
    Smith).
Wilkinson, G. and Jackson, P.M. (1981). "Public Sector
    Employment in the UK". July. Public Sector Economics
    Research Centre, University of Leicester.

New Forms of Flexible Utilization of Labour: Part-Time and Contract Work

R. DOMBOIS and M. OSTERLAND

The crisis-ridden economic development which the Federal Republic of Germany has experienced during the last twelve years or so has caused firms to extend their instruments of employment policy in an attempt to adapt to the changed economic circumstances.

Whereas in times of growth employers sought to hold on to their workforce using mass lay-offs to cope with recessionary periods, as for example in 1966-67, since the end of the 1960s there appears to have been a partial break with the customary practice of "hire and fire". Problems of labour development have arisen which within the constraints of traditional instruments of policy can be solved only at the expense of incurring high costs and the risk of conflict: for example, cyclical and seasonal fluctuations in the volume of work which result in either transitory shortages or surpluses of manpower; rationalizations of work processes which result in an increased division of labour and only temporary demands for certain qualified work; and safeguards for workers built into labour legislation and collective labour agreements. As a consequence of this employers are increasingly adopting new, differentiated variations of labour policy which are more in keeping with the necessity for a greater flexibility of labour deployment.

It is, of course, perfectly clear that these problems
vary in their intensity depending on the market relationships and the production schedules of the particular
branches of industry concerned and also from plant to plant
- and the methods availed of in order to tackle these
problems are correspondingly diverse (Schultz-Wild, 1978).
Thus, almost all branches of industry are increasingly
making use of the elastic devices of short-time working and
overtime work, both of which can perfectly well occur at one
and the same time in a single firm. Even the once oft-
bemoaned problem of a high turnover in labour - predominantly in standardized mass production manufacturing with a
large proportion of the workforce with low level qualifications - has in the meantime come to be utilized as an
instrument of labour policy. Branches like the car-making
industry, consumer electronics and fish processing are among
those which have already resorted to augmenting the "normal"
turnover of personnel when necessary, by means of severance
settlements and early retirement schemes, so as in this way
to be in a position to adjust manpower capacity to
fluctuations in production.

These forms of labour policy do not create any completely new situations, differentiations or risk-groups on
the labour market; they merely constitute more developed
variations of established procedures, which attempt to
guarantee the elasticity of employment without having to
resort to the practice of "hire and fire" when firms are
faced with legislation and rules aimed at stabilizing
employment relationships.

However, the use of sub-contract or part-time workers
as a means of ensuring flexible deployment of labour is
quite another story. These practices often involve neither
costs nor time expenditure for the recruitment of workers:
they ensure that labour is available at extremely short
notice and, into the bargain, labour possessing a broad
spectrum of qualifications. These forms of labour, which
differ from "normal" (full-time) employment in manifold
ways, are rapidly gaining significance on the labour market.
Their number has by now gone over the two million mark
according to official estimates and unofficial estimates are
considerably higher. Almost every tenth employee in the
Federal Republic is currently working in some form of
employment which no longer corresponds to what we term the
traditional employment relationship.

It is not only the numerical significance of workers
employed on either a part-time basis or as contract labour
which is of relevance for the discussion surrounding the
developments on labour markets in industrialized capitalist

nations; these forms of employment also give rise to
interesting theoretical questions.

Part-time workers and contract workers are not
necessarily endowed with the same characteristics usually
attributed to the especially risk-prone members of marginal
groups of the industrial workforce. This group embraces an
exceptionally broad spectrum of qualifications and is by no
means restricted to non-skilled occupations. It may well be
worth looking into the question of whether, in addition to
the traditional sectors of the labour market, to what extent
a differentiated, complementary labour market is emerging
for employment relationships which differ from those of a
firm's permanent workforce, not so much from the point of
view of employment safeguards and qualifications structure,
but above all from the point of view of working time
structure.

In the following we shall first take a closer look at
the structure and the function of part-time and contract
labour. Then some of the theoretical implications as well as
the consequences for labour market policy will be touched
on.

I. PART-TIME EMPLOYMENT

The number of part-time employees in the Federal Republic,
disregarding temporary fluctuations, has been consistently
rising since the 1960s. The years 1977-79 alone saw an
increase from roughly 1.7 to 1.9 million. This figure,
though, includes only those employees working on a "regular"
basis - thus excluding seasonal workers - and only those
who work from 15 hours a week upwards. Anyone working less
than 15 hours a week, the limit at which social insurance
becomes compulsory, is not included in the statistics [1];
this number is estimated to be about 900,000.

Almost 90% of all part-time employees are women.
Unquestionably, this type of employment is preferred by many
women as it allows them time for other duties in the family
and the household (Wochenberichte der DIW, 1980). It is in
accordance with the traditional pattern of work distribution
between the sexes that males are not only considerably less
often interested in part-time jobs, but also that employers
show little inclination to offer males employment involving
less than the standard working hours.

The fact, however, that it is especially the female sex
which is predominantly engaged in part-time employment can
be put down to very definite economic reasons, as is
illustrated by a glance at their distribution over the

various branches of the economy. Part-time employment, so
far as it involves at least 15 hours a week, is to be found
in particular where women constitute a large proportion of
the total workforce. In 1979, for instance, it accounted for
: 65.6% (68,000) of female employees of the Bundespost – the
German postal service; 36.5% (173,000) in higher education,
the arts and publishing; 28.4% (144,000) public services
(communal and municipal authorities); 24.1% (366,000) in the
retail trade (Wochenberichte der DIW, 1980).

These figures show clearly that part-time employment is
concentrated for the greater part in those sectors where the
work-load allows or encourages worktime organization which
can be met profitably by part-time employees – in the field
of commercial service industries, in the retail trade and in
public administration.

Part-time employment, however, is by no means
restricted to groups with a low qualification profile: for
example, it also embraces qualified secretarial and
administrative occupations, and jobs in education where it
very often serves the purpose of retaining experienced
female staff by reducing individual working hours as an
incentive to remain in employment. In spite of this, though,
it is the low level qualifications which predominate, if
simply for the reason that in the above mentioned sectors
women are invariably only to be found in positions belonging
to the lower sections of work (Olk et al., 1979), which
seemingly are particularly well-suited for flexible labour
deployment. The retail trade, in which almost 25% of all
statistically registered (i.e those with social insurance)
part-time female workers are engaged, serves as an example
to illustrate this point.

A. Part-Time Employment in Non-Skilled Work

1. The retail trade

Part-time employment in the retail trade includes, along
with various office activities, above all those jobs for
which either no or at most only modest qualifications are
required, and which can be performed after only short
periods of on-the-job training, for example, packers,
internal distribution and transport staff, cashiers, sales
staff for products requiring no in-depth knowledge.

The exceptionally variable volume of work resulting
from the peak periods common in the retail business make the
flexible deployment of the workforce in this branch an

obvious choice. Department stores, supermarkets and chain
stores are thus to an ever-increasing extent availing
themselves of the procedures known as KAPOVAZ (Rudolph et
al., 1981), i.e. capacity oriented variable working time.
This system is made use of in particular where the volume of
work is not only predictably subject to fluctuations
depending on the time of day, but also according to
individual days of the week and for certain periods of the
year (weekend trade, peak periods at sale time and before
public holidays – especially Christmas etc.).

The technical basis for the systematic development of
this practice and its extension into other areas of the
economy has been provided by the progress of electronic data
processing with its capability of providing the requisite
data on all employees at the touch of a button. The concept
of KAPOVAZ is aimed at creating a fully flexible and
temporally variable labour force potential. To this purpose
the first step is to ascertain over an extended period the
distribution of total turnover or volume of work at certain
periods of the year, week or day. On the basis of this it is
then possible to determine the personnel requirement for the
various time periods.

Typical results of surveys of customer demand in the
retail business are, for instance, that the peak hours occur
in the mornings between 11 and 12 o'clock, and between
4 o'clock and 6 o'clock in the afternoons; the early morning
hours (up to 10 am) and the time from 1.30 pm to 3.00 pm
account for only a comparatively small share of the total
turnover. It is quite possible that during peak hours a
self-service food store, for instance, needs to have eight
cash registers working against perhaps only one or two in
the slack periods and three or four at the times in between.
Weekend and holiday business, and especially the Christmas
trade, may necessitate the manning of additional cash desks.
According to the system of KAPOVAZ such a staff requirement
could be met by hiring only two full-time cashiers and
otherwise utilizing part-time employees. But the requirement
is not just for part-time work, but for working times which
have to be as flexible as possible, so that along with
morning and afternoon staff other employees would have to be
available for the times from 10 am to 12 noon, and or from
4 pm to 6pm (Bauer, 1980, p. 40). To take things one step
further, the ideal solution would, of course, be to have one
member of staff available who, in particular at peak hours,
could be called in at random by telephone, or someone
willing to work for only a few weeks of the year during the
especially busy seasonal trade, and not at all for the
other months.

In order to attain the greatest flexibility and variability in staff deployment, employees are engaged according
to requirements on a fixed monthly basis for anything from
40 to 140 hours. An optimum of fully variable labour deployment is aimed at by the system whereby the actual hours put
in are accurately recorded, and by working some weeks more,
some weeks less, the fixed monthly rate is eventually
accounted for.

This meticulously worked out part-time system
constitutes a logical and systematic further development of
the currently common practice of compensating for hourly,
daily and seasonal fluctuations in sales turnover - and
hence volume of work to be performed - by means of a
differentiated deployment of the workforce. Due to the fact
that so many women, because of family considerations, are
dependent on part-time employment it is evidently no great
problem for employers to be able to dictate conditions of
working hours. In its advanced form the system of KAPOVAZ in
reality leaves little scope for female employees to plan and
to organize their daily routine and at the same time to
allow for family considerations. They are subordinated to
being mere stand-ins in the service of the working day, on
call at all times.

More or less the same practices as those described
above, representing the most refined applications of KAPOVAZ
in the retail trade, are to be found in similar form in most
other sectors where such part-time practices are on the
increase. The advantages accruing to the employers are self
evident:

i) Part-time employment offers the possibility of
   being able to concentrate exactly the required
   number of personnel on the periods of peak
   business. In the retail trade, in service
   industries and in the administrative areas of
   public and private industry, but also in
   certain sectors of manufacturing subject to
   sudden fluctuations, the employment of full-
   time workers to the extent necessary to cope
   with peak work periods would involve - from
   the employers' standpoint - merely having to
   pay workers during periods of unproductive,
   idle time. Part-time employment makes it
   possible to either reduce considerably or even
   completely eliminate paying for "idle time". The
   permanent full-time staff can be minimized in
   this way, and its labour can subsequently be
   utilized with more continual intensity.

ii) Part-time employment enables the work done by the individual worker to be intensified. The loss of labour efficiency through tiredness and waning ability to concentrate after four or five hours worked is less than that experienced during a normal eight hour working day. This makes itself felt particularly when the work is organized in such a way that the peak workload coincides with the hours of greatest individual productivity and alertness, viz. before midday. The rest periods which would otherwise be essential can be minimized in this way.

iii) On top of this, by employing staff for less than 15 hours a week, the firm avoids having to pay any contribution to the otherwise compulsory social insurance scheme. In the event of part-time employment not exceeding either ten hours a week or 45 hours a month, the employer is also freed from the obligation to continue wage payment if the employee should fall sick. By stipulating a limited term of employment the firm would also free itself of the constraints of sick pay protection.

Even though the preceding summary deals solely with one particular aspect of the manifold forms of part-time employment, and its function and consequences were portrayed in a rather extreme example, there is good reason to assume that there are also similarities to be found in other branches. A group of workers has come into existence which is not covered by rules negotiated in collective bargaining and which occupies a unique status within the industrial workforce. It cannot, however, be classed unreservedly together with other classical marginal groups of workers. Although to date there have been only a few empirical surveys on the subject, this group – along with contract workers – is not only of significance solely from the viewpoint of the amount of working hours, but for the general discussion surrounding labour market policy.

II. CONTRACT LABOUR

Since the end of the 1960s contract labour has also been considerably on the increase in the FRG; persistent crisis and mass unemployment have not had the effect of stemming the growth of this particular labour market (Biedenkopf et al., 1979; Borgaes, 1980; Steinbach, 1980, p. 263 ff.).

Between the years 1975 and 1979 the number of legally licensed labour-contracting companies [2], rose from 831 to 1,311. The number of registered contract workers employed by these firms rose from 9,000 at the end of 1975 to over 30,000 by the end of 1979 (Amtliche Nachrichten der Bundesanstalt fur Arbeit, 1980). Their share of 0.15% of the country's total working population is, though, relatively insignificant. Of considerably greater importance, however, is the unlicensed contract labour which exists on the very verge of illegality and which uses bogus work contracts, thus evading the statutory obligation of registration and the officially limited three month work permit (Kruger et al., 1981; Bahl, 1979, p. 443 ff.).

Since the official end to the recruitment of immigrant labour, the illegal "slave trade" in foreign workers – who possess neither official work permits nor the requisite residence permits and who can subsequently be exploited at will – has been flourishing, especially in the construction industry: these workers are denied not only the usual employment and social safeguards, but invariably the minimum wage rates paid in the sector, too. Contract labour in all its various forms has for a long while operated on an international basis: the list of registered labour contractors compiled by the two regional labour offices (Landesarbeitsamten) alone contain the names of 62 English and Irish firms, together with over 120 French ones; one third of the registered male contract workers are foreigners. The number of firms engaged in contracting out foreign workers illegally is probably many times this number [3].

It is extremely difficult to assess the true extent of the unlicensed, and very often criminal, practice of hiring out contract labour. Investigations in selected industries and regions [4] have arrived at the following estimates of the extent of various forms of contract labour:

i) The metal-working industry: contract workers account for 7% of the total workforce; the ratio of registered to unregistered contract workers employed on bogus work contracts is 1:6.

ii) The construction industry: 20% contract labour, in some firms up to 50%. The ratio of legal to other forms here is 1:9.

iii) Shipbuilding: up to 10% contract labour for the industry as a whole, in some firms as much

as 25%. The ratio of licensed workers to
workers with bogus work contracts is around
1:5.

All in all, the illegal forms of contract labour have
probably achieved proportions which exceed the licensed ones
many times over (Veiter Bericht der Bundesregierung, 1979).
The extent of contract labour varies from industry to
industry. Quite clearly it accounts for a large contingent
in areas where the volume of work and the call for a
corresponding number of workers is subject to heavy
fluctuations, as in the building industry, in shipbuilding
and in the ports; on the other hand, in sectors with
comparatively constant levels, contract workers are employed
to offset temporary personnel shortages, e.g. at holiday
times (Prognos-Untersuchung, 1980; Borgaes, 1980). However,
it is not uncommon for contract workers to occupy long-term
positions, too (Broicher et al., 1980).
    The range of jobs covered by contract workers is
surprisingly comprehensive; even so, the statistics indicate
a concentration in certain areas. Among the male workers it
is those with a skilled trade who clearly dominate. A good
third of all male contract workers belong to the metal-
working industries (including fitters and mechanics); one
fifth works in the construction industry and another fifth
is engaged in labouring jobs. It is a different picture for
female workers: a good three quarters work in office jobs
(Amtliche Nachrichten der Bundesanstalt fur Arbeit, 1980).
    The example of one large licensed contractor in
Northern Germany serves to illustrate the great variety of
qualifications offered by labour contractors: the firm
employs and contracts out a total of 1,600 workers from more
than 17 branch offices: these include 100 engineers,
construction workers and technicians. More than half of the
workers have learned a trade; they are engaged in plant
construction, repairs and maintenance, but above all in
industrial installation (Osterland, 1981).
    The legal contract labour market is not so involved
with the placing of workers with low level qualifications
[5]. The contract labour market appears to be sub-divided
into different sectors, but the market for skilled personnel
seems to dominate.
    In the following section we will examine the structure
and function of this the largest sector of the market,
taking as our example the ship-building industry.

A. The Contract Labour Market for Skilled Workers in the
Shipbuilding Industry

The shipbuilding industry's protection process is
characterized by a high proportion of craftsmanship.
Compared with batch or mass production the degree of
mechanization and of specialization is relatively low and
the qualifications of the workforce are high. In the
individual "shops" specializing in the individual separate
phases of production one finds a group of craftsmen who all
belong to the one particular trade: shipwrights fit the
steel plate, pipe fitters make up and install the pipes,
carpenters take care of the interior installations, etc. In
some of the trades the distinction between skilled and
unskilled worker has been eroded: workers who have been
trained as shipwright's mate or pipe fitter's mate for three
years or more, today perform the same work as their
colleagues who have served apprenticeships, although they
remain in the minority. Overall there are few jobs which are
the preserve of unskilled labour. These jobs too usually
require lengthy experience, sometimes including training
courses – for example, in welding. The shipyard's labour
requirements are thus met mainly by the skilled sector of
the labour market.
    A further peculiarity of the shipbuilding industry lies
in the discontinuity of the workload. Work is performed at
irregular intervals and with a deadline; on top of this the
capacity of the "shops" themselves is used to varying
degrees, depending on the type of ship under construction,
and the stage of production which has been reached, as there
are only very limited possibilities for producing stock.
Flexibility in the deployment of labour through transferring
workers between shops is necessarily limited by the
different occupations and qualifications of the workforce.
As a consequence, the manpower requirement for the yard as a
whole, and individually for the various shops, fluctuates
considerably.
    The shipyards attempt to compensate for these
fluctuations internally by variations in depth of
production, accepting manufacturing orders other than for
ship construction, or by variations in working time, mostly
by means of overtime and short-time work. An additional
traditional means is the exchange of skilled workers and
welders amongst the shipyards themselves, including also the
hiring-out of permanent full-time personnel to other firms,
e.g. in the automotive industry. A large maintenance
shipyard in Bremerhaven, for instance, employs, during
peaks, workers from other yards to the extent that they

sometimes account for over 10% of the total workforce [6].

The mutual exchange of workers between the shipyards — which is not classified as contract labour — puts a firm in a position to be able to "borrow" on a temporary basis the specially qualified surplus employees of other yards and in this way to meet additional demand for labour arising in its own operations. The 6,500 workers employed at the five Bremerhaven shipyards belong, as it were, to a sort of shipbuilding industry pool, by means of which the discrepancies in supply and demand for labour among the individual yards can be evened out.

Since the beginning of the 1970s, and in particular during the crisis in the shipbuilding industry in the latter half of that decade, the yards have also been availing themselves of contract labour to a significant extent. Whereas right up to the 1960s contract labour was employed only in the areas requiring little skill and involving high stress-loads — cleaning work, for example — the contractor firms today function as a reserve labour pool from which the shipyards are able to satisfy additional needs arising for qualified workers. The flexible use of this reserve would appear to have replaced the laying-off of permanent full-time workers which was a frequent occurrence during the slack periods of the 1950s and 1960s.

Since 1974 the shipyards in the region have cut their workforce by almost a quarter; any further reduction of the permanent personnel would constitute a threat to continued production. It is due to this fact that the incidence of contract labour has grown substantially. For example, the proportion of contract labour as a percentage of the total workforce reached in some yards as much as 25% in the past year [7].

Altogether the market for contract labour probably accounts for a good tenth of the total permanent workforce employed in the shipbuilding industry. The number of contract workers employed in the yards at any one time varies considerably in accordance with the volumes of orders on hand.

The minimum term for contract work is usually just a couple of weeks. Contract workers as a rule, though, work on average for several months at a time, even for several years in the same shipyard. Our medium-sized contractor firm in Bremerhaven, for instance, has managed to place over a quarter of its employees for periods of several years with a number of its longstanding clients.

Of the 42 companies that we are aware of operating in the shipbuilding industry in Bremerhaven only seven hold a licence. By far the greater part of contract labour is based

on bogus and subsequently faked work contracts. Even the
licensed contractors often hire out labour using these types
of work contracts.

The contractors are often small and medium-sized
businesses, sometimes having their own small manufacturing
set-up, but relying primarily on the contract labour side of
their operations. They are mainly engaged in supplying the
shipyards in the region. The contract workers usually
possess the qualifications typical of the shipyards'
permanent workforce: they are for the most part skilled
workers. Indeed, they carry out exactly the same jobs as
permanent workers, quite often as members of a mixed team.

The contractor firms recruit their employees mainly
among previous shipyard workers, sometimes even luring other
workers away from a yard where they have employment. This is
due to the fact that workers possessing the high-grade
qualifications that are required - such as shipwrights, pipe
fitters and welders - can usually only be found within the
shipbuilding industry. Higher hourly rates, away-from-home
supplements and high overtime earnings for contract workers,
together with employment reductions in the yards themselves,
provide sufficient incentive for older as well as younger
workers to change their place of employment.

B. The Contract Labour Market - A Monopolistic Sector of the Labour Market?

The advantages accruing to a firm from the use of contract
labour are self-evident:

i) The permanent payroll can be kept down to a
   level sufficient for dealing with the minimum
   amount of work expected. At the same time, the
   workers can be kept working continuously and
   at a greater intensity. Additional demand for
   qualified manpower can be met on an ad hoc
   basis by hiring contract labour. However,
   contract workers in the shipyards and in other
   branches sometimes occupy permanent jobs. In
   this case contract labour is being utilized as
   a cushion against cyclical downturns rather
   than as a means of offsetting short-term
   fluctuations. Hence contract labour has come
   to be an important instrument of
   rationalization enabling firms to reduce their
   permanent payroll, particularly in crisis
   periods.

ii) The costs of engaging contract labour are
comparatively low [8]. By using contract
labour the expenses arising from recruiting,
training and vocational adjustment, sickness
pay and additional payments for seniority can
be avoided.

iii) In the event of either a reduction in the
volume of work, or if for any reason a firm is
not satisfied with an employee's work,
contract workers can be withdrawn without
incurring costs, conflict or the necessity of
having to give a period of notice. By
utilizing contract labour a firm can evade the
legal and collectively negotiated constraints
surrounding employment protection. The
contractor firm also benefits from the greater
disposability of workers. Among licensed
contractors labour turnover is enormously
high; for example, in 1979, a mere 1.6% of the
registered male contract workers had been with
the same contractor firm for a period of more
than a year. But even in firms with a
relatively stable permanent staff, such as
those specializing in skilled workers [9], the
contractor frequently uses a hire and fire
policy in order to offset fluctuations in
demand. In very few of these firms is there a
workers council which could take up a claim
arising from dismissal, and very few contract
workers indeed enjoy any kind of employment
protection from collective agreements.

iv) There is a further reason behind the
employment of some special groups of skilled
contract workers. It would appear that in
certain areas the contractor firms have a
virtual monopoly of particular sought-after
skilled tradesmen. A case study conducted by
ISO (Broicher et al., 1980, p. 114)
established that in certain regions
occupational groups like fitters and welders
can scarcely be found on the "free" labour
market, and are subsequently available solely
from contractor firms.
The shipyards, too, seem to have reached a
state of virtual dependency on contract labour
firms. This is sustained by the fact that they
experience great difficulty in recruiting
skilled workers of their own. Although the

permanent workforce has been drastically cut
in recent years, qualified workers such as
shipwrights and pipe fitters are under-
represented among the unemployed in the
industry. Clearly a number of workers have
moved out of the shipyards, some of them to
the contract labour firms and to sub-
contractors.

The spread of contract labour may well be attributable to
the organization of the labour market; only the contractor
firms maintain a pool of labour which is readily available,
whereas recruitment through the Labour Office involves a
number of uncertainties, for example, the number of workers
available, their work motivation, the duration for which
they are prepared to work.

In the FRG several segments of the labour market are
today supplemented by contract labour markets: the earnings
potential and the social and material risks accompanying
contract work can be assessed by examining the specific
structure and function of contract labour markets in
connection with their corresponding segment of the main
labour market.

The assumption that skilled contract workers can be
classified together with marginal, deprived groups is
inaccurate. They not infrequently possess qualifications
which are in short supply – the same qualifications as the
members of the permanent workforce in the complementary
labour market. Their earnings are usually higher than those
of the permanent workforce in the company where they are
employed, and instances of discrimination in job allocation
do not appear to be significant. Moreover, a job with a
contractor firm need not necessarily be insecure, since the
employment risks are then spread virtually over the entire
industry. On the other hand, a very high degree of working-
time flexibility and mobility is expected of contract
workers. The social safeguards are minimal and the risk of
dismissal is high.

Such conclusions do not, however, apply unconditionally
to all sectors where contract workers are to be found. In
the labour market for workers with low level qualifications
and especially for workers with no legal alternative
employment, conditions of poor pay, social insecurity and
exploitation coexist and reinforce each other.

C. Part-Time and Contract Labour – The Institutionalization of Buffer and Risk Groups?

Even though still comparatively little is really known about the manifold forms that contract labour and part-time employment assume, and its specific functions in the various segments of the labour market, it is nevertheless possible to draw certain cautious conclusions from our case studies which in turn suggest further lines of investigation.

The growth of contract labour and at least those forms of part-time employment which are adjusted to coincide with peak workloads are both expressions of the trend towards injecting more flexibility into the utilization of labour. Enterprises can minimize their "permanent payroll", at the same time as ensuring greater intensity and continuity of work, compensating for additional and probably fluctuating labour requirements through the use of special workers who are available on a temporary basis. Such workers often occupy jobs which would otherwise be held by permanent staff, but during a reduction of workload as a result of cyclical downturns, for instance, they can be withdrawn without cost.

Their very contracts of employment subject them to different conditions – and thereby greater risks – than the members of the permanent work-force: for instance, they have to work different hours, often receive only fixed-term contracts, and they have no prior claim to any particular type of work. Conditions of employment are negotiated individually and not collectively as is the case for the permanent workforce. In spite of the fact that work at the same place and probably even perform the same work, the norms and protective rules guaranteed in collective agreements for the permanent personnel do not apply to contract and part-time workers.

Their marginal status, which endows them with the function of an institutional buffer group, is intensified by their exclusion from collective bargaining institutions: they are either, like the vast majority of contract workers, without any form of representation whatsoever (e.g. works councils), or they have at best only a slim chance that their interests will be adequately represented in the institutional system. This is due to several factors: they are reluctant to join a trade union; there is often a lack of communication between them and the members of the permanent workforce and as a rule they have much shorter time-perspectives than the latter. In so far as they have no alternative possibilities for employment, their tolerance of conditions is also of necessity considerably higher. This,

along with their integration with the permanent workforce
which, in turn, elects the works council and the trade union
delegates and is thereby naturally the main focus for trade
union policy.

Even though as a result of their contracts of employment, part-time and contract workers have a different status
to the members of the permanent workforce and are thus
subject to additional risks, it is not possible to categor-
ize them unreservedly as discriminated-against groups:
formally they accept their conditions of employment voluntarily – sometimes because they see no alternative possi-
blity for work, sometimes because they are lured by the
offer of high earnings. If one excludes the group of illegal
workers, then it is possible to say that they are not
deprived of any formal rights.

Strategies for making the utilization of labour more
flexible create new buffer groups: the members of such
groups enter into special employment relationships and
inevitably take the risks involved.

What is the logic and the perspectives of such
strategies for the flexible utilization of labour? At the
present time it is not possible to say with any certainty
whether these strategies, which until now have been
developed in sectors with intermittent peak workloads, will
find general application and whether they will increasingly
be adapted to also include existing permanent jobs.

The new differentiation between permanent workforces
and marginal groups indicates a trend towards the externalization of employment risks, the shifting of risks onto the
shoulders of groups outside the firm and onto easily
externalized members of the workforce. The previous differentiation between permanent and temporary personnel –
formally with equal rights, but in reality constituting a
most unequal distribution of real risks – could become
replaced or augmented by the building up of an institutional
separate labour market which is in itself differentiated
into separate segments. These new relationships of employment provide not only a necessary flexibility buffer for the
complementary "main labour market" with its stable employment relationships, but at the same time it also reduces the
incidence and the costs of dismissal.

It is perfectly clear that these forms of increased
flexibility are a means of evading those legal and collectively agreed-upon protective rules which have been devised
in an attempt to stabilize the employment relationship, e.g.
rules surrounding employment protection and the co-
determination rights of works councils. The question arises
as to whether part-time and contract work in the forms

described here constitute a reaction of the employers to the increasing numbers of legal and collectively negotiated safeguards of employment, i.e. an attempt to undermine these rules and to create new zones of flexibility. Advocates of prohibiting contract work, a demand often voiced in German trade union circles, should take note of this correlation: in all probability such a ban would lead not to the relinquishing of a flexibility buffer, but rather to a shift from legal to illegal and semi-legal forms. One has to consider the possibility of counter measures and appraise the chances of being able to keep them under control.

NOTES

1. An exception are the civil servants (Beamten) who do not fall under the compulsory social insurance scheme. In 1979 they accounted for about 300,000 part-time workers; altogether 600,000 part-time workers were employed in public service. These and the following statistics have been taken from: Wochenberichte des Deutschen Wirtschaftsinstitut fur Wirtschaftsforschung, 1979; Wirtschaft und Statistik, 1978; W. Bauer, R Dombois, R. Wahsner, 1980. There are discrepancies in the published data; the official statistics talk of 1.4 million socially insured part-time employees in 1978 and 1.6 million for 1980. Cf Stat. Landesamt Bremen, 1981, p. 164 and G Backer, 1981, p. 194 f.

2. According to the provisions of the "Arbeitnehmer-uberlassungsgegesetz" of 1972 a firm may contract out workers for commercial purposes when in possession of a permit from the Bundesanstalt fur Arbeit. One provision is that the contract workers are in normal employment with the contractor. The contract of employment has to contain certain clauses and may only be for a fixed term for reasons specific to the employee. The period for which a contract worker is hired out may not exceed three months. C.f. M. Kittner, 1977, p. 52 f.

3. A recent development is the contracting out of qualified personnel from Great Britain - construction workers and nurses, for instance. For many years now a large group of shipwrights from Liverpool has been working in North German shipyards: the share of foreign workers among the registered male contract workers is over one third. The illegal trade has led to the organization of the contractor firm in rings. The Public Prosecutor in Bochom, for instance, is investi-

gating infringements of the laws governing contract labour in 350 sub-firms in the region of the Ruhrgebiet alone. The charges include the founding of a criminal association, breaches of the Auslandergesetz, tax evasion and the witholding of social insurance contributions: cf. the Oberstadtdirektor of Gelsenkirchen (1980) also Vierter Bericht der Bundesregierung uber Erfahrungen bei der Anwendung des AUG, 1979.

4. The ISO survey embraces contract work in a total of 16 firms in the construction and metal-working industries of three regions (Goesfeld, Dusseldorf, Hagen); see M. Broicher et al, 1980. The investigation being carried out by the Zentrale Wissenschaftliche Einrichtung "Arbeit und Betrieb" at the University of Bremen, on which we were also working, is on contract labour in the shipbuilding industry of Bremerhaven. This is the largest local branch with about 6,500 workers.

5. It most probably does not apply in the same way for illegal contract labour, which is concentrated especially in the construction branch. See also Vierter Berichte der Bundesregierung (1979).

6. To what extent the employment of borrowed workers from other yards varies is illustrated by the figures for four separate days last year: 155, 13, 87 and seven workers from other yards respectively were engaged in a yard with a permanent workforce of 1,200.

7. On four separate days in two Bremerhaven shipyards with a total of 2,100 personnel there were 440, 167, 131 and 109 contract workers respectively.

8. In 1980 one hour of contract work in Bremerhaven cost DM 28, whereas DM33 had to be paid for workers from other yards.

9. In one medium-sized contractor firm in Bremerhaven which mainly supplies the shipyards, 90% of their contract workers had been employed for more than one year and more than a third for over five years.

REFERENCES

Amtliche Nachrichten der Bundesanstalt für Arbeit (1980), No. 11.

Bäcker, G. (1981). Teilzeitarbeit und individuelle Arbeitszeitflexibilisierung, WSI-Mitteilungen, 4.

Bahl, V. (1979). Leiharbeit als flexible Arbeitsmarktreserve und Dumpingstrategie gegen die gewerkschaftliche Tarifpolitik. Gewerkschaftliche Monatshefte, 7.

Bauer, W., Dombois, R. and Wahsner, R. (1980). Flexibler

Arbeitseinsatz und variable Arbeitzeit – eine neue
beschäftigungspolitische Strategie der Arbeitgeber?,
Mitteilungsblatt der ZWE 'Arbeit und Betrieb', No. 1.
Biedenkopf, K.H. and Meigel, M. (1979). Gutachen über die
wirtschafts-, gesellschafts- und arbeitsmarktpolitische
Bedeutung der Zeitarbeit, o.J. Bundestags-Drucksache, 8.
Borgaes, H.-U. (1980). "Arbeitnehmerüberlassungsrecht,
Leiharbeitsmarkt, Wirkungsweise des AUG", Werkvertrag,
mimeographed script, Bremen.
Broicher, M., Möller, C. Schaible, F., Winkel, R., Zill, G.
(1980). "Leiharbeit – Formen und Auswirkungen".
Cologne.
Institut fur Arbeitsmarkt- und Berufsforschung, Mitteilungen
No. 3.
Kittner, M. (1977). "Arbeits- und Sozoalordnung", OTV-Druck,
Stuttgart.
Krüger, M. and Wahsner, R. (1981). Illegaler Arbeitskrafte-
verleih und Scheinwerkverträge. Methodische
Vorüberlegungen und Ergebnisse einer Betriebsbefragung
in der Chemiebranche. Mitteilungsblatt der ZWE 'Arbeit
und Betrieb', 2.
Oberstadtdirektor der Stadt Gelsenkirchen (1980). Das
Problem der illegalen Arbeitnehmerüberlassung, mim.
1980.
Olk, Th., Hohn, H.-W., Hinrichs, K. and Heinze, R.G. (1979).
Lohnarbeit und Arbeitszeit, Arbeitsmarktpolitik
zwischen Requalifizierung der Zeit und kapitalistischem
Zeitregime. Leviathan, 2 and 3.
Osterland, M. Struktur und Arbeitsweise des Arbeitskrafte-
verleihs – am Beispiel zweier Bremer Verleihfirmen,
Mittelungsblatt der ZWE 'Arbeit und Betrieb', 2.
Prognos-Untersuchung (1980). "Zeit-Arbeit II", Basel.
Rudolph, R., Duran, M., Klohn, M., Nassauer, M. and Naumann,
J. (1981). Chancen und Risiken neuer Arbeitszeitsysteme
– Zur Situation teilzeitarbeitender Frauen im Berliner
Einzelhandel. WSI-Mitteilungen, 4.
Schultz-Wild, R. (1978). "Betriebliche Beschaftigungspolitik
in der Krise". Frankfurt/New York.
Statistisches Landesamt Bremen (1981). "Statistische Monats-
berichte", Heft 5.
Steinbach, M. (1980). Gefährdungen der Arbeitnehmer durch
Leiharbeit. WSI-Mitteilungen, 5.
Vierter Bericht der Bundesregierung über Erfahrungen bei der
Anwendung des AUG (1979). Bundestags-Drucksache, 8.
Wirtschaft und Statistik. 3 and 9 (1978).
Wochenberichte des Deutsche Institut für Wirtschafts-
forschung (DIW), 47. Jg., 1980.

Policies of Workforce Reduction and Labour Market Structures in the American and German Automobile Industry*

W. SENGENBERGER and CH. KOHLER

I. INTRODUCTION

Labour market structures on the industry level tend to be shaped by rules and regulations which are the outcomes of conflicts and struggles over what are considered the major concerns in the industry for employers, workers and the state.

In the automobile industry a key concern has been the cyclical variation of demand for the product. Management has been confronted with the problem of how to cope with the alternating problems of labour shortage and excess labour. Workers and unions have been mainly concerned with the insecurity resulting from product market instabilities for employers and income.

This paper demonstrates that different policies have been designed and followed by management and worker organi-

*This article presents some results from a comprehensive study on employment structures and industrial relations in the automobile industry; the study is financed by the Sonderforschungsbereich 101 of the University of Munich. (For completion results, see: Kohler, Ch.; Sengenberger, W., 1982).

zations in the US and German automobile industries in
response to cyclical instability, and that disparities in
labour market structures can in large part be traced back to
these differences.
　　The analysis is couched in the notions of organizational flexibility and rigidity with regard to wages,
hours and other conditions of employment. It is shown that
while the relationship between flexibility and rigidity is
fairly stable in the short run, it is constantly altered in
the course of struggles to gain competitive advantage in the
product or labour markets.

II. POLICIES OF WORKFORCE REDUCTION: A COMPARISON

There are substantial differences between the United States
and West Germany in the policies and measures taken by
companies to handle workforce reductions or otherwise cope
with the problem of excess labour. In the United States
direct workforce reduction through temporary or indefinite
lay-offs has been the dominant measure of adjusting the
workforce to fluctuating demand. In Germany, there have been

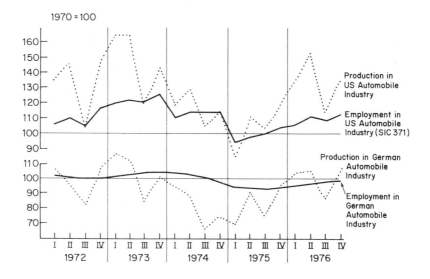

Fig. 1 Indicators of the number of motor vehicles produced
and the number of employees in the US and German Automobile
Industry, 1972-1976. Data Sources: BLS, "Employment and
Earnings"; Ward's "Automotive Yearbook"; Statisches
Bundesamt.

redundancies as well, but overall there has been much more
emphasis on policies to prevent dismissals and to lower
labour input in a more indirect fashion through measures
such as hiring stops, natural wastage, early retirements,
severance pay contracts and, above all, short-time working.

This proposition holds for the economy as a whole; it
is also true for the automobile industry – with which this
paper is mainly concerned. To give some empirical
illustration of the differences of workforce reduction
patterns, we compare changes of production and employment
during the economic recession of 1973–1975 in the US and
German automobile industries. As shown in Fig. 1, employment
in Germany in this period went down by a comparatively small
amount and with a considerable time lag after production. It
is also clear that employment would have decreased much
further if there had not been extensive short-time working,
which in early 1975 affected almost 200,000 workers or one
third of the automobile industry labour force.

In contrast, the US automobile industry shows more
pronounced swings in employment and much more rapid
adjustment of the employment level to production during the
economy cycle. Moreover, looking at monthly figures,
compared to Germany there is much more instability of the
employment level in the short run, partly due to lay-offs
during model changeovers.

To get estimates of employment adjustment over a longer
period of time, we computed elasticities [1] of the annual
rates of change of the number of employees, of weekly man-
hours and of total labour input (employees times hours per
employee) with respect to rates of change in the level of
output in the American and German automobile industry for
the past three decades [2]. The results are presented in
Tables I and II. The elasticity measures are not entirely
comparable due to differences in industry classification and
missing data. Yet, overall, the data problems appear to be
minor in relation to the striking differences shown in the
results of the estimations.

The main findings from this analysis may be summarized
as follows:

i) For both the US and German auto industry
there is evidence of effects described by
Okum's law, i.e. a less than proportionate
adjustment of employment to fluctuations in
production. For all labour input variables
and for all periods investigated, the
estimated coefficients of elasticity are less

Table I. Estimates of elasticities of employment (a) to production in the US automobile industry for various periods

Employment variable	Period	Production variable t-1	Production variable t-2	R^2	F	DW
Average number of production workers (SIC 371)	1948–1980	.06 (1.08)	.59 (11.76)	.84	72.13	1.88
	1961–1980	.12 (1.88)	.57 (9.92)	.84	46.47	1.53
	1971–1980	.21 (2.41)	.57 (7.23)	.89	28.86	2.04
Average weekly hours paid per production worker (SIC 371)	1948–1980	-.02 (-.92)	.14 (6.84)	.67	28.02	2.52
	1961–1980	-.03 (-1.20)	.18 (6.50)	.71	22.19	2.56
	1971–1980	.02 (.30)	.17 (3.83)	.68	7.37	2.18
Total labour input (SIC 371)	1948–1980	.03 (.66)	.73 (15.41)	.90	126.86	1.70
	1961–1980	.07 (1.18)	.75 (12.65)	.90	80.31	1.65
	1971–1980	.22 (3.43)	.74 (12.70)	.96	86.18	1.89

(a) Annual rates of change

Table II. Estimates of elasticities of employment (a) to production in the German automobile industry (b) for various periods

Employment variable	Period	Production variable		R^2	F	DW
		t-1	t-2			
Average number of production workers	1961–1980	.26 (4.12)	.33 (5.37)	.73	24.06	1.94
	1971–1980	.38 (5.01)	.28 (3.55)	.83	19.49	1.82
Average weekly hours paid per production worker	1961–1980	-.09 (-2.56)	.30 (8.92)	.82	42.05	1.66
	1971–1980	-.06 (-1.83)	.34 (9.51)	.92	46.37	1.84
Total labour input	1961–1980	.17 (2.55)	.62 (9.67)	.85	31.52	1.38
	1971–1980	.32 (4.10)	.62 (7.66)	.91	28.86	1.74

(a) Annual rates of change.
(b) Including motor cycles.

than unity.

ii) The flexibility of labour input is
accomplished in different ways in the two
countries. In the United States, the number
of employees is fairly elastic to changes in
output and the speed of adjustment is high
(indicated by the much higher regression
coefficients obtained for employment changes
in the same year compared to the ones for the
previous year).
The elasticities of working time as measured
by the number of paid weekly hours per worker
are significantly lower. From these findings
it may be concluded that flexibility in the
US automobile industry is derived primarily
from the variation of the level of employees
rather than from man-hours.

iii) In contrast, both the volume and speed of
adjustment of German automobile employment is
low. In other words, the level of employment
in terms of the number of employees is much
more stabilized, at least in the short run.
The lag of adjustment has further risen in
the 1970s as indicated by the higher
coefficients of employment with respect to
production levels in the previous year.
Flexibility in the German employment system,
both in terms of volume and speed of adjustment, largely stem from the variability of
weekly hours paid. As mentioned above, part
of this variation can be attributed to
significant amounts of (state-subsidized)
short-time work during periods of slack.
The elasticity coefficients of hours per
employee are more or less as high as the ones
for the number of employees. Evidently during
the 1970s working time flexibility increased.
Looking at the elasticity coefficients for
the 1971-1980 period a curious result
emerges: measured by the rate of change in
production levels within the same year
(indicated by the t-variable) the elasticity
of the number of employees in the German case
takes almost exactly half the size of the US
elasticity, whereas the elasticity of hours
per working in the German automobile industry
is twice as large as in the US. This result
vividly underlines the differences between

the two countries with respect to the sources
of labour flexibility.

iv) The elasticities of total labour input being
a composite measure of the number of workers
employed times the number of weekly hours per
employee are slightly higher for the US
automobile industry, but the differences are
not statistically significant.

The comparatively low production elasticity
of the total blue collar workforce employment
in the German automobile industry does,
however, conceal significant differences in
the elasticity of various skill groups. These
differences are presented in Table III.
According to the figures, semi-skilled
workers show much less continuous employment
patterns than skilled workers and the volume
of employment of unskilled workers is even
more sensitive to changes in production.
There are, furthermore, sizeable differences
among the three skill categories with respect
to the speed of adjustment. This is indicated
by the elasticity coefficient which measures
the reaction of employment to the production
level in the same year in relation to the
sensitivity of employment to production in
the previous year. Thus, for example, the
employment level of the skilled workforce is
very insensitive to changes in output in the
same year, but is more responsive to production changes in the previous year. The size
of the unskilled workforce is very elastic to
output change in the same as well as the
previous year. Given that the low-skilled
workers carry the bulk of workforce
adjustment it is hardly surprising that their
employment level adjusts for some time after
the change in output.

III. DISPARITIES IN THE SYSTEMS OF RULES AND REGULATIONS

Much of the stated differences between the two countries in
dealing with excess labour resources can be explained by the
disparities in the systems of rules and regulations on
employment which have evolved over the past decades.

To be reasonably effective and acceptable to both
employers and workers, institutionalized regulative systems

must resolve basic conflicts between the employer's interest
in flexible and low-cost adjustment to changing market
conditions and the interest of workers in job security and
income protection.

The way the conflicts tend to be resolved is by
preventing foreclosing or by raising the firm's cost of
particular options of adjustment and, at the same time,
facilitating, legitimizing or rewarding other actions. In
general, but not exclusively, prohibitive rules are set by
law and contractual agreement to limit certain strategies,
while "desirable" responses are elicited by monetary
incentives (such as subsidies, tax reductions etc.) provided
by the state.

There is not necessarily a reciprocal one-to-one
relationship between the rigidity resulting from the
regulation to the employer and the security afforded by the
rules to the worker. Nor does employer flexibility
inevitably threaten worker interests of security and
protection. It very much depends how organizational
flexibility is achieved, whether for example, by uninhibited
"hire and fire" policies or by "preventative" adjustment of
worker development, production and marketing measures
facilitated by a highly skilled "polyvalent" and flexible
workforce.

Moreover, the management and the workforce of a firm
may collaborate and both improve their position by
transferring the cost of organizational flexibility and
worker security on to other firms (for example, suppliers),
the state or the public at large.

A. Employment Protection

Job security and employment protection have been developed
in the two countries to different degrees. The differences
in protection relate to:

  i) The periods of advanced notice.
 ii) The terms and conditions under which a worker
     can be laid off.
iii) The compensation to be paid to the worker in
     case of lawful or unlawful dismissal.

Whereas in the US there are hardly any contractual or legal
constraints placed on the employer in running down the
workforce when and as much as he likes, it has become much
more difficult and much more costly to the German employer
to react as quickly and as drastically to product market

fluctuations.

First, <u>basic minimum notice periods</u> in Germany, which
are laid down by law and are often improved upon as a result
of collective or individual agreement, are as follows: up to
five years service = two weeks notice; five to ten years
service = one months notice; ten to 20 years service = 2
months notice; over 20 years service = 3 months notice.
Whilst in the US automobile industry, notice periods
specified by collective agreements amount to 24 hours.

Second, mass dismissal, which is now defined as
dismissal of 30 (previously 50) or more employees per month
in establishments of 500 or more workers, it is lawful only
if it is done for urgent economic reasons and if it cannot
be averted by other actions, such as internal training or
internal transfers. If an employer plans mass dismissal for
economic reasons, he is obliged to report his plans to the
employment office, stating the reasons for his actions and
the number and categories of workers to be laid off. The
notification is to be given at least one month in advance of
the planned reduction. the employment office cannot prevent
the lay-off as such, but it can delay the action for up to
two months to provide the time necessary to set up some
means of redeploying the displaced workers (through
training, relocation, etc.) elsewhere in the economy.

Third, the employer is obliged to negotiate with the
works council over a "balancing of interests", i.e. a
sharing of the burden or the cost of the workforce reduction
between employers and workers affected. Usually, this
negotiation results in a "Social Plan" which specifies a
number of measures with the intent of cushioning the
economic and social impact of redundancies. The works
council can veto any dismissal, no matter whether individual
or large-scale, if the dismissal action is regarded as
"socially unwarranted". In this case, a labour court will
make a final and binding decision on the case. During recent
years, about 20% of all dismissals were revoked after the
works council had intervened. Ten per cent of all dismissals
ended with a labour court ruling.

In addition to general protection there is special
employment protection afforded to particular groups, like
works councillors and pregnant women. Industry-wide
collective agreements afford special protection to older
workers.

The major effect of this employment protection has been
to place legal restrictions on employer discretion for
workforce cuts and, perhaps more significantly, it has
increased the costs of lay-off in terms of financial
compensation, indemnification payments, etc. These effects

have led employers more and more to offer severance pay
contracts with lump-sum separation payments to redundant
workers instead of going through the risky and time-
consuming legal procedures for mass dismissal. Besides, the
public short-time allowance has quite successfully induced
employers to keep the experienced workforce during the
recession. The allowance is granted if, through short-time
working, dismissal and unemployment are likely to be averted
or deferred and if all precautionary steps had already been
taken by the employer to forestall short-time working.

To some extent, the practice of workforce reduction
falls considerably short of the formal protection as
stipulated by law or collective contract. Several aspects
have to be mentioned in this respect: with a few exceptions,
the protective provisions have not averted redundancy as
such, at least not where production has fallen by large
margins. But they have forced employer policies to keep
redundancies at a minimum; and they have clearly advanced a
more long-run view in the company for human resource
planning [3]. Thus, the actual impact of protection has not
been to prevent redundancies, but to smoothen, for part of
the workforce at least, the adjustment of employment in
relation to production levels and to cushion the negative
impact on income.

On the other hand, employers have been very creative in
designing and carrying out measures of workforce adjustment
which are able to neutralize or evade costly and time-
consuming provisions of protection. Such measures include
fixed term contracts, sub-contracting, personnel leasing,
inter-firm agreements for labour exchange and the like.
These measures have sharpened the lines between stable and
unstable worker groups in the auto plants by introducing
more clearly a differential legal status of workers within
the companies' workforces.

Finally, employers during the last decade have been
quite successful in externalizing the adjustment costs by
placing them on the wider community and particularly on the
social security system. This type of reaction has been
particularly prominent with respect to early retirement,
which places the financial burden on unemployment insurance
and retirement funds.

There are also differences in job security in the two
countries for the redundant worker. For example, given
normal business fluctuations, unemployment benefits to the
redundant US auto worker compare quite favourably with the
German benefits; during heavy and more prolonged economic
downturns, however, the social security system in the US
automobile industry reveals major short-comings. Thus,

during the recent crisis in the US automobile industry a
substantial section of unemployed auto workers exhausted
their claims both for state unemployment and TRA benefits as
well as for SUB.

B. Selection of Employees to be Dismissed

The thrust of the US regulative system is not in protecting
the employment relationships but is in restricting the
freedom of the employer in selecting workers for lay-offs by
imposing seniority rules. Generally speaking, then, the US
managers in the automobile plants have much less discretion
whom to fire and to recall than the German managers do. This
does not mean that in the US automobile industry seniority
is, under all circumstances, the sole factor in determining
the selection of workers for downgrading and lay-off, but,
at least within the Big Three companies, seniority plays a
pretty decisive role for worker allocation in the internal
market. Therefore, managerial discretion in this area is
severely restricted.
    German management is also bound by selection criteria
as well, specified by differential protection from dismissal
of different workers. The criteria are established by
broadly defined selection guidelines negotiated with the
works council and by legal stipulations of social criteria
for selection [4]. Hence, German employers cannot, on the
whole, arbitrarily select employees to be included in
collective dismissal actions.
    Yet, compared to the determining force of the US
seniority rules, the German selection rules are much less
detailed, less binding, much more geared towards groups than
individuals and much more open for negotiation. De facto,
they do not place severe restrictions on the employer;
rather, they leave considerable discretion for management to
select workers.
    Within certain limits set by social criteria German
firms have been in a position to select much more according
to standards of achievement, effort and social conduct of
the worker. Workers to be dismissed may be hand-picked and,
thereby, conflicts over selection tend to be individualized
(Dombois, 1979). As a consequence, it is in the area of
worker allocation inside the firm in which German employers
enjoy the flexibility to select according to efficiency
principles. Managers have been able to structure the plant
workforces into stable core components (Stammbelegschaft)
and unstable peripheral components (Randbelegschaft). This

division, which relates to the differential protection of worker groups, does not merely help to ease and to lower the cost of workforce adjustments to varying demand of labour, but also serves the function of selecting from the fringe workforce the most promising workers for the core component.

In summary, the employment reduction patterns in the two countries reflect different strategies of control by corporate managers, worker organizations and, to a lesser extent, by the state to intervene in the process. In the US automobile industry management faces little restriction to hiring and firing, but is forced to observe contractual seniority rules over worker selection for lay-off and downgrading. Conversely, German management is hampered by legal restriction and costs of rapid adjustment of workforces but has a comparatively free hand in worker selection. As a consequence, economic advantages to the companies are secured through high rates of selectivity and effort extraction in Germany, whereas in the US there are smaller expenses to the firm from cyclical changes in the level of the workforce.

IV. THE DYNAMICS OF REGULATION: FLEXIBILITY AND RIGIDITY

So far we have highlighted redundancy policies and regulative frameworks in the two countries more or less from a static cross-sectional viewpoint. Now, we will look at the same subject from a more dynamic viewpoint.

Some labour market analysts have suggested that the labour market moves steadily away from being market regulated towards a state in which the labour market process is heavily institutionalized. Law and collective contract would increasingly govern the process. It may be true that the extent of regulation has grown over time, but this extension of regulation is not to be confused with an inevitable corresponding limitation of employer discretion and power to shape employment policies in accordance with his basic interests.

Taking the analytical concepts of flexibility and rigidity as a point of departure, we might say that while there is historical evolution of political intervention into the labour market there also is at any time both rigidity and flexibility in the labour market structure. Rigidity relates to areas of action in which employers are cons-trained in their freedom to act as they like in order to seek advantages and pursue interests. This rigidity may result from legal or judicial provisions initiated by unions or the state or may reflect well-established customs

initiated by the employers themselves [5]. <u>Flexibility</u>
relates to a high degree of freedom to act in accordance
with own interests.

What brings about changes in the regulative system? As
shown in a previous paper (Sengenberger, 1979), the
aggregate employment level is a most important force in
shaping the relationship between flexibility and rigidity
through offensive and defensive policies respectively. In
general, one might say that in periods of increasing and
high demand for labour when employers are in a relatively
unfavourable position on the market, they attempt to gain
flexibility by moving into new fields or dimensions in which
there is little regulation. Conversely, in periods of
economic depression or decline, employers tend to be on the
offensive, trying to press for roll-backs in areas in which
they have previously lost discretionary power. Obviously,
the objective of such strategies is to erode structural
rigidities.

Worker organizations, on the other hand, are in a
relatively favourable position, during periods of tight
labour markets, to make advances in regulation which would
interfere with worker competition, while during phases of
economic slump they are compelled to assume a defensive
posture.

The impact of aggregate economic activity on the
redistribution of basic power relations and on flexibility-
rigidity relations in the labour market does vary across
countries depending on, among other things, how far and in
which way the industrial reserve army mechanism has been
curtailed [6].

Labour market dynamics reflect a constant reshuffling
of the areas and degrees of rigidity and flexibility from
employer actions (as well as worker interventions). Although
there is a limited number of policy parameters (or dimensions), such as wages, working hours, worker effort, worker
allocation, market entry and market exit, and training, the
potential scope for re-shaping existing regulation appears
to be unlimited.

For example, in the German auto industry during the
1970s, employers faced increased rigidities in workforce
adjustment as a result of extended and tightened employment
protection. Simultaneously, the public subsidy to short-time
working introduced by the Labour Promotion Act of 1969
offered considerable scope for low-cost adjustment of weekly
working hours. Not surprisingly, therefore, the automobile
producers increasingly used the short-work week as an
instrument for reducing labour input. And, in lieu of direct
workforce reduction, which on a large scale could only be

accomplished by the expensive buy-out of protective laws and contract rules, firms attempted as much as possible to use more indirect means of workforce variation, such as natural wastage linked with hiring stops and internal transfers.

This shift in adjustment policies is reflected in the differences in the elasticity coefficient between the 1961-80 and 1971-80 periods in Table III. While the short-run elasticity of average weekly hours was higher in the 1970s than in the longer period of 1961-80, the short-run elasticity of the number of workers was lower in the 1971-80 period. Furthermore, in the 1970s the employment level of production level reacted more strongly to changes in output in the previous year. This may be interpreted as signalling delayed adjustment of the level of the workforce related to the legal barriers to direct and short-term reduction of the workforce.

To give some illustration of this point, the UAW made many significant advances on the bargaining table during boom phases. For example, both seniority rights and SUB were initiated when the state of product and labour markets were improving or otherwise to the favour of the UAW, and also, the speed and dates of augmentation of these gains depended very much on the market conditions. Similarly, in Germany, progress on job and income protection and active labour market policies came about or were extended or strengthened during the time of high economic activity, prosperity and generally tight labour markets, during which employers being under severe competitive pressures had conceded more security to workers to keep them attached to the company. Successively during the 1960s and the early 1970s, from a relative position of strength, labour was able to consolidate or extend protective policies.

In periods of economic crisis the situation tends to be reversed. The past three years in the US auto industry have demonstrated that the UAW has been under pressure to make concessions in areas in which it appeared to have a firm grip. Workers at Chrysler faced a roll-back of wages and fringe benefits eroding the traditional UAW wage strategy of equal wages and employment conditions through pattern set-ting and pattern following. The union is now under pressure to accept further encroachment into gains made in the past. Furthermore, while the UAW realizes the limitations of the seniority system to provide for security and SUB to provide for income maintenance, the prospects for legislation proposed by the union appear rather bleak at present.

At the same time as US automobile corporations try to erode essential standards of employment won by the UAW during the heydays of strength, they are in the process of

Table III. Estimates of elasticities of employment (a) to production in the German automobile industry (b) by skill groups and periods

Employment variable	Period	Production variable $t-1$	Production variable $t-2$	R^2	F	DW
Skilled workers	1961-1980	.19 (2.17)	.06 (.70)	.23	2.67	1.85
	1971-1980	.17 (1.40)	.07 (.54)	.23	1.36	1.83
Semi-skilled workers	1961-1980	.45 (4.48)	.45 (4.62)	.71	21.77	1.96
	1971-1980	.60 (5.91)	.42 (3.74)	.87	30.94	2.29
Unskilled workers	1961-1980	.66 (2.01)	.70 (2.16)	.34	1.96	2.13
	1971-1980	1.07 (2.19)	.77 (1.07)	.49	4.32	2.48

(a) Annual rates of change.
(b) Excluding motor cycles.

extending the perimeters of their operative flexibility
through opening up various new avenues, such as the
development of world cars and the concomitant global
strategy of parallel production and marketing. It is obvious
that this strategy could weaken the bargaining position of
the national union (Dombois and Sengenberger, 1981).

In Germany to date, the economic crisis in the
automobile industry has not reached the same magnitude. Yet,
both at the industry level as well as for the economy as a
whole, both the economic and the political environment is
clearly working in favour of employers. Earlier union moves
to cut weekly hours of work and to curtail inter-worker
competition in the plant are at a stalemate. At the same
time, the social security network, as well as general
standards of labour, are being scrutinized and cut-backs are
likely in view of the fiscal crisis of the state. Their
effect will be to "discipline" the labour force and to
reactivate the labour reserve mechanism.

To come to a conclusion on these points one might say
that under conditions of economic crisis flexibility-
rigidity relations in the labour market are re-structured at
the expense of labour in a double sense: worker
organizations do not succeed in gaining regulation or some
other form of control in areas which constitute areas of
flexibility for management and which expose workers to tough
competition. And with the deepening crisis it is likely that
seemingly well-established impediments to worker competition
tend to be eroded. Neither is there straight or unilateral
development in the labour market structure nor, as Sabel has
demonstrated (1981), is there the widely held tendency
towards institutional convergence between countries.

V. LABOUR MARKET STRUCTURES

Labour market structures tend to mirror past policies, both
offensive and defensive ones, that were followed by either
party to gain advantages in the product or labour market.
Here, we will mainly be concerned with patterns of
differentiation and segmentation resulting from the
respective policies in the two countries under
consideration.

To gain a fairly comprehensive view of the labour
market structure in an industry one would need to look at:

 i) The job structure and the allocation patterns
    of workers within the job structure.
ii) The distribution of employment opportunities

as well as the structure of <u>wages</u> and income
maintenance.
iii) <u>Intra–</u> as well as <u>inter–</u>plant distributions.

In the following we will not be able to present a complete
analysis of labour market structures in the two countries.
Instead we will highlight what we believe are some crucial
differences in the structural fabric of the German and
American labour markets in the automobile industry.

Our main propositions are that labour market
segmentation in the German automobile industry is manifested
primarily in the distribution of employment opportunities
(rather than in the wage area), and, furthermore, is
manifested in intra–plant (rather than inter–plant)
divisions. Conversely, in the US automobile industry
segmentation lines are characterized by inter–plant
divisions mainly in the wage structure.

A. Intra–Plant Structures

In German automobile plants during the 1970s intra–plant
divisions of the workforces into a skilled and fairly stable
component (Stammbelegschaft) and a low–skilled and unstable
component (Randbelegschaft) have grown and gradually become
institutionalized. This structuring process has largely
been occasioned by workforce reduction policies during
periods of economic slump.

The brunt of the reduction during the 1973–75 recession
was borne by the younger direct production workers and,
among them, by disproportionately high shares of foreigners
and women. In addition, a significant number of workers
approaching the age of retirement left the firms "voluntarily" on severance payment contracts providing more or
less full compensation for losses of earnings and retirement
benefits. Most of the early retirees were members of the
experienced core labour force.

The distribution of forced and voluntary worker
separations cannot sufficiently be explained by the
distribution of the reduction of jobs during the period of
decline. To a significant extent there has been downward
worker displacement. The bumping occurred largely in line
with skill and performance standards rated on an individual
worker basis. Within limits of quotas set for various skill
groups in some plants, skilled workers displaced semi-
skilled workers and semi–skilled workers displaced unskilled
workers; Germans displaced foreigners and men displaced
women.

The burden of the economic crisis, then, was
distributed very unevenly across different sections of the
workforce. The majority of redundancies were low-skilled or
low performance workers whose employment status was fairly
marginal. The established core workforces, on the other
hand, incurred comparatively small costs. As far as their
members were affected at all by the reductions, they were
either downgraded for some limited period of time or they
left the companies with little or no economic loss. As
mentioned above, the outcome of the selection process was a
sort of political compromise between different interests,
including the managerial interest of screening according to
skill, performance on behavioural standards, the differential legal and contractual protection of employment afforded
to different groups of workers and the interest in
management and the works council to resolve the conflict
over selection in a peaceful manner by taking consideration
of established differentials of power and status within the
plant labour force.

Because of works council intervention, management was
not always fully in control of the cut-back operation, but
nevertheless, the selection process worked pretty much to
its satisfaction. Exceptions to this occurred where demands
from works councils had to be met which gave workers a
choice of taking a severance pay contract. In this case, the
company lost some of the experienced workers to other firms
in the area. But other than that, management got the kind of
selection it wanted, allowing the firms to dismiss the least
productive and least motivated workers. By phasing out both
young and old workers the age structure of the plant
workforces did not get too much out of balance. By including
"voluntary" turnover through large lump sum payments the
threat from a potentially explosive situation of mass
dismissal was removed.

The works council, though it had a stake in the
selection process and had the right to veto every single
dismissal, did not come up with principles and decisions
fundamentally different from those applied by management.
Works councillors agreed to the principle that those workers
should be phased out first who had alternative employment or
income opportunities outside the plant, whereas primary wage
earners, i.e. middle aged men, should be retained. This
principle not only coincided with the managerial interest of
keeping the experienced labour force, but it also allowed
the worker representatives to retain its primary clientele
in the plant.

Selection policies during the recession have set the
stage for more clear-cut divisions within the auto plant

labour forces. The line dividing the stable and the unstable workforces has become even more accentuated in the aftermath of the 1973-75 recession when management, in response to protracted and expensive cutback operations, had turned down new forms of flexibility to adjust to cyclical variation. Fixed-term contracts, personnel leasing and inter-firm contracts for labour exchange are beyond the reach of the system of worker protection from dismissal. Through these measures, costly reduction programmes can be avoided. At the same time, the reciprocal relationship between the security of the fringe workers has been strengthened to the extent that now, more than before, cyclical variations in labour demand are buffered by the fringe workforces.

From this analysis one may conclude that while the German automobile plant labour markets are generally more closed than their American counterparts in terms of legal restrictions and the cost of making workers redundant, they are more open to the extent that there are exit positions (as well as entry positions) on different levels of the job hierarchy. These exit positions are not subject to written rules; rather they are subject to collective bargaining at plant level. In contrast, entry and exit, as well as internal movement of workers in the American automobile factory, is more strictly governed by a very extensive set of written rules based on seniority. The US automobile plant is more closed than the German one in terms of the number and location of entry and exit ports. The ports to the external market are largely restricted to job classification at the bottom of the skill hierarchy; as a consequence, when the workforce is reduced lay-offs are highly concentrated among the low seniority workers and there is more extensive bumping across jobs of different skill requirements. This pattern of internal reshuffling of workers follows the more or less rigid observation of plant seniority rules. As a result, the dynamics of worker lay-offs in the US automobile plant are not so closely related to the number of jobs.

Linked with the strictly limited locations of exchange between internal and external labour market in the US automobile industry, there is a correspondingly large volume of internal worker mobility. Mobility chains extend over the entire hierarchy of jobs from low-skill entry positions into the ranks of skilled workers. Though there is some external recruitment of skilled workers, the large majority of them are recruited from inside the plant.

In the US, more so than in Germany, it is the junior and low-skilled worker who is laid off when production shrinks. But, with the exception of recently hired workers, laid-off employees have recall rights which reduce their

competition with other workers on the external market. As
soon as an employee has accumulated seniority his likelihood
of being laid off in normal recession periods becomes very
small.

Job opportunities and mobility patterns in the German
automobile plant tend to be more discontinuous, one might
even say more polarized. The penetration ratio of semi-
skilled workers into skilled jobs is limited and, therefore,
the employment status of the semi-skilled worker is a more
permanent one.

B. Inter-Plant Structures

Inter-plant labour market segmentation is manifested in
differences of wages or security of employment and income
across regions, between parent and subsidiary firms or
between supplier and producer firms.

Overall, inter-firm differentials in the automobile
industry are larger in the US than in Germany. Ultimately,
this difference may be explained by some basic discrepancies
in the industrial relations system. Industrial relations in
Germany are widely regulated by law and statutory terms and
by fairly large and encompassing collective bargaining units
which make for a relatively small dispersion of wages and
terms of employment across occupations, industries and
regions. Under the law, union wage standards are legally
enforceable and employers must not fall short of them.
Unions in Germany have mostly given preference in their
basic representational strategy to the "wide front" rather
than to the "strong point". Owing to such fairly uniform
labour standards there is a comparatively small incentive
for firms in Germany to relocate production or shift plants
in order to gain control or to save labour costs.

In contrast, in the United States, where the industrial
relations system is much more fragmented and decentralized,
both wage levels and terms of employment are less
egalitarian and depend much more on union strength. The UAW
has been quite successful in standardizing wages and other
conditions of work across plants of the Big Three, but the
equalization has remained incomplete and has been challenged
during the recent crisis. There have remained "union-free"
regions as well as unorganized supplier firms which can be
used by employers to undercut the union's bargaining
strength in the established areas of automobile production.
Thus, for example, in the Detroit area, the heartland of
automobile manufacturing, the number of automobile plants

has declined from 200 in 1951 to about 140 at present. Part of this loss has been due to the "Southern Strategy" of the producers relocating production in the low wage and union-free belts [7].

There are forces of push and pull for management to resort to inter-plant flexibility. Push forces are operative, for example, where there is widely varying union strength. In this case, management may attempt to undermine the labour relations in plants in which the union has a firm grip. Pull forces are created by favourable environments for plant location or capital formation. In the US, the Right to Work movement represents one example. Another would be the economic incentives provided by states and municipalities in order to attract new business to their locality. Among other things, there have been offers of investment subsidies, tax cuts or tax abatements, eroding worker or environmental protection and the like. In periods of overall economic stagnation and unemployment such competition for jobs is destructive to the extent that it leads to nothing more than a geographical redistribution of employment, often with the result of undermining established labour standards. The UAW, at a recent convention, denounced such practices as "economic cannibalism".

In recent years there have been indications of such destructive inter-regional competition for the automobile plants in Germany as well. Whenever an automobile company announces a plan to build a new plant state governments begin to outbid each other in coming up with attractive financial offers to get the new jobs. Firms gain not only cheap capital formation and the most modern capital equipment in the new plant, but also the prospect of escaping the tough and entrenched labour relations climate in the old plant. This example demonstrates that even in a country with fairly well-established wage and employment standardization, there can be new avenues for differen-tiation in the industrial structure.

C. Segmentation Patterns Compared

Table IV draws together some of the main points raised on the patterns of segmentation in the American and German automobile industry.

Changes in labour market structures echo the changes in labour market politics which are fed both by macro-related developments in the national industrial relations system and specific politics at the industry level.

Table IV. Segmented labour market structures in the US and
German automobile industry

	Intra-plant segmentation	Inter-plant segmentation
Employment	US: Continuous hierarchical job opportunity structure Germany: more discontinuous, dichotomous opportunity structure	
Wages		US: Comparatively high wage differentials across regions and plant-type Germany: Comparatively low wage differentials

VI. CONCLUSION

In this paper we have demonstrated that there are
significant differences between the US and German auto
industry with respect to employment policies, systems of
regulation and labour market structures. Although the
ultimate objective of the regulative systems is to reduce
worker competition (from a union viewpoint), or to foster
worker competition (from a managerial viewpoint), the basic
strategies and instruments in accomplishing these objectives
are different in the two countries. While the US regulative
system centres heavily on the seniority system and contains
almost no direct elements of protecting the employment
relationship, the German system depends heavily on the
latter instrument. As a consequence, the employment policies
that can be observed in adjusting to fluctuating demand are
quite different.

We have also shown that although there is something
like structural stability in the labour market, in the
short-run the structure is subject to continuous change. The
prime movers of this change are cyclical switches in the
power relations between capital and labour in line with

shifts in aggregate levels of employment; and changes in the battlefield or "theatre" (to borrow a term from the glossary of modern military strategy), in which the major conflicts between the actors are staged. We have tried to show that depending on their relative strength, employers, at times, may retreat or "escape" to new areas in order to secure new opportunities for flexibility and, during favourable periods, they tend to roll back established rules and institutions which they regard as barriers to their manoeuvrability. Similarly, unions, (and to a varying extent worker allied state governments) move forward or are forced to make concessions depending on their economically derived bargaining position.

NOTES

1. The percentage change in the measure of labour input associated with a 1% change in output.
2. In the comprehensive report we also present regression results based on monthly and quarterly figures. In addition, we show estimates for four-digit industries of the automobile industry and for various categories of labour.
3. A similar effect has been reported in the UK, emanating from the Employment Protection Act (Daniel and Stilgoe, 1978, p. 40).
4. An employee can make a judicial claim that his/her dismissal is socially unjustified if the employer in the selection process has not taken into account social aspects such as age, length of service and family responsibility.
5. It is important to realise that employers, though principally interested in as much autonomy and manoeuvrability as possible, come up with actions and measures which, if sufficiently generalized and diffused in the labour market, show a structural impact which may turn out to be (external) constraints to the range of employer actions. For example, the widespread and ongoing practice of "weeding out" the least attractive workers in periods of low demand for labour tends to produce hard core unemployment with the result of reducing effective labour reserve on the external market. Such self-created rigidities explain why there are structured labour markets even in the absence of unionism or state regulations.
6. We do not propose here a simple type of reductionism, which looks at power relations in the labour market

merely as a function of the demand for labour. We see
"political" conjunctures as being of great importance
as well. We do believe, however, that the labour
movement as a whole, and unions in particular, cannot
entirely shield themselves from basic economic
conditions.
7.   However, during recent years the North-South wage
differentials have vanished. The UAW contract with GMC,
for example, assures equal wage rates for all GM plants
in the country.

REFERENCES

Bluestone, B. and Harrison, B. (1980). "Capital and
Communities: The Causes and Consequences of Private
Disinvestment". The Progressive Alliance, Washington,
D.C.
Daniel, W.W. and Stilgoe, E. (1978). "The Impact of
Employment Protection Laws". Policy Studies Institute,
XVIV, No. 577, London.
Deutschmann, C. (1982) "Der Einfluss der Produktion-
sentwicklung auf die Beschäftigungsdynamik in der
Industrie - Eine ökonometrische Untersuchung der
Struktur der Nachfrage nach Arbeitskräften in der
Industrie insgesamt sowie in ausgewählten im Zeitraum
1969 bis 1978 in der Bundesrepublik Deutschland".
Arbeitspapiere aus dem Arbeitskreis Sozialwissen-
schaftliche Arbeitsmarktforschung.
Dombois, R.(1976). Massenentlassungen bei VW, Individuali-
sierung der Krise. Leviathan, 4.
Dombois, R. (1979). Stammarbeiter und Krisenbetroffenheit,
Fallanalysen zu Krisenbetroffenheit angelernter
Arbeiter. PROKLA, 36.
Dombois, R. and Sengenberger, W. (1981). Die Automobilar-
beitergewerkschaft UAW und die Krise in der US
Autoindustrie. Gewerkschaftlichte Monatshefte, 8.
Kohler, Ch. (1981). Betrieblicher Arbeitsmarkt und Gewerk-
schaftspolitik - Innerbetriebliche Mobilitat in der
amerikanischen Automobilindustrie. Forschungsberichte
aus dem ISF München, Frankfurt.
Kohler, Ch. and Sengenberger, W. (1982). Wenn der Absatz
schrumpft Beschäftigung, Personalabbau und Arbeitsmarkt
in der deutschen und amerikanischen. Automobilindustrie, Campus-Verlag, Frankfurt/München.
Mendius, H.G. and Sengenberger, W. (1976). Konjunktur-
schwankungen und betriebliche Politik: zur Entstehung
und Verfestigung von Arbeitsmarktsegmentation. In ISF

(Hrsg.), Betrieb – Arbeitsmarkt – Qualifikation, Bd. I, Frankfurt.

Mendius, H.G. and Schultz-Wild, R. (1976). Betriebsräte und Personalabbau. Leviathan, 4.

Rubery, J. (1978). Structured labour markets, worker organisation and low pay. Cambridge Journal of Economics, 2.

Sabel, C. (1981). "The Division of Labour". (Manuscript).

Schultz-Wild, R. (1978). "Betriebliche Beschaftigungspolitik in der Krise". Frankfurt.

Sengenberger, W. (1981). Labour market segmentation and the business cycle. In "The Dynamics of Labour Market Segmentation", (F. Wilkinson, ed.). Academic Press, London and Orlando.

Sengenberger, W. (1981). "Protection of Workers in Case of Work Force Reduction in the Undertaking – The Case of the Federal Republic of Germany". ILO.

UAW (1980). "Where We Stand: Resolutions Adopted". 26th UAW Constitutional Convention, June 1-6, 1980. Anaheim, California.

UAW et al. (1979). "Economic Dislocation: Plant Closings, Plant Relocations and Plant Conversion". Joint Report of Labour Union Study Tour Participants, May 1, 1979.

Labour Market Segmentation and Workers' Careers: The Case of the Italian Knitwear Industry*

G. SOLINAS*

I. INTRODUCTION

This paper reports on empirical research into the labour
market in the knitwear and ready-to-wear industry in the
province of Modena (Emilia). In particular, it looks at the
careers of three categories of workers: homeworkers, those
employed on the production lines of larger firms, and
artisans [1].

Italy, in common with many other industrialized
capitalist economies has witnessed a growing decentralization of production. This tendency has been differently
interpreted but a consensus is emerging that such developments are not evidence of economic backwardness [2]. On the
contrary, an industrial structure consisting of firms of

*University of Modena. This article is a revised version of
a paper presented at the Third Conference of the
International Working Party on Labour Market Segmentation,
September 1981. I wish to thank Sebastiano Brusco, Paola
Villa and the referees and editors of Cambridge Journal of
Economics for their valuable suggestions and comments. My
thanks also to Paola Pagliarini for collaborating with me on
the early stages of my research.

different sizes but with a large number of small and even
"microscopic" enterprises is increasingly being recognized
as one possible avenue of economic development. Taking this
for granted, the aim of these notes is to investigate the
structure of the labour market in a prosperous area typified
by economic growth with the small firm as its base element.

Sections II and III describe the industrial structure
and the manufacturing processes; sections IV and V analyse
the different strata of the labour market and sections Vl
and VII examine the factors determining earnings and the
allocation of the workforce to various jobs. Section VIII
gives my conclusions.

II. KNITWEAR AND READY-MADE GARMENTS: THE INDUSTRIAL STRUCTURE

A. The Industrial District

The knitwear and ready-made garment industry is concentrated
in Carpi and its surrounding boroughs which also constitute
the local market within which workers are willing to move
and do move comparatively freely. In this area the large
majority of firms produce knitwear and ready-made garments;
in these industries the level of vertical integration is low
and so firms tend to specialize in one particular stage of
production. Carpi and its surrounding area is a prime
example of what Becattini calls an industrial "district",
for:

> the elements uniting those firms making up the
> district ... are a complex weave of external
> economies and diseconomies, interrelated costs
> and historical and cultural links which
> influence both business and personal
> relationships (Becattini, 1979, p. 20) [3].

These factors give cost advantages to the firm by virtue of
favourable location, and form the basis for the development
and maintenance of skills and specialized knowledge
essential for the industrial system. In turn the concentration of skill and "know-how" provides the foundation from
which small businesses spring up, and from which "that
certain extra productivity" from labour derives (Becattini,
1979; Paci, 1978).

Such "monocultural" areas characterized by a fragmented
industrial structure have proved to have a remarkable
capacity for resistance during times of crisis. This is due

in no small part to the speed with which the industrial
framework adjusts to changes in demand. In the last ten
years Carpi's knitwear industry has demonstrated a marked
vitality, despite wide fluctuations in manufacturing
activity. Gross product and investment in fixed assets have
increased and the industry has maintained its position in
both the home and international market despite rapidly
growing competition from third world countries. This success
has preserved full employment.

B. Industrial Organization

The firms can be divided into three major categories:

   i) Firms with a comparatively high degree of
      vertical integration which produce directly
      for the consumer, which undertake all the main
      stages of production and which are only
      dependent on outside labour to a small degree.
  ii) Sub-contracting firms which undertake a
      single, intermediate stage of manufacture.
 iii) Firms which have access to the consumer
      market, which produce individual styles and
      control the quality of the finished product
      within the plant but which commission outside
      labour for the larger proportion, and often
      the whole, of manufacture.

By Woodward's classification (1965) firms in groups (i) and
(ii) produce in large batches and small batches respectively
whilst firms in group (iii) produce "prototypes" used to
solicit orders which are then "made up". The greater
majority of the firms in group (i) are large (over 100
employees) whilst those in groups (ii) and (iii) are medium-
sized or small [4].

C. Market Organization

The larger firms make standardized, generally good quality
articles and operate as much in international as national
markets. The small firms can be divided into two groups. The
first group, firms which produce samples for the trade,
receive orders and commission the manufacture externally,
and also a fair number of sub-contracting firms, have three
notable characteristics. First, by continuously redesigning

products and diversifying production they show a marked
capability of creating their own demand. These firms:

> invent new needs and satisfy them at the same
> time ... The secret of this trick lies in the
> particulars of the firm's internal
> organization, its close relations with its
> clients and its collaboration with other firms
> in the sector (Brusco and Sabel, 1981, p. 106).

Second, they use advanced techniques which are comparable to
those of the most successful large firms and are often
equipped with the best machines available (Ervet, 1979).
Moreover, in industries such as knitwear and garment making
where the manufacturing process may be fragmented without
resorting to inferior techniques, small production units may
benefit from the economies of scale. Becattini, quoting
Marshall, argues:

> the advantages of production on a large scale
> can in general be as well attained by the
> aggregation of a large number of small masters
> into one district as by the erection of a few
> large works ... In fact with regard to many
> classes of commodities it is possible to
> divide the process of production into several
> stages, each one of which can be performed
> with the maximum of economy in a small
> establishment (Becattini, 1979, p. 19).

The threshold level of operating efficiency at single stages
of production is low enough in the knitwear and ready-to-
wear industry to admit very small workshops (see Brusco,
Giovannetti and Malagoli, 1979). For example, many knitting,
stitching and finishing workshops employ from four to six
workers.

Finally, small firms are not necessarily nor usually
subordinate either in the market for their supplies or in
their product markets. As Brusco observes:

> if subordination is to be judged by the
> "capacity of one firm to limit the profits –
> and indirectly, in certain circumstances – the
> wages of another", then the study of the firms
> functioning by filling orders, and the
> examination of their relations with the
> commissioning companies suggests that this

>really is not a widespread phenomenon. The
>sub-contracting firms do not in fact usually
>operate in a monopsonistic market, where the
>power of the commissioning buyer is very
>strong, but rather in a market, which, though
>by no means perfect, is basically a competitive
>one (Brusco, 1975, p. 36).

This argument is also valid for the consumer market. Since,
for the most part, the smaller production units have no
direct channels to the market, their products bear the
brandnames or trademarks of the wholesalers. Even here the
opportunities are small for the commercial middle-man to
dominate the producers. The large numbers of wholesalers
mean that they have little control over the market, and
cannot "make the price".

The second group of small firms – small in number and
much less representative – produce for the home market (in
certain cases only for the local market) and manufacture
lower quality articles. A not inconsiderable number of sub-
contracting firms also turn out lower quality components.
These use a much lower level of technology and are in some
instances merely "offshoots" of other businesses. Frequently
these firms operate on a margin of the market, springing up
and vanishing with product market fluctuations.

D. Industrial Relations

Industrial relations and working conditions vary widely with
the size of firms and are determined by the degree of union
organization and by aspects of Italy's labour legislation.
In firms employing 30 employees or more union membership is
high, the union is very strong, and has factory-level
organization (Capecchi and Pugliese, 1978; FLM, 1975). From
this well-organized position the unions can ensure comp-
liance with social welfare provisions (sickness, pensions
etc.), to enforce the "Statuto dei Lavoratori", and obtain
noticeable improvements upon the levels of pay and conditions agreed nationally. Moreover, in medium to large
factories workers have achieved significant control over the
labour process and employment. Thus:

>the presence of the union, and its involvement
>at every turn makes it extremely difficult for
>the management to dismiss workers. In fact,
>every time there is any difficulty it tends to
>become a political issue, the conditions for a

strike are created, depositions made to the
Department of Employment, there is inter-
vention by government agencies, etc.
(Capecchi, 1980, p. 30).

In the smaller enterprises the picture is totally different:
most have no shopfloor union organization, the legislation
against unfair dismissals offers no protection in firms
engaging less than 15 persons, and workers are laid off at
the first sign of a crisis. In many instances, agreements
between individual workers and the employer take precedence
over collective contract, welfare norms are evaded, and
variations in the workload and in working hours occur more
frequently than in larger firms. The homeworking section is
even less well protected.

E. Relations with Other Areas

Well-established Carpi firms frequently build new factories
outside the region and direct a flow of orders to sub-
contractors in other areas, even at a distance from Carpi.
In fact, decentralization extends into the provinces of
Mantua, Verona, Ferrara, Rovigo, Ancona, etc. Brusco (1982)
has stressed a "core-periphery" relationship develops
between areas where firms are long-established, and those of
recent establishment. The vast majority of firms, especially
the smaller ones, have no access to the consumer market, are
not usually equipped with sophisticated machinery, and carry
out those stages of production with low value added. For the
most part they make use of cheap labour: for example, 10% of
the employees of artisans in Modena are apprentices, whereas
in other areas this proportion rises to 50% (Malagoli and
Mengoli, 1979). Similarly, the homeworkers are engaged in
jobs calling for a lesser degree of qualification and (even
where the job content is the same) are paid much less than
their counterparts in Carpi. The periphery therefore
provides core firms with the means of increasing profits and
gives the industrial structure an added degree of flexibility. In the event of a falling product market artisan
sub-contractors and homeworkers in Ferraro or Rovigo see a
decline in the volume of orders well before outworkers in
Carpi. This shifting of risk to the periphery protects the
core firms and allows greater security of employment and
stability in labour relations even in small and "mini"
enterprises, and more continuity in the flow of orders to
artisan businesses and homeworkers.

III. THE MANUFACTURING PROCESS AND THE ACQUISITION OF SKILLS

Once the prototype has been developed and the patterns made, the manufacturing process can be separated into knitting, shaping the knitted panels, making-up, finishing and pressing, quality control and packing. Not all the stages are indispensable and the number of single operations combining into a single production stage may vary according to the type and quality of the product. For example, in so-called "diminishing-stitch" knitwear the cutting/shaping stage is eliminated; the making up of "fully-fashioned" garments invariably requires a greater number of single operations; and not every kind of product requires buttonholing and attachment of buttons. The product's physical properties, its seasonal demand, and the varying kinds of manufacturing techniques necessary for adapting to

Table I. Stage of production, degree of automation and worker qualifications

Production	Automation	Worker Qualification
Sample	No	Craft
Knitting	Yes	Craft Skilled operatives
Cutting/ Shaping	Yes/No	Craft Skilled operatives
Making-up	No	Craft Skilled operatives Semi-skilled operatives
Finishing	Yes/No	Craft Skilled operatives Semi-skilled operatives
Pressing	No	Skilled operatives
Control/ Packaging	No	Semi-skilled operatives

changes in fashion and to differing qualities of materials
are such that even the larger firms, with their longer
production runs, are obliged to adopt remarkably flexible
work organization. A change of product may require the
rearrangement of what is usually termed the "plant balance"
and therefore involves worker mobility between machines
within the same department and between departments [5].
Consequently it is not possible to define precise divisions
between the different professional spheres. The scale of
mechanization varies between the different stages of
production. Only in the making-up operations and certain of
the finishing operations are the machines engaged in
different operations arranged in sequence so that production
methods approximate to those of assembly lines. Most of the
other processes use similar machines but not assembly line
methods. Mechanization has gone furthest in knitting,
certain kinds of finishing (embroidery) and, in some cases,
cutting. Three types of automatic loom, the straight, the
circular and the cotton loom are used for knitting. Since
cotton looms can be used effectively only for large batch
production they are generally found in larger factories.
Artisans and small enterprises mostly make use of circular
machines and, above all, of straight looms [6]. All
production line work uses more traditional fixed-cycle and
single function power machines. This stage of the
manufacturing process has not lent itself to automation,
because of the special characteristics of material and of
semi-finished products, and because of the physical
properties of the final product, the profusion of styles and
patterns and low levels of investment [7]. Two features of
the operation of industrial sewing machines have an
important bearing on the job content. About 70% of the total
work time is "dead" time as the operator positions the work
piece. On the other hand, when run at maximum speed the
sewing machines produce six to eight thousand stitches per
minute, so the "real" work time is extremely intense. The
successful operation of sewing machines therefore requires
considerable manual dexterity and the demands of the machine
limit the application of production line techniques and
hence the degree of de-skilling of the labour force.
However, the relationship between mechanization and job
qualification is by no means rigid (See Table I). The case
of knitting is typical: even programmed machines will not
run themselves. They require close attention and a great
deal of intervention on the part of the operator and hence
considerable knowledge of how the machine operates. Thus
"the intelligence of production has neither been built
entirely into the machinery nor taken off the shopfloor. It

remains in the possession of the workforce" (Noble, 1979, p. 42).

But the question of skill is not confined to the relationship between the operator and the machine. In an industry where the organization of production is so flexible, both inside and outside the factory, the question of professional skill does not centre on manual ability and experience in the use of one particular machine, but rather on the capability to operate a variety of machines and produce a range of qualities of weave. With this in mind, manual labour in the knitwear industry can be divided into three grades:

i) Craft workers: workers with complete knowledge of the manufacturing process, who may be utilized in any department, and who are capable of filling any position on the production line and perform any kind of stitching, and workers who style, design and check products and who therefore have high skill and heavy responsibility.

ii) Skilled machine operators: these include skilled production line workers and such non-production line workers as loom operators and pressers.

iii) Semi-skilled machine operators: production line workers carrying out simple finishing and operating only one power machine, plus workers engaged in quality control and packing of the finished product.

Such skills cannot be regarded as firm-specific since the same product can be manufactured either by a large firm or by a group of co-ordinated small firms. Nevertheless, the features distinguishing types of firms are of central importance in determining the skill and knowledge of the workers. The large firms employ a heterogeneous workforce, with semi-skilled and skilled operators and craft workers within the same establishment. On the other hand the smaller firms' workforces are more homogeneous, and the degree of skill and experience is dependent upon both the quality of the product and the types of production techniques adopted. Sub-contractors which carry out quality knitting or making-up employ skilled operatives and craft workers, whilst workers employed in firms where the finished products are inspected and packaged, or those carrying out special types of finishing (pleating, embroidering, etc.) are generally semi-skilled. It should also be noted that production line

workers in smaller firms have greater manual ability and
superior knowledge of the manufacturing process than do
their counterparts in the larger firms. Small firms have
less rigid demarcation practices, require a greater degree
of individual responsibility and process a wider variety of
materials than large firms. However, in both large and small
firms skills are acquired by a long period of "on-the-job
training", although the learning process is more rapid in
small firms where production runs are shorter and hence
experience is more varied. Finally, firms which put out mass
production of their prototype samples employ highly skilled
workers. These firms have no production line and the workers
collaborate closely in the designing of new models;
moreover, the smaller the firm, the greater the individual
contribution made by each worker. Each worker, if not
actually designing products, knows every aspect of the job
in the creation and adaptation of new models with the
consequence that dividing lines between manual labour and
intellectual effort tend to disappear. (Brusco and Sabel,
1981).

Although the principal means by which professional
abilities are acquired is by working in a factory, it is
not, however, the only way. In such a "monocultural" area,
skills can be learned from the worker's mother, friend or
relative who may be a home or factory worker. By this kind
of apprenticeship sufficient skill will be acquired for a
limited number of single tasks, but not an extensive expert
knowledge of the manufacturing process.

Finally, the skills required in the knitwear and ready-
to-wear clothing industry tend to be industry-specific. The
tools and machines used in factory production differ
markedly from those in the made-to-measure clothing trade
and there is no continuity between the skills in the latter
and those of factory workers. Even more tenuous is the link
between household and industrial production, or between
experience acquired in other industrial sectors and that
needed in the knitwear and ready-to-wear clothing industry.

IV. HOMEWORKERS, PRODUCTION LINE WORKERS AND ARTISANS

There are considerable differences in the age and sex
composition of the three categories. Production line workers
and homeworkers are generally women whilst a large
proportion of artisans are men. Furthermore, only a small
fraction of the artisans and homeworkers are less than 25
years old, although the great majority of factory workers

are in this category. Lastly, women of 40 to 45 years of age
more often than not work at home rather than in the factory.

Homeworkers, production line workers and artisans are
mainly local labour or long-established immigrants and with
the exception of certain young artisans are low both in
scholastic achievement and social means. Recruitment into
the industry can be divided into two main periods. In the
1950s and the first half of the 1960s the source of labour
was the exodus from the rural areas, resulting from the
combined effects of the crisis in the sharecropping farming
system, and the increasing industrialization of the region.
From the second half of the 1960s the main source of labour
was from within the industry, and the inflow of labour from
other sectors slowed down markedly. The shape of the
industry during the first period differs in many ways from
that existing today [8]. The 1950s and early 1960s was an
era of high unemployment and underemployment. In this period
there was limited mobility between the different segments of
the labour market particularly between different sized
firms, and most job changes resulted from dismissal. From
the mid 1960s the industry increasingly adopted the
"contours" which it has retained. An important difference
between the periods before and after the mid 1960s is the
growing evidence from the latter period of the willingness
of workers to move around within and between the different
sub-markets: from large to small firms, and from the firms
into self-employment. It is on this second period that the
analysis will be particularly centred.

In terms of pay, conditions of work, job characteristics and career patterns there is considerable overlap
between homeworkers, factory workers and artisans. Features
such as "cash-in-hand" arrangements, underpayment, absence
of union protection and collective sickness and insurance
benefits are not exclusive to the sphere of homeworkers.
More than 50% of production line workers, and a comparable
proportion of artisans, have completed at least two years in
a factory without any form of legal contract. Similarly, the
termination of apprenticeship by dismissal, or the extension
of apprenticeship beyond the normally accepted duration, was
widespread even quite recently. Voluntary quitting is a
common occurrence and the search for employment is not made
through official channels (employment bureaux and the like)
or union organizations: knowledge of the market and the
nature of job opportunities is widespread and employment is
sought amongst friends, relatives and through other social
networks (Rees, 1966). Employers, especially small
operators, make full use of similar channels when recruiting
labour, by utilizing the grapevine existing between their

own employees and acquaintances or by other informal methods
(Mackay et al., 1971). It is also not uncommon for firms to
employ workers who apply directly (Reynolds, 1951).
Furthermore, the tightness of the labour market means that
the periods of unemployment are very short especially when
the worker quits voluntarily.

A consideration of the work histories of production
line workers, homeworkers and artisans shows considerable
mobility between home-based work, employment in small firms
and in large firms. Of those surveyed, one homeworker in
four had been employed in large or medium-to-large sized
firms (more than 49 employees) and one production line
worker in three had worked at home; small and very small
firms (less than 20 employees) recruited 30% of workers from
either production line employment or home-based work; and
amongst the artisans 20% had been employed in large firms,
23% in small firms, and 27% had worked at home. Of the
female artisans, more than 50% had previously been
homeworkers.

There is no regular progression from homework and small
firms to large firms. A study of the last ten years shows no
evidence of any "one-way" mobility carrying workers away
from labour sub-markets unprotected by unions into sub-
markets offering such protection. It is by no means rare for
workers to quit large firms for employment in small firms.
Such moves have been made by factory workers, homeworkers
and particularly artisans. From interviews with the latter
it emerges that no less than one in five artisans moved from
large to small firms. In addition, "homework" - which for
most workers was the last stage in their career - also
served as a stop-gap between factory jobs. It is also not
uncommon to find spells of homework separated by stints of
factory employment.

The routes by which skill is acquired are no more
clearly defined than are the mobility chains. Progress from
semi-skilled to the craft level may be achieved by advance
within a large firm, or between small firms, or by a
sequence of changes between firms of different size.
Nevertheless, a comparison of the careers of production line
workers compared with those of the homeworkers and artisans
allows three broad conclusions.

    i) It is unusual for a movement between jobs to
       involve a loss of skill. Mobility is generally
       along skill bands or infrequently to higher
       skill levels.
   ii) "Ports of entry" into production work can be

through large firms, or small sub-contracting
firms. The latter will, however, only hire
inexperienced workers if very young. The
specialized sample-producing firms normally
only take on skilled and craft workers [9].
iii) Only large firms provide vertical mobility
between each grade. But even in a large firm
progress to the higher grades will be gained
only by a small proportion of employees. The
semi-skilled areas of large firms are "transit
zones" from which workers will be moved on
after a relatively short time.

Thus there are two barriers to vertical mobility. The first,
the most important, operates between small production units,
and denies access to workers who are either unqualified, or
no longer young, seeking entry into firms carrying out
sophisticated and complex manufacturing procedures. The
second operates within large firms, and constitutes a
discriminatory barrier between the bulk of skilled
operatives and workers who hold key positions in the factory
(for example, sample producers and foremen).
     There are, then, two transitional steps from the lowest
to the highest professional level: one which takes the semi-
skilled worker from the small to large firm; the other which
leads the skilled worker from the large firm towards the
smaller, and particularly towards firms producing samples.
Both steps require higher skill levels and consequently
represent a promotion in the job ladder.
     Since labour recruitment among the small firms is not
subject to any kind of union-imposed constraints, the firms
are free to base their recruitment policy on the match
between experience or skill and the company's manufacturing
characteristics. Consequently, the relatively unskilled or
the less able gravitate towards those firms carrying out
functions in which the actual labour content is lower
(embroidery, quality control and packaging, pleating, stitching of low quality materials, etc.). For such workers, the
best opportunity to acquire professional knowledge and
skills will be employment in a large firm. Indeed, in large
firms union control means the management will be less
selective in its hiring policy and ensures that most
employees will manage some professional progress. Progress
from packaging - the "transit zone" for recently-engaged
unskilled workers - depends on workers' and union control
over the labour process rather than, as in the case of the
allocation of workers between small firms, skill and
experience. Once on the production line, workers acquire

skill by movement between jobs within and between
departments. Only a small proportion of workers are promoted
to key positions in the manufacturing process, and to the
sample production department; moreover, such transfers are
managerial prerogatives with unions exercising little, if
any, control. Thus, the achievement of the highest skill
levels within large firms does not depend on a formal
promotion system or on specific manning. Therefore, access
to the higher rungs of the job ladder for the large majority
of production line workers is gained by winning entry into
the "upper stratum" of small firms. Mobility towards the
smaller enterprises furnishes the worker with the ability to
circumvent those obstacles to promotion resulting from
managerial control of the top jobs in large firms.

    The worker's career therefore evolves out of a succes-
sion of changes from one firm to another of differing size,
as shown in Fig. 1. This results not only from the particular industrial structure and the specialist nature of the
smaller firm, but also from the "industrial relations
system" governing the working relationship within small and
large factories, and from policies of restraint pursued by
larger firms in the sphere of craft labour.

    Periods of working at home, while prolonging the time
taken to rise to higher skill level, do not usually break

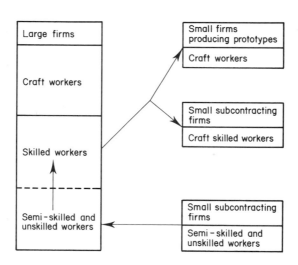

Fig. 1 Directions of labour motility
and the acquisition of skill

the factory career. It is rare to find examples where the
move from home to factory work involves a downgrading of
jobs. Generally the homeworking and factory jobs are on a
similar skill level.

V. THE INTERNAL COMPOSITION OF THE CATEGORIES

A. Classification of Homeworkers

Homeworkers can be classified into two groups on the basis
of their "career line", on the length of time spent working
in a factory, and the kind of firm by which they were
employed.

Thirty four per cent of homeworkers surveyed were ex-
factory production line workers with a long history of
skilled labour. Nearly all became homeworkers between the
age of 25 and 30 years of age. In the course of eight or
more years of factory employment they became highly skilled
in at least one operation and usually mastered a range of
operations calling for a medium-high degree of skill. Almost
all of them are familiar with many aspects of the
manufacturing process; they have operated many different
kinds of machine, worked either with knitwear or with
fabric, and performed various tasks on the production line.
Their main attributes are ability and versatility, enabling
them to adjust readily to changes in demand. They have
little difficulty in switching to different kinds of work
when new products and styles are in demand and when articles
require special types of manufacture. Their ability to
diversify also allows them to change buyers easily, and they
are not necessarily formally fired by a firm. But this does
not imply a lack of bargaining power. In fact, female
workers who enjoy the security of a working husband often
have no interest whatsoever in "formalizing" their labour
relations. There are also many cases where there is mutual
agreement to avoid formal employment relations so that the
employer pays no welfare contributions and the worker avoids
tax (Capecchi, 1980; Fua, 1976).

Sixty-six per cent of the sample of homeworkers had
never been factory workers or had not acquired significant
degrees of skill whilst in factory employment. Most of the
workers aged 40 years and more are in this group, which can
be divided into two main sections. Those who have been
employed in the factory are generally ex-stitchers employed
on production lines for only short periods or ex-packers,
labellers and fixers who have spent insufficient time in
factory employment to acquire high levels of skill or who

have been employed on relatively unskilled work. The lower
levels of skill can be explained by frequent job changes or
more usually by employment in a sub-contracting firm where
low-skill processes are undertaken.

Those who have never been employed in firms in the
sector are mainly ex-labourers and farm-hands. Many of these
were homeworkers in the 1950s and 1960s, whilst still
employed in agriculture. This traditional Emilian worker –
homeworking during winter, and then rice and fruit picking
labouring or odd-jobbing in summer – was the principal
source of low-cost labour in the early development of
Carpi's knitwear industry. The traditional homeworkers often
perform the sort of jobs commissioned "out" by the buying
firms in the early period but which, either because of
changes in the product or in production techniques, are
gradually dying out. The remainder of homeworkers without
factory experience is made up of immigrants with no previous
job experience, or manual workers coming in from other
sectors without any experience of knitwear.

Homeworkers in the second category are normally engaged
in jobs demanding a low degree of skill. Only the small
minority move from simple to more complex operations.
Furthermore, because of limited skill and experience, the
relatively unskilled homeworkers are unable to adjust
rapidly to changes in demand. The disadvantages of low skill
levels and lack of adaptability place the second category of
homeworkers at the mercy of the buyer. They are not hired by
the commissioning firm because of their lack of bargaining
power. Their employment is also susceptible to variations in
demand, both seasonal and cyclical, and therefore in every
sense they are marginal workers.

B. Classification of Production Line Workers

Production line workers employed in the larger firms can be
broadly classified into three groups by the length of time
spent at work in the knitwear and ready-made section, and by
age.

Workers who have completed no more than five years in
the sector accounted for 29% of the sample. Of these the
highest proportion are under 25 years old. These are young
girls working in their first job or who have been apprentices in the "lower strata" of the small sub-contracting
firms. Few have ever worked at home. There is little
difference between youngsters from small firms and those
with no previous work experience except that the former who
can stitch are put straight onto the production line, whilst

the latter work on the control and packaging stations, or
act as assistants for other workers. These girls carry out
simple operations which require little skill but where
great speed is essential (attachment of hooks, buttons and
labels, etc.). Similar tasks are assigned to young women who
are unskilled or have come into the industry from another
sector.

Women of between 25 and 40 years of age who have not
less than six to eight years experience in the industry made
up 62% of the sample. These include long service workers in
large firms, workers from small sub-contracting firms and
workers who have experienced both factory and home working.
The different types of experience have no substantial effect
on the workers' role in the factory. Those with continuous
employment with large firms do the same jobs as those from
small firms and as ex-homeworkers. However, nearly all have
changed jobs and have worked in different departments. These
are the most mobile element - production line workers
capable of carrying out a wide range of operations which, on
occasion, call for a high degree of manual dexterity. In
firms specializing in making-up ready-to-wear articles the
organization hinges upon this section of the workforce.

The rest of the sample - around 9% - are 40 years old
or more and have usually worked for 20 or more years in
industry. They may be ex-homeworkers, employed in larger
firms, and they have a thorough knowledge of the manufacturing process. However, they no longer possess the speed
required for flow production and the majority have been
transferred to other departments (especially pressing) while
those who remain on making-up are given special jobs. In
fact, most skilled and specialist workers in this age group
either instruct apprentices, or do those jobs requiring a
great deal of craft but where speed is less essential, for
example, "making good" and finishing off especially fine
garments (attachment of trimmings, picking up threads,
etc.).

C. Classification of Artisans

Artisans can be divided into two groups by the length of
time since setting up in business. Twenty per cent of
artisans set up in business during the 1950s and the early
1960s. In this group, men outnumber women by two to one. The
typical case history here would be of a salesman, travelling
in knitwear, ready-to-wear or similar types of garments.
This "trader-entrepreneur" became independent by
commissioning orders from the homeworkers - usually from his

wife – before taking on his own first employees. Also
typical of this era were tailors who were proprietors of
small "workshops" with one or two employed helpers but who
made the transition from the rapidly declining "bespoke"
tailoring. Examples can also be found of workers without
knowledge of either the market or the manufacturing process
who nevertheless established small firms.

The early artisans were amongst the founders of the
area's knitwear and ready-made garment business. Their
particular traits were the ability to create a market for
their own product, to develop new articles, and to organize
a "circle" of homeworkers. Moreover, the oldest of artisan
firms in this group were established in the same years as
some of the bigger firms and both types of entrepreneurs
have similar professional backgrounds.

These "artisanal" firms normally employ six to eight
workers, and control a considerable volume of out-work. They
turn out high-quality goods, mainly for the consumer market,
and have a turnover which is estimated to vary between
£430,000 and £738,000 (at 1978 prices) and realize a margin
over costs of not less than 30–35%.

A "second generation" of artisans set up shop from the
second half of the 1960s onwards and provided 80% of the
sample. Unlike the first group, these are a product of the
development of the sector and consist of men and women in
equal proportion. For analytical purposes it will be useful
to distinguish between those who are ex-homeworkers and
those who are ex-factory employees.

In more than half of the cases canvassed, the ex-
homeworkers had factory experience but had become intermediaries between one, or more, firms and had a "circle" of
homeworkers. Partly on their own initiative, and partly
under pressure from the commissioning firms – particularly
in the case of firms registered since the passing of legislation regarding homeworking and the imposition of VAT – the
parasitical "middleman" or "ring-leader" without legal
status has been transformed into a small entrepreneur. Many
of these firms continue to maintain a structure reminiscent
of the homeworker "circle", employing few internal employees
and a tight-knit network of homeworkers to produce for other
firms.

The most representative of the new generation of
artisans who quit the factory to become self-employed, are
the specialist workers or foremen. These may come from small
or large firms or may have "stepped-up" the ladder by moving
from a big to a small factory. One typical example is the
woman who first of all worked for home for ten years, then
was employed for six years on the production lines of two

large knitwear factories, before "upgrading" her skill level
by moving to a small sub-contracting firm. Finally she
became foreman with an even smaller fashion business; from
there her career advanced in two stages to the head of
department in successively larger firms.

Other typical male artisans were originally employed in
the mechanical engineering industry and associated textile
machinery sector. These were skilled in the production and
maintenance of knitwear manufacturing machinery and established small production units supplying knitted cloth to the
trade, a progression which has its own rationale. The supervision of the production of one or more powerlooms requires
more in the way of the ability to keep the machine running
efficiently than skill and dexterity in its operation.

Only a very small minority of the self-employed are not
former skilled workers, or are not knowledgeable about the
manufacturing process. In these cases it is usual for the
artisan to have either entered into partnership in an
existing business, or been employed in the knitwear industry
(as, for example, a driver or warehouseman). In a firm
engaged in making-up, these are the people in direct contact
with the out-work. Not infrequently this grade of worker was
delegated overseer of a circle of homeworkers and from there
progressed to self-employment.

Amongst the younger self-employed are those who have
stepped from white collar jobs to artisan positions. They
come mostly from the smaller firms and are familiar with
technical and administrative organization and have a central
role in maintaining contact with suppliers, and clients, as
well as co-ordinating the out-work.

Finally, a sizeable proportion of the "second generation" of male artisans owe their status to being the sons or
husbands of ex-"ringleaders", of ex-homeworkers, or of ex-
factory workers. Some are "heirs" who, before taking over
the business, will train by securing employment with another
firm, usually as a white-collar worker. The husbands who
became artisans were usually workers in various industries
who continued to be employed until their wives' businesses
were sufficiently well-established to guarantee sufficient
income to allow the husband to give up his employment to
take over managerial responsibility. In a sector where the
workforce is predominantly female and where skills are
traditionally "female property" the woman has a leading role
in production whilst the husband has mainly administrative
responsibility.

Between second generation artisanal firms prosperity
varies widely. Some enterprises produce for the consumer
market, others for the trade market. Within this overall

picture, a fairly typical stitching sub-contractor with a
staff of about six will have a turnover of something between
£184,000 and £307,000, yielding a margin over cost of not
less than 20-30%, and an average of three to five
commissioning buyers in any one year. However, many firms
have levels of turnover comparable with long-established
firms while others are very small indeed.

VI. FACTORS DETERMINING THE ALLOCATION OF LABOUR ACROSS THE MARKET

This section considers the factors determining differences
in career pattern, variation in experiences within the skill
strata and the allocation of workers to the various segments
of the labour market. An important first question is what
influences the choice between home and factory work?

Up to 20 years ago there was an extensive industrial
reserve army in the Emilia region of Italy made up of
labourers, poor smallholders, peasants, farmhands and
others. Then, the factors determining the allocation to
factory or homework were different. The demand for labour in
the firms was directed predominantly towards women who had
acquired some degree of skill through having worked at home.
Thus for the great majority of older women, as indeed for
many of the younger workers, homeworking constituted the
only possibility for employment. The firms - in those years
especially the larger firms - "creamed off" the more
productive and professionally skilled element in the female
workforce whilst the "weaker" element gravitated towards the
homeworking sector. Furthermore, many women who had a
principally "rural" background worked at home on a strictly
part-time basis and regarded this activity as complementary
to their rural waged labour. These women had a relationship
with the industry which gave them no incentive to acquire
professional skills and, in many cases, they did not seek
factory employment (Sabel, 1979). However, the development
of the knitwear and ready-to-wear industry has created an
"indigenous" labour force.

An examination of the careers and the family households
of homeworkers, factory workers and artisans suggests that
in half the cases spells of homeworking coincide with two
sets of circumstances. Homework was usual where the woman
had one or more children of pre-school age or the family
included an aged relative or someone requiring constant
attention and where there was no other woman within the
family who could take over these domestic responsibilities.
Conversely, those interviewed had worked in the factory when

they were still living with their original family and when,
although married, they had either no children or children
who were sufficiently grown up to be left alone. Where there
were small children the tendency was for mothers to work in
a factory only when an extended family household included
another woman – mother or mother-in-law – who either did not
work or was herself a homeworker.

Women working in the factory, then, are for the most
part those without heavy domestic responsibilities or from
households where there were sufficient women to allow
factory work and home duties to coexist peacefully. As C.
Saraceno observes:

> the inclusion of mother or mother-in-law within
> the family provides the domestic labour (including
> care of children) which would otherwise become
> precarious or impossible as a result of the
> wife's going out to work. By contrast, where such
> an inclusion is not possible ... the economic
> necessity may draw the woman into working at home
> (Saraceno, 1976, p. 105).

It is worth noting that inter-generational family ties in
the sense of "mutual assistance" and economic relations
which do not necessarily depend on cohabitation are of
considerable importance. For example, there are many women
who, although belonging to a simple family unit with small
children, can continue in factory employment by delegating
household duties to "grannies" who live elsewhere [10].

The research thus leads to the conclusion that the
main factor regulating the allocation of women workers
between homework and factory work is differentiation of
family labour supply determined by the characteristics
of its individual members, the family structure, and
those inter-family relationships [11].

The family position of women is an important determinant of their careers. Although many women do not interrupt their working career and many others return to the
factory once their domestic situation permits, the job
trajectory of most women is characteristically a progression
from the factory towards homeworking.

> Thus the women's career line seems to be an
> inversion of the men's which typically sees a
> progression at least until 45–50 years of age, to
> jobs of higher skill and status. In contrast,
> women reach the highest level in their career

whilst young ...; then with the marriage and the
arrival of the children ... they move away from
the central sector of the labour market ... to
return at length ... into the marginal areas ...
(May, 1977, p. 62).

The age of workers is the second factor determining the
allocation of labour to homework. Large, and to an even
greater extent, smaller firms operating a production line
are very reluctant to take on workers of over 40 years of
age. Their efficiency, measured in terms of speed, is lower
than average and after a certain age opportunities for
factory employment dwindle.

The allocation of women to homeworking is therefore a
product both of "selection" within the market of the weaker
strata of the labour force and of out-market factors
determined by family responsibility. In this respect there
is a close connection between the employment policy of the
firms and the organization of working class families. The
firm discriminates against the older woman on the grounds of
productivity and their family assigns to them domestic
responsibilities. The younger women have secondary roles
within the family and, being more in demand in the labour
market, pursue full-time employment.

There is, however, a third reason which prompts certain
women to abandon factory employment for homework which is
independent of their relative efficiency and household
responsibilities. Some women choose to work at home because
of the greater degree of autonomy they enjoy in being able
to organize their work. The homeworker is obliged to follow
the required methods and to meet deadlines. Nonetheless,
homeworking allows her to escape — in no small way — the
control exercised by the "bosses" in small firms, and by the
"hierarchy" in larger firms. These women forego the
advantages of direct employment in the factory in favour of
a greater freedom to decide how much, how long and how to
work.

The principal factor which differentiates artisans from
both homeworkers and factory workers is their degree of
professional ability. The analysis of the previous section
shows that workers who leave the factory in order to set up
in business on their own generally have a thorough knowledge
of the manufacturing process and, moreover, are capable of
organizing and managing production. Whether owners of a firm
producing for the consumer market or of one producing
intermediate goods, the artisans are the most skilled among
their own employees, and they have organizing and other

responsibilities comparable with those of heads of department or production managers in the larger fims. They
undertake the more complex manufacturing operations,
organize the production line and manage the labour force.
There are other bases for developing small businesses
including administrative experience and the knowledge of the
operation of the out-work system of the warehouseman. On the
other hand, access to skill, the knowledge of the manufacturing process, the internal structure of the firm and of
the out-work system have been, and still are, generally the
necessary conditions for establishing a small firm. Given
these requirements, in a sector where technological barriers
to entry are very low and demand in the production market is
high, the decision to open a small business production unit
is essentially a matter of willingness to do so. In these
circumstances "what is striking is not how many become artisans, but how many of those who are able do not" (Brusco,
1982, p. 175).

   Finally it will be clear that the kind of tight
personal and social relationships, the concentration of
firms producing similar commodities, and the tradition of a
ready movement from worker to artisan status must be taken
very seriously when considering the differentiation of the
supply of labour.

   Professional skill not only provides a yardstick for
determining the borderline between artisans and the other
two categories of workers, but also provides a method of
classifying homeworkers and production line workers.
However, the conditions for acquiring that skill also play a
major role in allocating workers between labour market
segments. Skill acquisition depends upon the chances of
employment with one of the small innovating firms, the type
of work being carried out there and, in larger firms, the
relative bargaining power of workers. Since skill and know-
how are products of on-the-job experience and the worker's
position within the factory, and since these depend largely
upon the age of the worker and the skill acquired by that
age, critical importance must be attached to the "point of
departure" of the career line. For example, a woman who
comes into knitwear and ready-made from another industry
will be employed on simple semi-skilled work; should she be
forced to leave the factory for any reason with little
experience she will become an extremely "weak" homeworker,
easily pressured by the buyer, and probably not formally
employed by the commissioning firm - in every case a
marginal worker.

VII. FACTORS DETERMINING INCOME

The income of the artisan has two components: profit and
wages (Sylos Labini, 1974). Profit can be regarded as being
determined by the degree of technology incorporated into the
machinery, the product market, the type and quality of the
product and the methods of production undertaken, and the
level of wages. The possible variety in these variables
means wide income differentials. At one extreme some
artisans earn little more than a "rich" homeworker, whereas
other artisans earn as much as the owners of substantial
firms.

The second component – wages – is a product of skill,
effort and time. Skills being equal, even artisans belonging
to the lowest group earn more than craft workers and foremen
employed in the larger firms, although much of this
difference may be accounted for by the longer hours worked
by artisans. Even where the profit is at a minimum – in a
family business with one or two dependents and a low level
of investment in machinery – a high income can be obtained
at the cost of hard, continuous work.

Homeworkers are paid by the piece. Their remuneration
is determined by the type of work, their physical efficiency
(determined at least partly by age) and the length of the
working day. The highest paid workers are those whose jobs
demand the highest level of skill, for example, cutting,
sample production, making-up involving complicated
operations; the worst-paid are those who do hand-finishing
and other semi-skilled jobs. Relative earnings are therefore
determined mainly by skills, but the product market is an
important influence on the level of pay. Changes in demand
are rapidly reflected both in type and quality of articles,
in the kind of out-work commissioned and consequently in the
homeworkers' earnings. In these circumstances the ability to
switch from one kind of work to another is an important
determinant of earnings. The more versatile homeworkers
receive hourly pay 25–30% higher than the less experienced.
The third important determinant of homeworker earnings is
age. Moreover, limited chances of employment in the firms
for older workers and weaker competition among firms for
less productive homeworkers will be translated into lower
earnings. Homeworkers over 40 years of age earn roughly a
third less than their younger counterparts. The combination
of differences in age and skill gives rise to wide wage
differentials and an older worker carrying out a simple task
may draw a wage as much as seven times less than a young
skilled worker. The latter will at times receive higher
hourly earnings than a similarly skilled worker employed in

a large firm. Normally, homeworkers work around the same
number of hours as factory workers but opportunities exist
for longer working hours and hence higher pay than is taken
home from the factory. Lastly, there is no evidence of any
significant wage differentiation between workers directly
employed by the commissioning firm and the homeworkers who
are not directly employed.

Earnings of workers employed in small firms are
determined by the same variables as homeworker earnings.
those who are experienced, versatile, fast and willing to
put in long hours have higher, and at times very much
higher, levels of wages than comparable workers in the
larger firms, whilst the reverse is true in the case of
older or less able workers.

Production line workers' wages are determined by
national agreements. The wage differentials (for example
those relating to skills) are the products of a continuing
bargaining process and have been eroded by the egalitarian
policies pursued by unions during the 1970s. The presence of
the unions within the large factory ensures that the
national labour contract is applied, and also that the
"work-place margin" from production bonuses and other local
additions will be at least partly controlled at both
national and company level. As a result, pay differentials
within the large firms are narrower than outside and those
factors which result in such wide earnings disparities
between homeworkers and the employees of small firms, whilst
present, are much less important in large firms. There, wage
differentials between the top and bottom grade of 10-15% are
not unusual. Moreover, the classification into the various
pay grades does not depend exclusively on skill. More
usually grading of workers was determined by the company
contract, the terms of which varied according to the
strength of union organization amongst workers in the
different firms. In the larger firms, then, age, skill and
the willingness to work long hours do not substantially
affect the level and the structure of pay.

This brief analysis allows us to arrive at three
important conclusions.

  i) Whether employed in well unionized or weakly
     unionized firms, or whether working in a
     factory or at home, it is possible to get a
     relatively high wage.
 ii) In the large firm, high wages are gained
     through the strength of workers'
     organization; in the "unprotected" sector
     they are tied to a worker's productivity and

individual bargaining power which depends on
scarcity.
iii) Thus, for skilled workers with wide
experience and at the height of their power,
allocation among the various submarkets –
especially the movement from large firms
to small, and from thence to homeworking –
does not necessarily reduce earnings and may
well increase them; on the other hand,
relatively high earnings of older workers and
those with lower levels of skill and little
experience depend very much on employment in
large firms.

VIII. SUMMARY AND CONCLUSIONS

The main features of the labour market in Carpi are outlined
in Table II. The first distinction that can be made is
between large and small firms. The main feature of the large
firm sector is the high degree to which workers are
safeguarded both by legislation, which is effectively
implemented, and trade union organization. In the small firm
sector, some parts of the labour legislation do not apply
and, moreover, evasion is more common; the majority of
workers are not effectively unionized and employment is less
secure than in larger firms.

In the larger factories there are wide skill differences, but unionization and union policy prevent wide wage
differentials. However in the small firm sector wage
differences depend on the one hand on the characteristics of
the firm (technology, product and product market condition)
and on the other on worker characteristics (skill, age and
social and family position). Workers employed in firms which
produce prototypes and subcontract production and in the
"non-subordinate" subcontracting firms turning out high
quality pieces and using advanced technology, have a
thorough knowledge of manufacturing methods, receive high
pay, more often than skilled workers employed in the large
firms. In the smaller "subordinate" and/or less technologically well equipped firms, earnings for less well
qualified workers are substantially lower than those for
comparable workers in large firms. The outworker labour
force is similarly segmented, job insecurity, exploitation
and low pay coexisting with high levels of professional
capability, job security and pay (Capecchi, 1980).

Significant differences also exist in the career
patterns of the worker in the large and small firm sector

Table II. Characteristics (a) in different types of firms.

	Large factories	Small firms producing prototypes or small non-"subordinate" sub-contracting firms with "good technology"	Small "subordinate" sub-contracting firms or firms with poor technology	Artisans	Homeworkers: upper stratum	Homeworkers: lower stratum
Union protection	+	-	-	(b)	-	-
Job Security	+	+ / -	-	+	+ / -	-
Degree of skill	+ / -	+	-	+	+	-
Career prospects	+ / -	+	-	+	+ / -	-
Level of income	+	+	-	+	+	-

(a) The plus and minus signs indicate the relative job quality and the job characteristic. Where both plus and minus signs appear it means that the quality of the job characteristic varies both within and between firms.
(b) Artisans are not usually union members, but belong to their own associations.

(Fig. 2). In small firms, access to the higher rungs on the
professional ladder is achieved by voluntary worker mobility
towards firms offering good terms and conditions of
employment. In larger firms career advancement is dependent
upon control over the labour process exercised by unions and
management.

The workers who are free of family commitments, young,
able to work full-time and highly mobile between submarkets,
progress toward higher paid and more prestigious jobs and
often travel from employment in a large firm to employment
in a small firm and between different types of small firm.
Moreover the only objective barrier to "setting up in
business" is lack of knowledge of the manufacturing process.
Conversely, older women and those with family responsibilities tend to be trapped and are therefore excluded from
the mobility chains to the better jobs.

It is clear that the structure of the labour market is
determined by factors influencing the demand for, and the
supply of, labour. The employment and wage conditions in
large firms are guarded by secure product conditions. In the
small firm sector, the quest for cheap labour, the

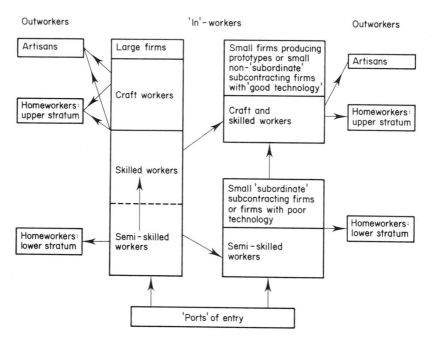

Fig 2. Job mobility and patterns of promotion

flexibility in the organization of manufacture and the
characteristics of firms operating within differing market
segments (for example, type and quality of product, degree
of vertical integration, existence or not of dependence on
other firms and methods of controlling and organizing the
production process) are factors of prime importance in
structuring the labour market. However, these demand-side
factors only provide a partial explanation of the system of
pay determination or of how labour is allocated between
firms. The varying degrees of union bargaining power within
the different submarkets, age and sex, the structure of the
family, opportunities to acquire skill and experience and
the network of personal and family ties all influence the
strength or weakness of particular workers in the labour
market. The structure of the labour market can only be fully
understood if account is taken of how these demand and
supply factors interact and in turn are modified. These
results, then, would seem to confirm that:

> segmentation requires multi-causal explanations
> and that the various explanatory hypotheses –
> based on the structure of technology, product
> markets control over the labour process and labour
> supply – are complementary rather than competitive
> (Rubery and Wilkinson, 1981, pp. 115-116)

The striking features of the Carpi knitwear labour market is
that a large proportion of the workforce are able to assure
themselves of "good jobs" even within highly competitive
small firms where union protection is minimal and government
legislation more frequently avoided. It depends upon three
closely interrelated kinds of influence:

  i) the characteristics of the industrial
     district.
 ii) the subordination of both subcontracting
     firms and individual out-workers located
     outside Carpi's industrial "enclave" to
     Carpi-based firms.
iii) full employment which stems from a success in
     both national and international product
     markets.

The high concentration of firms within the area ensures that
the market for intermediate produce from subcontracting
firms is competitive. This protects the artisan from the
monopsonistic power of the producers of the final products.
More importantly the industrial districts form "compost"

from which develop small innovative firms which are able to
solve the clients' individual problems (Brusco and Sabel,
1981). As Marshall pointed out:

> when the total number of men interested in the
> matter is very large there are to be found among
> them many who, by their intellect and temper, are
> fitted to originate new ideas. Each new idea is
> canvassed and improved upon by many minds; each
> new accidental experience and each deliberate
> experiment will afford food for reflection and for
> new suggestions, not to a few persons but to many
> (Whitaker (ed), 1975, Vol.II, p. 198, as quoted in
> Becattini, 1979, p. 19).

However, the survival and growth of innovative firms are
conditioned by the utilization of sophisticated machinery
(as emphasized by Brusco and Sabel) and also by the
availability of highly-skilled professional labour.
Competition for these workers ensures that they are well
paid.
   The above circumstances are likely to be found in the
provinces to which production is decentralised from Carpi.
In most cases they have no access to the final consumer
market, and in addition to their using somewhat inefficient
production techniques, they are subject to the monopsonistic
power of the commissioner-buyer. It is amongst these small
sub-contracting firms and homeworker circles that the most
disadvantaged elements in the labour supply are concentrated. This distribution of low "value-added" production
stages and jobs with lower skill content along the
decentralization route away from Carpi (to Mantova, Rovigo,
Ferrara, etc.) increases the proportion of good jobs in
Carpi. Consequently, the low incomes of the homeworkers and
artisans operating in the "peripheral areas" enhance the
income profits of Carpi entrepreneurs and workers.
   Lastly, high levels of demand for Carpi knitted
products means a high level of employment of both worker
ability and worker time. Furthermore, the more the labour
market is stretched, the more wages tend to rise particularly for those with scarce skills and knowledge of the
manufacturing process. With growing experiences of high
employment, "risk factors" connected with job uncertainty
lose much of their potency, mobility increases within and
between the various submarkets, between large and small
firms to self-employment. In this important sense the supply
of skilled labour is demand determined. The growing number
of good jobs provide the opportunities for acquiring both

additional skills and experience; the experience of job
security encourages workers to move in search of higher
wages, better conditions and, particularly, more skills and
experience.

NOTES

1. The bulk of the data to which reference is made is the
    product of direct interviewing. Since the aim of the
    research was not to deal with the actual dimensions of
    the strata of different workers, but rather to look at
    their characteristic features, and given the set of
    difficulties in defining a representative sample we
    chose to interview 100 workers for each group
    (production line workers, homeworkers and artisans).
    For each group interviewed we analysed the workers by
    age. In particular artisans and homeworkers were
    divided up thus: 25-34 years, 35-44 years, over 44
    years; factory workers were divided differently: up to
    25 years, 25-34 years, over 34 years. The survey
    relates to the second half of 1978.
    In a decentralized industrial system such as this one,
    there will be an abundance and variety of outworkers
    amongst whom it becomes difficult to distinguish
    artisans from homeworkers. For the sake of convenience,
    we classify workers on the basis of the way they
    consider their own work. Therefore we define as
    homeworkers those who: i) make no use of dependent
    labour; ii) do not utilize machinery or, at least, use
    only "traditional" kinds of machine. Conversely, we
    classify as artisans those workers who: i) avail
    themselves of dependent labour; ii) even when making no
    use of dependent labour whatever, utilize sophisticated
    machinery (automatic power looms or bobbin winders,
    etc.).
    It is worth noting that in Italian law a firm is
    defined as artisanal if it employs no more than ten
    workers (owners included) and up to five apprentices.
2. See Bagnasco (1977); Bagnasco and Messori (1975);
    Brusco (1975, 1982); Capecchi (ed.) 1978; Frey (ed.)
    1975; Paci (1975); Piore (1977, 1980); Rubery and
    Wilkinson (1981); Sabel (1982); Sallez (1979); Vianello
    (1975).
3. All quotations in Italian have been translated by the
    author.
4. It is useful to point out that of the firms with less

than 20 employees about 40% produce for the consumer market.

5. "...one may define the 'balance' as being a process which aims at 'optimizing' — in terms of time and cost — a set of individual jobs whose sequence is submitted...to specific constraints of precedence, and/or current contingencies..." (Coriat, 1979, p.121).

6. Looking at the relationship between technology and the structure of industry, the ascendancy of the straight loom over the "cotton" would seem to be the most significant consequence of production decentralization and fragmentation.

7. For similar reasons it has been difficult to automate the making-up of footwear (Bright, 1958).

8. The industrial structure in the 1950s and early 1960s, in comparison with that of the present day, is essentially characterized as follows: in terms of job density, large firms outweighing the small; the more general diffusion of homeworking; and the existence of true "intermediaries", that is "links" between firms and outworkers.
    Against a background of growing international competition for standardized products, and a strengthening of trade union organization within the factories, many firms have tended to push out the middle stages of the manufacturing process. The imposition of VAT (1971) and the passing of legislation concerning homeworkers (1973) have meant that the route to "undeclared" home labour (i.e. unprotected in terms of welfare) has become much more tortuous. The combined effects of these factors have brought about intense modifications in the structure of the industry. On the one hand, it has enlarged the proportion of firms developing prototypes and on the other — equally important — it has changed the general structure of out-work: intermediaries have more or less disappeared; homeworkers have reduced considerably; a large number of small sub-contracting firms has sprung up (Malagoli and Mengoli, 1979; Solinas, 1981).

9. The fact that sub-contracting firms carrying out knitting or making-up will take on unskilled labour, but only very young (preferably under 18 years of age), would seem to be due to the lower cost, and the higher "potential" productivity of that labour supply. Not only, in fact, will they be taken on as apprentices and therefore paid less, but they will also be easily "pressured", and likely to succumb to the paternalistic kind of climate that is inherent in those

small manufacturing units (Vianello, 1975). These
advantages, however, cannot compensate for lack of
skill in a firm of the kind which produces samples.

10. It is the writer's conviction that the presence of
    extended family households in the region and, what is
    more, the continuance of strong ties between families
    of differing generations is the main factor on the
    labour supply side allowing a high rate of female
    activity (as far as direct employment in factories is
    concerned). In such circumstances, it is clear that the
    hardest-hit women will be the immigrants, those who
    have no means of turning to their families of origin
    for support. It is in this area that one should look
    for answers as to why women from outlying provinces and
    central and southern Italy are obliged to work at home,
    rather than in discriminatory practices on the part of
    employers.

11. Other surveys carried out in Italy in recent years come
    to somewhat similar conclusions (Ascoli, 1977; Balbo,
    1973, 1978; Comba and Pizzini, 1975; Del Boca and
    Turvani, 1979; Saraceno (ed.), 1980).

REFERENCES

Ascoli, U. (1977). Rigidita dei ruoli familiari e offerta di
    lavoro femminile. Inchiesta, 28

Bagnasco, A. (1977). "Tre Italie: la Problematica
    Territoriale dello Sviluppa". Il Mulino, Bologna.

Bagnasco, A. and Messori, M. (1975). "Tendenze dell'
    Economia Periferica". Valentino, Torino.

Balbo, L. (1973). Le condizioni strutturali della vita
    familiare. Inchiesta, 9.

Balbo, L. (1978). La doppia presenza. Inchiesta, 32

Becattini, G. (1979). Dal 'settore' industriale al
    'distretto' industriale: alcune considerazioni sull'
    unita di indagine dell' economia industriale. Revista
    di economica e politica industriale, 1.

Bright, J.R. (1958). "Automation and Management". Harvard
    University, Boston.

Brusco, S. (1975). Organizzazione del lavoro e decentramento
    produttivo nel settore metalmeccanico. "Sindacato e
    Piccola Impressa" (a cura della FLM di Bergamo), De
    Donato, Bari.

Brusco, S. (1982). The Emilian model: productive
    decentralization and social integration. Cambridge
    Journal of Economics, 2.

Brusco, S. Giovannetti, E. and Malagoli, W. (1979). La
    relazione tra dimensione e daggio di sviluppo nelle
    imprese industriali: una ricerca empirica. Studi e
    ricerche dell' Instituto Economico. Modena.
Brusco, S. and Sabel, C.F. (1981). Artisan production and
    economic growth. In "The Dynamics of Labour Market
    Segmentation" (F. Wilkinson, ed.). Academic Press,
    London and Orlando.
Capecchi, V. (1978). Sviluppo economico emiliano, ruolo
    dell' industria metalmeccanica, problema del
    mezzogiorno. In "La Piccola Impresa nell' Economia
    Italiana". (V. Capecchi, ed.). De Donato, Bari.
Capecchi, V. (1980). Lavoro e condizione giovanile. Problemi
    della transizione, 4.
Capecchi, V. and Pugliese, E. (1978). Bologna e Napoli: due
    citta a confronto. Inchiesta, 34-36.
Comba, L. and Pizzini, P. (1975). La donna che lavora e la
    famiglia, Inchiesta, 18.
Coriat, B. (1979). "La Fabbrica e il Cronometro". (Itlalian
    edition of "L'atelier et le Chronometre"). Feltrinelli,
    Milano.
Del Boca, D. and Turvani, M. (1979). "Famiglia e Mercato del
    Lavoro". Il Mulino, Bologna.
ERVET (1979). "Indagene sullo Stato e le Prospettive della
    Tecnologia del Settore Maglieria nel Comprensorio
    Carpi-Correggio". Ente Regionale per la Valorizzazione
    Economica del Territorio, Bologna.
FLM (Federazione provinciale di Bologna) (1977).
    "Occupazione, Sviluppo Economico, Territorio". Edizioni
    SEUSI, Roma.
Frey, L. (ed.) (1975). Lavoro a Domicilio e Decentramento
    dell' Attivita Produttiva nei Settori Tessile e dell'
    Abbigliamento in Italia". Angeli, Milano.
Fua, G. (1976). "Occupazione e Capacita Produttiva: La
    Realta Italiano". Il Mulino, Bologna.
Mackay, D.I., Boddy, D., Brack, J., Diack, J.A. and Jones,
    N. (1971). "Labour Markets Under Different Employment
    Conditions". Allen and Unwin, London.
Malagoli, W. and Mengoli, P. (1979). Lavoro a domicilio e
    artigianato nel comparto della maglieria. Citta e
    regione, 5.
May, M.P. (1977). Il mercato del lavoro femminile in Italia.
    Inchiesta, 25.
Noble, D.F. (1979). Social choice in machine design: the
    case of automatically controlled machine tools. In
    "Case Studies on the Labour Process" (A. Zimbalist,
    ed.). Monthly Review Press, New York.
Paci, M. (1975). Crisi, ristrutturazione e piccola imprese.

Inchiesta, 20
Paci, M. (1978). Le condizioni sociale dello sviluppo della
    piccola industria. In "La Piccola Impresa nell'
    Economica Italiana" (V. Capecchi, ed.). De Donato,
    Bari.
Piore, M.J. (1977). Alcune note sul dualismo nel nercato del
    lavoro. Rivista di economia e politica industriale, 2.
Piore, M.J. (1980). The technological foundations of
    dualism and discontinuity. In "Dualism and
    Discontinuity in Industrial Societies" (S. Berger and
    M.J. Piore eds.). Cambridge University Press,
    Cambridge.
Rees, A. (1966). Information networks in labor markets.
    American Economic Review, 2.
Reynolds, L.G. (1971). "The Structure of Labour Markets"
    (1st ed. 1951). Greenwood Press, Westport.
Rubery, J. and Wilkinson, F. (1981). Outwork and segmented
    labour markets. In "The Dynamics of Labour Market
    Segmentation" (F. Wilkinson, ed.). Academic Press,
    London and Orlando.
Sabel, C.F. (1979). Marginal workers in industrial society.
    Challenge, March-April.
Sabel, C.F. (1982). "Work and Politics: the Division of
    Labour in Industry". Cambridge University Press,
    Cambridge.
Sallez, A. (1979). Subforniture, produttivita del sistema
    industriale e sviluppo economico regionale. In
    "Ristrutturazioni Industriali e Rapporti tra le
    Imprese" (R. Varaldo, ed.). Angeli, Milano.
Saraceno, C. (1976). "Anatomia della Famiglia". De Donato,
    Bari.
Saraceno, C. (ed.) (1980). "Il Lavoro mal Diviso". De
    Donato, Bari.
Solinas, G. (1981). Il mercato del laboro nell' industria
    della magliera e delle confezioni in serie nella
    provincia di Modena. Quaderni di Rassegna Sindicale,
    88.
Sylos Labini, P. (1974). "Saggio sulle Classi Sociali".
    Laterza, Bari.
Vianello, F. (1975). I meccanismi di recupero del profitto:
    l'esperienza italiana 1963-1973. In "Crisi e
    Ristrutturazione dell' Economie Italiana" (A,
    Graziani, ed.). Einaudi, Torino.
Whitaker, J.K. (ed.) (1975). "The Early Economic Writings of
    Alfred Marshall: 1867-1890", Vol. II. Macmillan,
    London.
Woodward, J. (1965). "Industrial Organization: Theory and
    Practice". Oxford University Press, London.

Systems of Flexible Working in the Italian Steel Industry

P. VILLA

I. INTRODUCTION

Trade union organization attempts to limit capitalist's discretion in the utilization of labour power; both with respect to the labour market and to the labour process itself [1]. A very good example of this is provided by the increasing power and changing organization of the Italian trade union movement in the 1970s. The process of union decentralization, the development of labour organization at the workplace and the diffusion of plant and shopfloor bargaining imposed strong constraints on the capitalist control of the production process. This paper examines the impact of these changes, and management response, on the flexibility/rigidity in the use of labour in the Italian steel industry.

This case study shows how the changes in the labour-union-management relations produced a radical transformation in the system of social organization of major steel enterprises away from a highly hierarchical system (based on a detailed division of labour; individual differences by job post, by length of service, by position along the job ladder, and by grade; and career patterns related to internal mobility) to a non-hierarchical system (based on the definition of collective tasks, where individual

differences in job post held, those by grade and length of
service disappear, therefore making redundant the concept
itself of internal career). These results have a special
relevance to the labour market segmentation debate since the
steel industry has been considered from the very beginning
as a typical example of internal labour market (Stone, 1975;
Elbaum, 1983). In particular, the hierarchical organization
found in the steel industry was stressed as the major
characteristic of internal markets, and the origins of it
were traced to managerial strategies developed to motivate
to work and to discipline a workforce made increasingly
homogeneous by technical innovation. The Italian case shows
how changes in the social relations within the factories led
to the elimination of the hierarchy without modifying the
structure of control based on the division between control
and execution. The strengthening of union organization
imposed constraints on management in the organization of the
labour process making the hierarchical system inefficient
and costly. As unions imposed control the system continued
to produce benefits in terms of upgrading and career
advancement for the workforce, but increasingly failed to
induce intensification of labour and to allow the flexible
use of workers to offset the rigidities imposed by
technology. By the new non-hierarchical system, management
has secured the necessary flexible use of labour through a
"collective" system of control.

II. TECHNOLOGICAL STRUCTURE AND THE INTERNAL LABOUR MARKET

The steel industry is a process industry. The transformation
of raw materials (iron ore, scrap, limestone, coal) into
finished products (plates, sheets, bars and so on) occurs
through a series of physical and chemical processes in a
fixed and rigid sequence. For an integrated steel plant
three main stages of the production process are
identifiable; reduction of iron ore into pig iron, refining
of pig iron into steel, and rolling of steel ingots into
semi-finished and finished products. Successive stages take
place in process departments (blast furnaces, converters and
rolling trains) supported by the service sections of which
maintenance services are the most important.
    Three basic features of the production process affect
the organization of the internal labour market. The first is
the technological rigidity of the production process which
is continuous, set out in a rigid sequence and with a high
degree of integration and interdependence between stages.
The second is that the volatility of the chemical/physical

transformation during the production process and its
complexity require a continuous monitoring of control and
regulation of the processes and machinery. The third relates
to the large scale and complexity of capital equipment, and
the differences between process departments (pig iron, steel
making and rolling department) and services (maintenance,
transport and auxiliary services).

The technological rigidity and the variability of the
process requires a certain degree of flexibility and
adaptability of labour. The labour force is divided into two
main groups: process and maintenance. Process workers are
organized in small teams by department and stage of the
process. Therefore, they are classified by the position they
occupy with respect to the production process, as well as by
the experience they accumulate there. On the contrary,
maintenance workers are organized in teams by trade
(electricians, engineers, fitters, bricklayers and so on),
and are classified by their craft skill.

III. THE SOCIAL ORGANIZATION OF THE STEEL INDUSTRY IN THE
1950s AND 1960s [2]

In the early post-war period, the Italian steel industry was
at a low level of development and technologically outdated.
Mechanization and instrumentation were at a low level so
that both the quality and quantity of steel depended on the
workers' performance. In the process departments large
numbers of relatively unskilled labourers were required, for
the most part employed in heavy manual jobs. The low level
of mechanization meant that few maintenance workers were
employed (together with workers employed in the other
auxiliary services, they accounted for no more than 25-30%
of total employment). Generally, the proportion of skilled
workers was 10-13% of total employment, and those were
unequally distributed between the maintenance department
where 20-30% were skilled and the process department where
the proportion was 2-5% (Pozzobon and Mari, 1978, pp. 220-1;
Broglia and Galbo, 1961).

A. Process Workers

In the process department the majority of workers were
employed in jobs requiring little technical skill but which
needed physical integrity, strength, resistance to fatigue,
the ability to withstand very uncomfortable working
conditions and courage to face unforeseen and dangerous

situations.

The labour process was organized around the features of the technological cycle: small teams of workers were in charge of complete sections of the productive process. Within each work team, the division of labour was based on a long and well structured hierarchical and pyramidal structure, founded on informal job ladders, asserted by tradition on the basis of the technologically determined job posts. The workers in the top positions were the most experienced. They controlled, regulated and supervised the production process by rule of thumb, taking decisions when needed and co-ordinating the activities of the work team. This led them to have considerable discretionary power over the other workers not only in the carrying out of the process, but also in the organization of the labour process itself, i.e. taking decisions over job allocation, mobility, careers, promotions, personal bonuses and disciplines [3], therefore with a wide measure of control over other workers' career patterns. This consisted of climbing up the hierarchical job structure, step by step; a long process of 15-20 years of service to get to the highest position, the outcome of which was quite uncertain.

Career advancement was at the foreman's discretion and in no way controlled by the workers, least of all by the union. The foreman's control over other workers' careers was based on a mixture of "prizes" (promotions, mobility, upgrading, personal bonuses, incentives) and "punishments" (downgrading, obstacles to career development, fines). This stick and carrot system was used by management to reinforce the workings of the factory system and to organize the production process, securing the necessary co-operation and consent of the labour force. Everything was functional to the idea of career: mobility, training, promotions, loyalty and good behaviour (Botta, 1978, pp.380-3; Vallini, 1957, pp. 93 and 147; Pozzobon and Mari, 1978, p. 136).

In this system of social organization internal mobility was used to resolve the problems posed by the technology in use. Given the need to maintain continuity in production, a certain flexibility in the utilization of the labour force was required to ensure the plant was continuously manned. This was achieved by internal mobility, consisting of moving workers between job posts, within departments and within teams [4]. Mobility could be either permanent or temporary, horizontal or vertical, upward or downward. Temporary mobility was used to fill temporary vacancies, and also as a form of on-the-job training: the worker, after having moved to a certain position for some time, was trained and therefore ready to be upgraded when that particular job post

was permanently vacant. Permanent mobility could take place
either upward or downward. The worker with the longest
length of service would be moved up on the job ladder when a
job post in a higher grade became permanently vacant. But
since many jobs implied considerable physical effort and
exposure to hard working conditions, it was often the case
that workers no longer fit for certain jobs were downgraded
to marginal and secondary jobs, involving a loss of wages,
status and hierarchical position (Vallini, 1957, pp. 20-21;
Pozzobon and Mari, 1978, p. 188).

The formalization of this organization was based on a
classification system, "paghe di posto", peculiar to the
steel industry, by which process workers were graded and
paid according to their job. Jobs were ranked and each job
post, or "piazza", of the process departments had an
associated wage rate, established not through collective
bargaining but by tradition. A process worker's skill was
defined by and depended on the position he occupied in the
production process. In other words, it was the job, and not
the worker, that was classified and graded. Process workers
were supposed to move both temporarily and/or permanently
between job posts, with their earnings changing according to
their mobility patterns.

Basic rates associated with job posts reflect only the
hierarchical structure of jobs within each department, so
that those involving greater responsibility were better
paid, but also the role played by every single job with
respect to the production flow. The "key job posts", i.e.
those affecting production more directly, were generally
better paid (Parenti, 1958, Part V, Tables 2,3, and 4).
Moreover, piecework was extensively used and accounted for
over 30% of total earnings. This part of earnings was
directly related to output, usually taking the form of a
team tonnage bonus. Given the state of technology,
production depended to a large extent on the direct
intervention of the labour force. This required
collaboration, understanding and joint effort by the work
team and developed on the one hand, team spirit, and on the
other, strong competition between teams. As the division of
labour was based on tasks that had to be carried out by
small work teams, inter-team competition provided the
stimulus to produce more. Management was well aware of this
and used the team tonnage bonus to increase control within
the teams and competition between them (Botta, 1978, pp.
378-82). Finally, to increase the variability of earnings
between job posts, there was a large number of allowances,
directly related to the conditions in which the job was
performed. Most of these allowances were related to

conditions prejudicial to the worker's health, such as heat, noise, exposure to smoke and fumes, risks and so on. The fact that wages depended on many different elements and the fact that mobility was high produced a very fragmented and differentiated wage structure [5].

B. Maintenance Workers

The basic principles of the social organization of maintenance workers (as well as all other workers employed in non-productive activities) were not very different from what was found in other industrial sectors where the labour force employed was craft-skilled. In the steel industry, maintenance workers were craftsmen, specialized by trade (electricians, engineers, carpenters, fitters and so on) and were organized by trade in small teams, whether in the process departments for maintenance work on the capital equipment, or in the workshops for the preparation of the spare parts. In either case, maintenance workers acted more as individuals than as a team, and the actual division of labour among them depended on their individual skills and abilities to do complex work.

Maintenance workers were hired by trade, and within each trade, they were classified, graded and paid according to their level of craft skill. The formalization of this organization was based on the "sistema delle qualifiche", the prevailing classification system in use in Italy. According to this system, a worker hired to perform a specific job within his trade could not be asked to perform a job different from the one he was hired for, unless he was promoted, and all trades were divided into skilled (Operaio Specializzato), semi-skilled (Operaio Qualificato, Operaio Comune), and unskilled (Manovale Specializzato, Manovale Comune) sectors. Therefore, the career advancement, expressed in terms of the acknowledgement of a higher classification grade, was directly related to the acquisition and improvement of the worker's craft skill. It was therefore linked to innate abilities, individual training and experience, and the improvement and demonstration of aptitude and skills. It was a sort of individual process of learning by doing, rewarded with higher grades and higher wage rates.

C. The Role of Management and Unions

The labour market structure was also influenced by managerial authoritarianism and paternalism and by union

weakness, particularly at the workplace. The principal
manifestations of trade union weakness were the divisions
along ideological lines, the centralization of their
organizational structure, the centralization of the level of
decision-making (both in disputes and in bargaining processes), their lack of organization at the workplace and the
low level of membership (Regalia et al., 1978, pp. 137-9;
Beccalli, 1972, p. 199). Collective bargaining was highly
centralized and based on national, inter-industry and
industrial sector agreements. Plant bargaining was not very
common and it was limited to the implementation of national
agreements. Thus, up to the late 1960s, any form of control
on the workers' side over the workplace and the labour
process was either indirect and mediated through general
agreements bargained outside the workplace, or very informal
and not very effective.

Management's discretionary power was virtually
unlimited within the factories. The change in the political
climate after the 1948 elections had allowed the entrepreneurs to regain control over the factories, a control
that was pursued, both by the private and the public sector,
through the combination of apparently contradictory mechanisms, which were all designed to discipline the working
class: paternalism, discipline, discretionary and
discriminatory practices. These measures included
experiments with social assistance to steel workers and
their families for the provision of housing, holiday facilities for their children, the creation of a fund for their
education and so on (Pozzobon and Mari, 1978, pp. 115-25;
Neufeld, 1954, pp. 42-9). This welfare policy was matched by
a toughening of factory discipline . Fines, punishments,
lay-offs, suspensions from work and the allocation of
workers to "confine departments" [6] were used to discourage
trade union activity, to control the labour force and to
organize the labour process. In the process departments,
temporary employment contracts were used to weaken worker
unity as the so-called "seasonal workers" were continually
threatened with the possibility of not having their contracts renewed if they went on strike or did not respect the
discipline of the factory (Vallini, 1957, pp. 131-4, 93-4
and 158). Moreover, unilateral and discretionary policies
were used for all issues related to allocation, promotion
and payment. This included favouring the "loyal" workers by
internal mobility and promotions, and extending to them a
large variety of monetary incentives and personal bonuses;
and discriminating against the others with the threat of
lay-offs, temporary contracts, or allocation to the "confine
department".

   To understand the extent of managements' power within
the factories also requires a consideration of the
characteristics of the labour force. The vast majority of
process workers were peasant workers from outside the area
surrounding the factory, who lived in the countryside or
mountainous areas nearby, and worked the land in their spare
time (Pozzobon and Mari, 1978, pp. 132-9; Dal Ferro, 1967,
pp. 192-4; Aucona, 1957). A large number of them were from
the same villages, not only commuting together but also
working in the same department, team and shift. Their poor
education (many of them were illiterate), the fact that they
had spent most of their working life in the same department
and their attachment to their peasant origin contributed in
isolating them from the external world. Moreover, process
workers' skills were industry and firm-specific, therefore
the possibility for career advancement was necessarily
related to the workers' permanence within the steel plant.
All this helps to explain their acceptance of the
paternalistic authoritarianism of management, as well as
the tendency to develop small group interests.
   Maintenance workers were craft skilled, usually with
some previous industrial experience and better education.
They also lived in the area around the factory and were well
integrated into the social milieu. They represented the
aristocracy of the steel workers, and it was among them that
trade union activists were found. But given on the one hand,
the political climate of those years and, on the other hand,
the socio-cultural origin of the majority of the labour
force, their efforts to counter internal management policies
had very little impact.

D. The Job Analysis and Job Evaluation System

This double system, based on the job ranking for process
workers and on the "sistema delle qualifiche" for
maintenance workers, was employed up to the early 1970s
throughout the private sector and in some public sector
steel enterprises. Up to the early 1960s, the only
noticeable exception was the integrated steel plant of
Cornigliano, where the job analysis and job evaluation (JA
and JE) system was introduced at the time of its
construction in 1951-53.
   The integrated plant of Cornigliano was built by the
public sector as the starting point of a very ambitious
project for the development and modernization of the Italian
steel industry. These works were considered at that time the
most up-to-date plant in Italy and one of the most modern in

Europe, equipped with the first example in Italy of a
continuous rolling mill for the production of plates, sheets
and strips. The new continuous rolling train represented a
remarkable increase in the level of mechanization of the
rolling process, involving not only much higher
productivity, but also a radical change in the organization
of the production process. Manpower requirements were
reduced, particularly for manual labour; the possibilities
for direct intervention of labour in the rolling process was
much less than in traditional mills, while jobs associated
with control and regulation and maintenance work were
considerably increased. Table I summarizes the main changes
brought about by continuous rolling by comparing with a
manual and a semi-manual rolling train.

Public managers introduced at Cornigliano not only the
best available installations and techniques for the
production of steel, but also what they thought to be the
best techniques in use for the organization of the enterprise as a whole and particularly for the management of the
labour force (Cai, 1976, pp. 29-31). The policy was to build
an ideal type of factory, based on up-to-date, highly
productive equipment, and also on the most advanced techniques available for the management of the production
process, the control of output, the division of labour and
labour relations. The solution proposed for the management
of labour was a combination of four main policies: i) a very
detailed description of division of labour (job analysis);
ii) a precise definition of the criteria for the determination of wages (job evaluation); iii) wide use of internal
mobility to allow for the increased rigidity and integration
of the processes; and iv) the recruitment of a "new working
class".

Job analysis formalized the division of labour,
specifying the tasks and operations involved for each job
and was used to define the wage structure. Each job was
classified by certain characteristics, and these were
evaluated to determine the wage rates. In this way some of
the previous formal distinctions between maintenance and
process workers disappeard; however, these two groups of
workers were differentiated by the type of division of
labour, training process, skill, level of education, degree
of internal mobility and pattern of advancement. Therefore,
the labour force still consisted of numerous groups of
workers with distinct characteristics and differentiated
interests, and the main innovation of the JA and JE system
was to make the distinctions betwen jobs more precise. But
this did not change the basic principles of work
organization, so that it is possible to describe the JA and

JE system introduced at Cornigliano in 1953 as a rationalization of the traditional job ranking system: workers were
classified, graded and paid by the job rather than by
capabilities [7]. In particular, as far as process workers
are concerned, production continued to be characterized by
technological rigidity — now even greater because of the
higher automation of the processes — and by the collective
nature of work activities based on team work. This, and the
very detailed division of labour introduced by job analysis,
called for large internal mobility and this high mobility
was related to on-the-job training and to career structure.
Finally, a new working class, i.e. one with no steel
tradition, was recruited.

       To understand the recruitment policy it is crucial to
realize that the building of Cornigliano steel works was
part of the restructuring plan for the public sector steel
industry, involving the closing down of several outdated
steel works. In the Liguria region, where the Cornigliano
works were located, three steel plants belonging to the ILVA
holding were shut down, making 2,901 workers redundant. By
1959, only 421 were found re-employed in the steel industry
and 824 were still unemployed (D'Alamo, 1960; Vento, 1981,
p. 152). Management did not hire the workers freed by the
restructuring of the other factories, preferring to hire
young workers (25–30 years old), with no previous experience
in steel factories, with various, non-industrial working
experience (as peasants, craft-workers, pedlars, barbers and
so on) and from nearby rural areas. Management put forward
"technical" arguments for their employment policy: as the
works, the processes and the organization of the factory
were new, then the structure of the labour force had to be
new too (Botta, 1981, pp. 107–10). But the underlying
reasons were more "social": management wanted a workforce
willing to co-operate without conflict with the construction
and organization of a factory where everything could be
predetermined on the basis of "objective" criteria. The
workforce of the steel works closed down in the region was
not suited to such a project: it had a very strong trade
union tradition, characterized by an allegiance to the
Communist Party (Botta, 1981, pp. 78–91 and p. 120). Hirings
for the new works took place with the aid of careful
"political" screening carried out by the parish churches, as
well as political and personal connections. It was only for
the top grades (foremen, supervisors and engineers) and for
the highest manual positions in the process departments that
employees freed from restructuring in the other steel plants
were hired. In this last case, the experienced and older
workers were employed only for a few years until their

retirement age, to train the labour force. As they retired,
they were replaced with technicians, and their jobs were
transformed into white collar jobs.

When, in 1960, Cornigliano and ILVA, the two largest
companies of the public sector, merged into a new
corporation, Italsider [8], management decided to extend the
JA and JE system in use at Cornigliano to all its plants. An
agreement was reached with the unions [9], and some changes
were introduced, but they were irrelevant to the principles
on which the system itself was based (Cai, 1976, pp. 35-38)
[10]. All other steel enterprises, both in the public sector
and in the private sector, continued to organize the labour
process around the job ranking system inherited from the
past [11].

IV. THE IMPACT OF CHANGES IN THE ITALIAN LABOUR MOVEMENT ON THE ORGANIZATION OF THE LABOUR PROCESS

In the large integrated plants the standardization and scale
of output led to higher levels of mechanization and the
introduction of computer control. These technical
innovations brought out some of the contradictions implicit
in the JA and JE system. First, the steady increase in
productivity due to technical innovation led, on the one
hand, to continuous attempts by management to re-adjust
incentives by "objective efficiency criteria", and, on the
other hand, to trade union opposition to the system of
incentives as they became aware that all the factors determining piece rates were directly decided by management (the
features of the equipment, their production plans and manpower requirements) (Cai, 1976, pp. 40-41). Second, technical change progressively modified the division of labour,
eliminating some tasks, creating new ones and changed the
skill content of jobs. This necessarily called for modifications in the evaluation system. However, because of the
principles on which it was based, the JA and JE system
turned out to be very rigid so that the modifications required by technical change proved very difficult. Finally, with
increased automation, labour became progressively de-skilled
in the traditional sense, different qualifications were
required and the concept of skill itself, as perceived by
the workers, began to change.

Meanwhile, in the scrap based steel plants, the
mechanization of the rolling mills and the modernization of
the electric furnaces had been set in motion. But given the
different technological features of the scrap based plant,

the process of mechanization was less advanced and technical
changes were easily and smoothly absorbed.

A. Changes in the Italian Labour Movement

The intense labour conflicts which developed in the
factories from 1967 onwards, with the emergence of labour
organization at the workplace and the rapid spread of plant
bargaining, changed the pattern of the industrial relations
system. The struggles of this period overturned the power
relations within the factories and succeeded in bringing
some constraints on the discretionary power of management,
thereby reducing flexibility in the use of labour. The
acknowledgement of workers' rights [12], and the establishment of a trade union organization within the factories
gave rise to a process of decentralization of decision-
making and bargaining activity that changed the prevailing
pattern of industrial relations.
    A plethora of new demands began to emerge from the rank
and file: they wanted generalized upgrading, flat wage
increases, abolition or strict limitation of incentives and
piece work systems, reduction of the pace of work and the
workload, the ending of the acceptance of dangerous and
risky jobs in return for money, ending or strict limitation
of overtime, and finally, reduction in working hours. These
demands, for the most part the spontaneous result of the
needs of certain groups of workers, stood in marked contrast
to the tradition of trade union bargaining, which tied wages
to skill level and to the growth of productivity. Facing the
problem of developing a policy that could link different
rank-and-file demands into a more general and non-sectional
strategy, the unions put forward an overall long-term
strategy centred on two issues: equality and control over
the organization of production. The demands for greater
equality, identified as a sign of the crisis of the
prevailing system of classification, and the demands for
greater control over work organization, identified as a
critique of the traditional system of the organization of
production (based on a division of labour unilaterally
imposed by management), were reflected in a variety of
solutions within the factories. Gradually, new common groups
emerged from the initially differing positions with the
union proposal of so-called "Inquadramento Unico" (IU) - a
single grading scale for manual workers, foremen and non-
manual workers. The new classification system interlaced the
wage structure of the three categories of employees; it
reduced the number of grades; it reduced wage differentials

between the highest and lowest grades; and finally, it
introduced some dynamics with respect to the problem of
career and qualifications.

The IU was first introduced at Italsider in 1970, after
a very long and hard struggle started at the Cornigliano
works to replace the JA and JE system, which was highly
criticized, particularly by the less skilled workers. But
the idea of the new scale developed at Italsider rapidly
became an arena of common debate in the Italian union movement, and the IU began to be negotiated in other steel
enterprises and in other industrial sectors. From 1973
onwards it was introduced in all major national collective
agreements, starting with the metal sector.

Intense bargaining activity, at plant and shop floor
level, followed the introduction of the new classification.
Disputes over IU became the focus for struggle for the
control of the organization of production. And, as a result
of the bargaining activity that followed, the workers increased their control over a large number of areas.

B. Changes in the Steel Industry

The idea of the IU was first developed by trade union
officials at Italsider in 1970, following the campaign
mounted by workers to do away with the JA and JE system
which categorized workers into 24 job classes. The latter
system was heavily criticized for its pseudo-objectivity:
the workers saw it as a way by which they were artificially
divided and immobilized (Lettieri, 1971, p. 114; Coppola,
1971, p. 257). They criticized the career structure implicit
in the system, since it was only for a small number of
workers that the idea of a career had any real meaning. Over
60% of manual workers were graded in the ten lowest classes
(out of 24), and less than 2% in the seven highest classes
(Pesce, 1970, p. 5; Torneo, 1970, p. 254). Finally, the
system was criticized for its rigidity in terms of wage
negotiations: it did not allow for the upgrading of workers
in the less skilled jobs, in spite of the fact that this was
happening in all the major enterprises in the other
industrial sectors. With its fixed criteria on the basis of
which each job post was analysed and evaluated with respect
to the others, the system prevented wage demands from
serving as a rallying point for any large group of workers,
since each demand had to be justified between the various
sections of the labour force (Cai, 1976, p. 39).

The explicit aim of the proposed new system was to
unify the pressure group generated by different groups. The

new classification was a way of grouping all employees in
very few categories based on professional qualifications and
work experience. At the same time it introduced a new
dynamic, in direct conflict with the JA and JE, which was
related directly to the workers' personal experience. The
central idea on which the new system was based was the
concept of "professionalita", as it was explained by one of
the leaders of the struggles at Italsider [13]:

> New professionalism means turning the
> principle of the job evaluation system upside
> down. The achievement of this new criterion is
> perceived by the workers as an overturning of
> the old practice of de-skilling, as a
> collective fact that helps to unify the
> workers, to assure mobility outside the cages
> created by the job evaluation. The new
> professionalism, moreover, takes as its point
> of reference, in broad terms, the capacity to
> work: capacity to know the production cycle
> and to intervene on it. In this sense, the new
> professionalism is identified as a collective
> fat, and it tends towards homogeneity even if
> this homogeneity is not immediate, but is
> realized through the development of experience
> that springs from a concrete socialization of
> work (Lettieri, 1971, pp. 115-116).

The general strategy underlying this concept of a new
professionalism was quite radical, and the struggles for the
IU soon became a battle for control over the organization of
production, decisively shaped by intellectual and overtly
ideological influence (Lettieri, 1970, pp. 148-9). To this
end, the unions pursued two different but parallel
approaches. As well as attempting to control the production
process by imposing a series of constraints on the
organization of production, which resulted in a system of
formalized guarantees preventing any unilateral decision on
important issues, the unions began to work in the somewhat
ambiguous direction of an alternative and different division
of labour. The starting point for the latter approach was
the concept of the new professionalism. The impact of the
changes introduced through plant and shop floor bargaining
was profound and far-reaching. But the results achieved were
contradictory, with respect to the initial ideas and
purposes (Della Rocca, 1982, pp. 160-1; Chiaromonte et al.,
1982, pp. 15-18; Quaderm di Rassepna Dindacale, 1982).

C. Changes in the Organization of the Labour Process in the Steel Industry

1. The division of labour

The final agreements on the implementation of the new classification system did not produce substantial changes in the division of labour. Both process and maintenance workers continued to perform the same jobs they were performing before, albeit with real differences in their classification and payment, so that the wage structure became very flat and many differences were abolished. The production process was still organized in terms of the definition of job posts that needed to be filled, and process workers were still supposed to move between posts when required. The new classification system called for a re-classification of all manual job posts, within each shopfloor, from the previous 1-24 classes of the JA and JE at Italsider and the large number of "paghe di posto" of the other steel factories to the 1-5 levels of the IU, with the result that very different jobs could now be classified at the same level. Wages were still related to the job posts process workers filled, with the difference that now workers acquired the right to a higher grade after a certain number of rotations and replacements, although continuing to be employed in a job classified at a lower grade. For maintenance workers the IU implied their grading according to their level of qualification. And since technical innovation has led to more complex equipment, both their number and their role had increased; as a result, they tended to be graded at a higher level than process workers, therefore the maintenance/ process worker difference was re-established.

2. The classification system and the grading structure

After the settlement of the IU agreements, first at Italsider and in the following couple of years in the other steel enterprises, a quite complex process of classification was carried out in a very long and diffuse bargaining process [14]. The workers had to define, through a process of collective discussion, their own scale of classification for each shop floor, on the basis of what had been settled in the general agreement. This process involved all employees and it took place first at the level of the work team and the workshop, and then at the factory level. But the discussion over the grading structure soon became a discussion over job posts and job tasks, with a tendency to continue to evaluate the job rather than the worker, and therefore in conflict with the trade union policy itself. Difficulties and conflicts between process and maintenance workers, as well as among different groups of process workers, and between the trade union officials and the workers, started to appear when the new classification had to be implemented. The process of discussion ended, in many cases, with the re-emergence of sectional pressures, a weakening of working class unity and a return to group claims [15]. In other words, the discussion among workers, instead of eliminating differences, produced a continuous process of comparison based on existing differences, and as a result was destined to re-establish them, with the trade union officials in the position of mediating the conflict in an effort to devise some general strategy. The distribution of workers across the new grading structure was therefore the result of several different forces at work: the balance of forces between the many groups of workers, as well as between management and workers, management policy and trade union policy within the factory. This explains the noticeable differences found in the distribution of workers throughout the grading structure, both between different steel plants, and within the same plant, between different departments (Villa, 1985, Ch. 4).

3. The wage structure

In the years that followed the introduction of the IU the wage structure became flatter and flatter. All the differences that had existed with the previous systems – both job ranking and job evaluation – were eliminated, and wage differentials widely reduced. A large number of wage elements previously related to the individual and/or specific conditions (such as personal bonuses, premiums, individual incentives, rewards for dangerous and heavy work, and so on) were abolished. Wages depended now, by and large, on the "professional level" attributed to the workers employed in certain jobs. At the same time, as a result of automatic mechanisms introduced for the workers' professional development, the distribution of the labour force within the grading structure changed over time, emptying the lowest grades (grades 1, 2 and 3). That is, the acknowledgement of higher grades after a certain number of rotations and replacements, in recognition of increased qualifications expressed in terms of the ability to work and the experience acquired through temporary mobility on different jobs, allowed workers to be graded at a level higher than that

attached to their jobs. Moreover, in the first years after
the introduction of the IU, higher grades were granted
through shopfloor collective bargaining, as a consequence of
the struggles and the demands of single groups of workers.
This process tended to regenerate itself by imitation,
developing a general tendency towards upgrading which
replaced wage bargaining. The result of this tendency, given
the upper limit for the grading of manual workers established at the fifth level, was a very flat wage structure.
In most of the large steel enterprises the grade 1 level is
never used, grades 2 and 3 are entry levels for process
workers and maintenance workers, respectively; blue collar
workers are, by and large, concentrated in two grades only,
the fourth and fifth.

4. Mobility, skill, career

As has already been said, agreements on the IU reversed the
criteria for classification: it was the worker and not the
jobs that had to be graded, and the basic concept for
workers' grading was their "professionalita". Moreover, this
system was supposed to introduce some devices to account for
the development of individual professional abilities, and
this modified quite drastically the upgrading system in use
for process workers. The mechanisms introduced through
collective bargaining (job rotations, job enrichment, job
enlargement, training and re-training) were supposed to both
increase individual abilities and to take better account of
them. Therefore, criteria for upgrading were associated with
them. The general agreements, at the enterprise level,
determined the basic rules for upgrading by establishing,
for example, the minimum length of service, the number of
rotations, the number of days of replacement required to get
to a higher level, and so on. Decentralized bargaining, by
plant and shopfloor, singled out the different solutions for
each department. The outcome of this decentralized
bargaining activity was a large number of minute agreements,
defining detailed career patterns for all sections of the
steel factory and for all jobs. This implied:

i) The definition of mobility paths, within each
sub-section of the production process, in
terms of the jobs to which a work, hired and
allocated to a certain position , is supposed
to move, both vertically and horizontally.

ii) The definition of the rewards of that
mobility, in terms of the acknowledgement of a

```
       higher grade after a specified number of
       rotations and replacements
iii) The definition of criteria for a permanent
     move to a higher graded job.
```

To conclude, mobility, skill and career were still
interrelated, as they had been previously. But collective
bargaining limited the almost absolute discretionary power
of the foreman over mobility and career by establishing
procedures and criteria for promotions. As a result, the
career process becomes <u>clearer</u> <u>and</u> <u>more</u> <u>certain</u>, because of
the introduction of negotiated criteria and procedures for
the regulation of career advancement; <u>flatter</u>, because of
the reduced number of grades and therefore the flattening of
the hierarchical structure within each team; and finally,
<u>quicker</u>, because of the automatic mechanisms introduced and
because upgrading was no longer restricted by the
availability of vacancies. At the same time, career as such
lost most of its original meaning not only in terms of wage
differentials, but also in terms of the workers' position
within the hierarchical structure and the power relationship
attached to it.

5. Hierarchical structure

The long and well-defined hierarchical structure inherited
from the past, on the basis of which the whole labour
process had been organized, became subject to substantial
changes both in its pattern and its function. Now that all
job posts had been compressed into no more than three or
four grades, the hierarchical structure was considerably
simplified by the reduction in the number of grades and
steps. Fig. 1 shows the changes that occurred in the
hierarchical structure for Cornigliano when the JE system
was replaced with the IU.
     Moreover, the role of the hierarchy, and particularly
the role played by the foremen and supervisors, was
considerably reduced. The legitimization of this role had
previously been based on a detailed division of labour,
expressed in terms of a precise separation of taxes,
knowledge and responsibilities, and thus on the authority
granted to the hierarchy from such an organizational
structure. The hierarchy and the authority associated with
it were accepted by the workers as they accepted the career
structure, the promotion system associated with it and the
right of the foreman to choose. The introduction and spread
of automation, through the installation of process computers

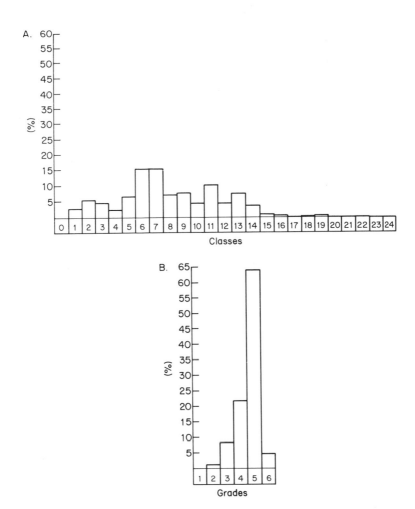

Fig. 1 Manual workers by classification grade at Italsider,
Cornigliano works in 1956 and 1980 (% distribution). A. The
"job evaluation system", March 1956
(total employment = 3889).
B. The "inquadramento unico", December 1980 (total
employment = 6910)

on real time in the process departments, partly reduced the
role of the foremen; some of their role in controlling and
co-ordinating the production process was incorporated into
the new equipment. In fact, in an emergency or in cases
where the control system run by the computer was in error,

the workers now preferred to ask for the intervention of the computer technicians rather than the decision of the foreman (Collettivo Tecnici Italsider, 1979, p. 38). This change in technology occurred at the same time as the struggles of 1968-73, rejecting the foreman's authority. The foreman's power in terms of decision over workers' careers, mobility, promotion and downgrading as well as disciplinary actions (fines, suspensions, dismissals) was restricted by the replacement of their discretionary power by clear rules and procedures negotiated with management; and decentralized bargaining power between shopfloor delegates and managers responsible for labour relations.

V. PROBLEMS OF RIGIDITY AND THE NEED FOR FLEXIBILITY

The changes imposed by this new level of labour organization upon the labour market structure raised three major problems for management.

1. Higher labour costs

The replacement of the previous systems with the IU resulted in a general upgrading of the labour force. This was the combined result of the different criteria used to classify workers and of the processes introduced to guarantee them some "professional development" (i.e. job rotation, job enrichment and job enlargement). Given the widespread use of internal mobility typical of the steel industry, the acknowledgement of these processes as indicators of the acquisition of a certain level of qualifications, and as a basis on which to award higher grades, produced a general tendency towards upgrading (with a limit of grade 5 for manual workers) and an upward flattening of the wage structure. This, of course, produced higher labour costs per head, and therefore higher total labour costs.

Moreover, with the new classification, there is no longer a stable relationship between the job performed and the worker's grade, since this depends not only on the job post filled, but on his own experience. Thus, management can no longer control productivity and labour costs through the control over the division of labour. This is quite clearly perceived by Italsider management [16].

> The relationship between skill/division of
> labour/productivity, which in the past was
> assured by the stable relationship between the
> classification system and the rewards, repre-

sented by the job evaluation and the analytical incentive system in use, has become now
quite critical (Fantoli, 1980, p. 201).

2. Rigidities in the employment of labour

The idea underlying the struggles of the late 1960s was that
the organization of production, at the factory level, was
the expression of a power relationship between management
and workers, and as a result everything was open to
negotiation. The intense and widespread bargaining activity
that followed imposed a system of control over a large
number of issues, such as the classification system, grading
structure, wages policy, internal mobility, upgrading and
promotions, overtime, pace of work, workload, resting times
and so on. This in turn produced a new series of rigidities
in the use of labour.
    As far as mobility in particular was concerned, the
bargaining activity which followed the introduction of the
new classification system changed its procedures quite
considerably. The new link between mobility and upgrading
produced a contradictory situation. On the one hand, there
was the workers' demand for higher internal mobility as it
is here expressed by a foreman and worker:

suddenly, everyone wanted to rotate and we
have been accused of not producing
opportunities for professional development
(foreman)

the oldest workers act as a brake on us, if
they don't rotate, they restrict our career
prospects: thus the foreman should give us
other ways out (worker) (Segatori and
Torresini, 1979, p. 45).

On the other hand, this new attitude sometimes produces an
impasse, where workers were not willing to move, to rotate,
or to replace with a fellow, when required, if this did not
count towards or result in a higher grade.

workers rotate only to get the grade, not to
learn (foreman)

if I have the fifth grade, why should I work

in job posts with less professional content?
(worker) (ibid.).

This was quite a general situation in all enterprises
examined, but the problem was far more acute where the
workings of the IU did not leave any space for manoeuvre,
either on the management or on the union side. And this was
the case at Italsider and Dalmine, where the upgrading
process was very far advanced with over 89.1% and 87.9% pf
workers respectively classified in the highest grades in
1977 (Segatori and Torresini, 1977).

3. Inefficiency

The traditional management techniques for the organization
of the labour process were based on a complex and informal
system of meritocratic premiums and punishments, assigned in
a discretionary fashion through the hierarchical structure.
On this basis, management was able to assure the collaboration of the labour force. Everything was functional and
related to the career structure: on-the-job training,
mobility, replacements, loyalty, responsible behaviour,
promotions and upgrading. The idea of career lost much of
its original meaning with the changes introduced via the IU
and its automatic mechanisms. At the same time, the
hierarchy at the workplace lost control over career
processes. All this rendered inefficient and worthless what
was left of the traditional techniques: a detailed division
of labour; the organization of the productive process into a
large number of jobs, positions and grades; and finally, a
hierarchical structure emptied of its previous role [17].

A. The Possible Solutions

The problem of rigidities imposed by the increased power of
the workers at the workplace was perceived from the very
beginning by the entrepreneurs. In some industrial sectors,
the enterprises have regained flexibility by sub-contracting
to smaller firms, where in general unions are weaker. but
given the characteristics of the technology in use
(continuous and integrated process) and the economies of
scale typical of the steel industry, decentralization was
not a feasible solution. Instead, some steel enterprises,
like AFL Falck and Breda Siderurgica, tried to minimize the
impact of workers' demands, and adopted a sort of "defensive
policy", in which mobility, promotions and grades were still
used to organize the labour process. In fact, in these

enterprises, the distribution of the labour force within the grading structure was far less concentrated and, particularly, the upward flattening process less marked than in other steel companies (Villa, 1985, Ch. 4). On the other hand, the policy pursued by other steel companies, including Italsider and Dalmine, were quite different: they developed new solutions in terms of the division of labour and the organization of the labour process. In this way, the initiative was taken by employers as a way of reaffirming their prestige and position.

As management did not have an alternative model of work organization, research projects and experimentation were instituted. At Italisider some innovations were introduced in specific areas and in a few plants after 1972, in order to single out possible solutions. Experiments continued in a large number of plants, but always carried out in small and well-delineated areas of the production process [18]. In 1978, a company agreement was made to carry out new forms of work organization, plant by plant and department by department, outlining the main criteria and principles on the basis of which innovations should be introduced. Other public sector steel companies (Dalmine, Terni) have carried out similar experiments on work organization, introducing innovations gradually and then generalizing them through plant collective bargaining. Both the content of the agreements and the tendencies in work organization are quite similar among steel firms: they focus upon the utilization of work groups. In this respect, it is important to note that the changes introduced into the steel factories are quite distinct from those introduced in other enterprises over the same period. The steel industry was the first to introduce experimentation, in reaction to the challenge of the trade union movement; diffusion of research and experimental activity was much wider than in any other sector [19]; innovations had a real impact upon the division of labour and the organization of the labour process [20]; and finally, the innovations, based on the diffusion of work groups, built on traditional forms of collective work which had continued to operate if informally (D'Andrea, 1976; Butera, 1979).

B. The Work Group

Despite large differences in the methodology adopted, all the projects on work organization carried out in the public sector steel industry in the 1970s are quite similar in their underlying ideas, with a common trend towards the

utilization of work groups, the so-called "Operative Unit"
(OU, which have a technical and a social basis. Technically
speaking, the OUs are complete sections of the production
process and within these the work-group is responsible for
all the functions of analysis, control and regulation of the
production process and output, including also some
maintenance work, emergency intervention, service
activities, care of equipment and so on. Thus, the OU should
be technically autonomous, with no external technical
interference in the management of the process of that
specific segment of the production cycle. The social
implication refers to the fact that the operative unit is
responsible for the organization of the labour process
within it. That is, the distribution of jobs, tasks and
operations, shifts and planned absences from work, holidays,
training and on-the-job training, and so on are all
delegated to the work-group as a whole.

   Experiments with work organization conducted by
Italsider, and the other steel enterprises in the 1970s,
were without doubt induced by the problems posed by the
increased rigidity of labour both for the production process
and for the management of the labour force itself (Della
Rocca, 1974, pp. 179-80; Fantoli, 1980, p. 201). It was,
therefore, necessary to find new forms of work organization
that would permit a form of control over the production
process no longer based on an individual and capillary
control of the labour force. They needed a form of control
of the labour process based on the workers' consent, and
therefore in line with the demands advanced by workers'
struggles. Moreover, as Italsider was facing a critical
situation both financially and in terms of its position in
the product market (Ministero dell'Industria, 1979; Mondo
Economico, 1981), there was an urgent need to regain
technical and economic efficiency. Innovations introduced in
work organization through collective bargaining were, in the
first instance, motivated on the one hand by the need to
recover and/or improve efficiency and productivity, and on
the other hand, to develop a better use of workers'
qualifications (experience, knowledge, capacity to learn)
(Italsider agreement 21.3.78, Premessa, punto 2, and Parte
1, punto 1). Thus, the main and explicit target for
management was the improvement of production, both in
quantitative and qualitative terms.

   This is nothing new: it is the usual aim of management.
What was new was the way in which this aim was pursued.
Control is no longer exercised through a detailed and
diffuse system of directives and supervision over the labour
process - based on a very detailed division of labour and on

an individual hierarchical form of control through the
foremen and supervisors. With the introduction of the new
classification, such a system has become useless, costly and
difficult to implement, given the changes in the social
relations within the factory (Del Lungo, 1976, pp. 250-3).
In this context, the redesign of work organization around
the idea of the operative unit is intended to regain
economic and technical efficiency through a more general and
global system of control, more directly related to output.

The solution itself - the relatively autonomous
operative unit for the organization of the labour process
operating within a well defined segment of the production
cycle - is suggested by the technology and its introduction
is facilitated by the recent technical innovations. The fact
that the production process is continuous and organized in
integrated but distinguished stages, where each stage is
assigned to small groups of workers, would seem to suggest
the possibility of some form of collective work. Moreover,
the empirical work done on the division of labour in the
steel industry (D'Andrea, 1976; Butera, 1979) has noted
that, in fact, despite the precise division of labour within
each team, and the definition of tasks and operations for
each single job post, a tendency to transcend this strict
division of labour was already in existence: a large degree
of co-operation and understanding, mutual assistance, and
interchangeability between jobs were already employed by
process workers producing - informally - some forms of
"autoregulated co-operation". As a result, the new form of
organization, based on work-groups, has incorporated,
expanded and formalized some of the concepts and ideas
already established. The existence of forms of co-operation
within the teams has made it easier to overcome a strict
division of labour, and this helps to explain the
development and the diffusion of forms of work organization
based on work-groups in the steel industry.

At the same time, technical changes introduced in the
1970s, and particularly the employment of process computers
in the main process departments (Collettivo Tecnici
Italsider, 1979), has facilitated the shift from the old
form of work organization to the new one. The mechanization
and the partial automation introduced into the production
process have reduced considerably the direct intervention of
manual labour, compared with the post-war situation. The
production flow is tied to the time required by the
installations to complete the processes of chemical/physical
transformation. It cannot, therefore, be speeded up or
slowed down, as in the past, by the pace of work imposed by
the team employed there. Nevertheless, the intervention of

the team is still crucial in ensuring that all operations
are properly executed and that they are on time, so as to
allow for a regular flow of production. The main problem for
management, in the organization of the production process,
is therefore related to the achievement of a regular flow of
production. With the previous system of work organization,
based on a detailed division of labour, a hierarchical
structure and an internal labour market structure linking
mobility, training, promotions and careers, workers were
induced to conform with a certain type of behaviour in order
to ensure a regular flow of production. The struggles of the
late 1960s and the bargaining activity which followed
rejected that system and imposed several constraints on it.
As a result, the division of labour which had given rise to
many separate jobs survived, and with it some part of the
hierarchy (foremen and supervisors), though these had little
control over the labour process. There was, therefore, a
contradiction between the formal system of control and the
actual mechanism of control itself. The diffusion of process
computers in all the main stages of the production process,
and the automatic control of production in all its variables
induced through them, suggested the solution. The idea was
that the role previously played by the hierarchical
structure within the labour process could be played by
technology itself, mainly through the diffusion of process
computers. In this respect it is interesting to turn to the
speech given by Mr Sette, President of Italsider at that
time, immediately after the introduction of the new
classification system, when entrepreneurs started to
consider possible responses to the workers' challenge:

> in an integrated steel plant, where coal and
> iron ore are shipped, discharged and treated
> by sintering, the coke plant transforms coal
> for the blast furnaces which produce pig iron,
> that is refined into steel, that is then
> rolled giving finished products: in a
> production process of this type, I would say
> that the possibility that output is produced
> regularly and integrally is given by the cycle
> and production flow ... In such a productive
> organization capital could regain control,
> from the point of view of production, could
> recover what will be lost in terms of
> individual piece work through an organization
> of the production flow more correct and more
> precise, more timed, more controlled, more
> synchronized ... And today one of the elements

that can make this possible in a more rational
way is the introduction ... of data management
computers and process computers on all
installations. Once the production flow has
been determined and organized in a certain way
the computer can assure the time optimization
of the production flow: the computer with its
terminals can reach the departments and
determine, fix, clock the times and the
methods that optimize, and reduce the time
losses for the whole production flow from the
store of raw materials and semi-finished
products, to the store of the finished
products and forwarding (Sette, 1973, p. 233).

C. Effects on the Labour Process

I will briefly discuss the main effects of the innovations
introduced through work-groups upon the labour process, on
the basis of preliminary experimentation at Italsider
Cornigliano after 1978 [21].

1. The division of labour

The workers of a defined and complete segment of the
production cycle (such as for the steel making department:
raw materials, the converter, anti-pollution and auxiliary
installations) are collectively responsible for its
management, overcoming the logic of the division of labour
into individual jobs. With the OU, the whole group of
workers and activities are "taken back to a unity" from two
aggregate factors: targets and operative autonomy.
    The OU targets are negotiated at the department level
and they refer to production, safety and workers'
qualifications. The crucial target is the productive one,
and this is agreed as the concrete and measurable result of
a complete segment of the production cycle, involving the
work of the whole operative unit . For example, for the
converter operative unit the productive target is defined in
terms of tons of liquid steel produced in a defined period
of time.
    The OU operative autonomy refers to the freedom to
auto-determine the allocation of the work activities
attributed to the group in order to achieve predetermined
targets. With respect to the organizational superstructure
this implies non-interference; with respect to the work-

group itself it implies the distribution of tasks and
operations among the members of the OU. And all this
implies, in turn, co-operation between workers and interchangeability between posts.

To conclude, plant collective agreements determine and
specify by department: the production targets (both in
quantitative and qualitative terms); the activities that
have to be performed by the operative unit as a whole; the
working conditions; and finally, the manning requirements,
per OU and per shift. Then the group of workers within each
OU is responsible for the management of that section of the
production cycle, therefore with complete autonomy over all
issues related to the division of labour, mobility,
vacancies, shifts, holidays, training and so on.

2. The division of labour, skill, mobility

With the overcoming of the division of labour based on
detailed individual positions and jobs, the concept of skill
itself cannot be related to the single individual worker any
longer. Instead, it becomes more like a collective concept,
related to the totality of the technical requirements of
that part of the production process under the control of the
work-group. As a result, the idea of mobility (i.e. shifts,
rotation and even promotion from one single job to another)
becomes obsolete as well. Within the single work-group there
are no differences between the workers with respect to the
posts: they are all defined simply with reference to the OU
within which they are employed: "operatori" (operators).

3. Grading system and structure

Differentiated activities and posts are still defined and
outlined within each OU, but this definition of the work
performed by the OU is not reflected in a distinction
between separate jobs. therefore, the distinction of jobs by
grade disappears too. The same grade, the fifth (the highest
for blue collar workers), is granted to all workers within
the same operative unit. Grades are used only with reference
to training: the newly hired worker is graded at the third
level. The work-group itself is in charge of his on-the-job
training, and within a limited period of time (precisely
four and a half years) the worker will be upgraded to the
fifth level, that is, when his training process is
completed. Now, the distribution of workers along the
grading structure depends only on hirings and the training

process (Carlini, 1981). Moreover, within each OU the agreements have singled out the possibility of grading some workers at a higher level, the sixth, for a limited number of cases within each OU. This has been introduced where the activities of the unit itself call for a more experienced worker; it also allows the oldest and more skilled workers to get better treatment.

4. Hierarchical structure and career

The most remarkable result, if compared with the work organization system in use in the post-war period, is the vertical disintegration process within each work team, so that no hierarchical structure is left within the OU. The "first operator", i.e. the worker graded at the sixth level, is distinguished from the other workers of the group by the fulfilment of some specific tasks and operations, usually involving higher responsibility and experience, but he plays no role in the co-ordination or control of the work-group, since this is demanded of the OU itself. The role of foremen and supervisors disappears and is replaced by a new hierarchical position - "assistente". This is a white collar position with the specific functions of planning, co-ordinating and controlling the productive results of the OU. The "assistente" is therefore responsible for the correct conduct of the process, and his functions of control are related to the technology in use and its correct management, and not to the labour process. Career is meaningless, as far as manual workers are concerned: the acquisition of grades is simply a matter of training and time, and is collectively negotiated. The possibility of having a career would remain only if promotion to a white collar position were possible, but a clear distinction between blue collar and white collar jobs still holds.

5. Wage system and wage structure

Wages are basically related to grades: therefore the wage structure is almost completely flat within the group. But differences are possible between work-groups, since the 1981 agreement has introduced a bonus system related to the achievement of productive targets, and this is settled in the shopfloor agreements.

6. Flexibility

With the work organization based on the OU, all the problems
of worker flexibility, with respect to the needs of the
production process, are completely shifted on to the group
itself. Training, mobility, replacements, vacancies, the
division of labour, holidays, overtime, everything is
decided by the work-group. On the one hand, this seems to
reflect a positive judgement on the new work organization
system, particularly with reference to the original demands
advanced in the early struggles. It overcomes the idea of
individual skill and it gives autonomy to the workers, in
the sense of a real auto-determination of the distribution
of tasks and jobs. At the same time, it can be looked at
more critically [22]. The new form of work organization
overcomes the problem of rigidity, particularly with respect
to the problem of internal mobility. This is no longer
imposed, but autonomously determined within the OU by the
workers themselves. In other words, what is left in the
workers' hands is the management of their own internal
mobility between posts, tasks, roles and functions; which
means, in turn, delegating to the workers the responsibility
for their own flexibility. The separation between control
and execution still holds: this is also formalized by
keeping the distinction between manual and non-manual
workers, technicians and workers, and it is possible by
technical changes [23].

VI. CONCLUSIONS

The rapid diffusion of workers' representatives at the
factory level, the process of trade union decentralization
and the diffusion of plant and shopfloor bargaining have
been particularly incisive, with respect to the labour
process, in two ways. First, the changes introduced imposed
a system of control, either unilaterally or through
negotiations, over the various aspects of the labour
process, while in the past managers' power was both
extremely extensive and discretionary. This allowed workers
- for the first time - direct control over the organization
of production, thus representing a drastic change of
direction. Second, the intense labour conflicts which
developed from 1967 onwards and the decentralized bargaining
activity which followed were concerned with a highly
innovative array of issues, with respect to traditional
trade union bargaining policy. The focus of contention
became the labour process itself, thus shifting the arena of

the class struggle and increasingly imposing limits and constraints on management's prerogative in the organization of the labour process.

Workers began to claim that everything could be negotiated, since everything was the outcome of power relationships. In the early 1970s, workers' power was extremely high within the steel factories; and they succeeded in increasing wages, in increasing control over the labour process and in reversing some of the mechanisms in use for the organization of the labour process. The outcome of the struggles was not only higher labour costs and a drastic reduction in management discretionary power, but also the fact that discipline, supervision, hierarchical structure, the relationship between mobility/skill/career, and the other processes used to organize the labour process became redundant, since they could not, as before, be used to push for greater effort, that is for increased output through increased labour input. Thus, workers' actions rendered inefficient some traditional forms of organization: the old mechanisms could no longer reach the targets they were designed for, in the sense that they could not induce workers to follow a certain behavioural pattern within the factory.

But the result of trade union action has been, on the whole, more negative than positive. That is, it has served to obstruct the old system of the division of labour rather than suggesting anything different, despite the ambitious original idea of overcoming the actual division of labour. Management has re-taken control of the labour process by introducing changes in the organization of work. It has regained flexibility within the labour process by switching from a very detailed division of labour, based on a minute system of control implemented through the hierarchical structure, to a form of work organization based on a global system of control. Here the work-group is responsible for the organization of the labour process, and what is controlled are not the activities of the work-group but the result of those activities. What is interesting to note is the fact that even with this new system of work organization what remains crucial is the distinction between control and execution. In fact, the new work organization introduced at Italsider is based on a very precise and clear distinction between the control structure and the executive structure, as clearly stated by management:

> The control structure is related to the co-ordination, planning, improvement and control of the productive results through which the

enterprise ensures that the whole range of
executive activities are effectually and
efficiently oriented towards the achievement
of the targets planned. The executive structure is related to the whole range of
activities oriented toward the realization of
the targets planned (Fantoli, 1980, p. 208).

NOTES

1. For example see Kahn, 1976; Wilkinson, 1977; Friedman,
    1977; Rubery, 1978; Elbaum et al, 1979; Lorenz, 1983.
2. There is almost no work done on the labour history of
    the Italian steel industry. This section draws most of
    its information from the oral history available. This
    includes Vallini (1957), collecting ten autobiographies
    of steel workers (pp. 9-25, 62-72, 89-113, 131-137,
    145-170, 236-259, 269-276); Manzini (1976), on the
    working life of a trade union activist employed at
    Falck Unione since 1937; Botta (1978) based on 15
    interviews with retired steel workers from ILVA Novi,
    focusing on the period 1930-55; Crespo (1979),
    containing 9 autobiographies of steel workers at Falck
    and Breda (pp. 41-104, 119-180, 263-274); and Contini
    (1980), based on a long interview with a retired steel
    worker employed at ILVA Piombino, focusing on the
    period 1935-60.
3. Behind this hierarchical structure, there also lay the
    need to prevent industrial accidents; a team-discipline
    ruled by the oldest and most experienced worker
    facilitated the smooth management of the production
    process and also made it possible to avoid the much
    tougher punishments of the department-supervisor in
    cases, for example, where the casting of the steel was
    defective. The foreman was not excluded from the
    punishment, and it was therefore in his own interest to
    discipline his subordinates (Pozzobon and Mari, 1978,
    p. 136).
4. Giugni (1964, pp. 18, p. 87 and pp. 98-99), in his
    analysis of the industrial relations system in the iron
    and steel industry, acknowledged a very high level of
    internal mobility.
5. For instance, at Dalmine there were over 1,200 job
    wages for about 7,000 process workers, out of 12,000
    total employees.
6. When a maintenance worker was found to be a union
    activist, he was removed from his job in the process

departments and allocated to a specific workshop, thus limiting his contacts with the other workers. These workshops were called by the workers as "confine departments", as they were used to prevent union activists moving around the plant and contacting other workers.

7. The principle was the same, while the factors of evaluation and their weight were different (Bonel, 1967, p. 201). Given the changes in technology, what was required was not to induce workers to work harder, but to ensure a regular flow of production, given the increased mechanization of the works. This explains the large weight given to factors of responsibility, and the little role played by piece work, found in the JA and JE system.

8. This included ten steel plants, five of which were integrated, employing over 30,000 employees (see De Rosa, 1978, pp. 269–272; Castronovo, 1978, pp. 290–294).

9. An agreement (9.12.60) was signed for the introduction of three separate systems: one for manual workers (30.4.61), one for foremen (6.6.62) and one for non-manual workers (9.5.63). They differed both in terms of the factors considered for evaluation and in the weight given to them. Blue collar jobs were evaluated on the basis of 12 factors (previous experience, training, intellectual abilities, manual dexterity, responsibilities towards goods, equipment, production process, other workers' safety, mental and visual effort, working conditions, risks) and classified in 24 classes. For all employees there were, in all, 54 different classes.

10. The replacement of the job ranking system with the JA and JE system in the ex-ILVA steel factories was quite smooth and provoked no conflicts. This can be explained partly by the fact that – at least for process workers – the JA and JE represented a sort of rationalization of the existing job ranking system; and partly by the fact that the level of wages was higher than with the old job ranking systems (Giugni, 1964, p. 87).

11. JA and JE systems have not received much attention in Italy. They represent a quite limited experiment within the overall Italian context (Broglia, 1962), with the most significant examples in the steel industry, at Italsider, and in the petro-chemical industry, at ENI.

12. The Act passed in 1970, known as the "Statuto dei Lavoratori" was a Workers' Charter, establishing principles for the regulation of both industrial

disputes and trade union organization within factories and workshops as well as for the protection of workers' rights at the workplace. The Charter, a sort of workers' Bill of Rights, was the direct result of the upheavals of the 1968-69 (see Regalia et al, 1978, p. 152).

13. Antonio Lettieri, a national union official of the FIOM CGIL, was responsible for drawing up the demands made by the rank-and-file.

14. This process has been relatively easy for all workers previously graded according to the "sistema delle qualifiche", as it was required simple to re-classify the old grades into the new levels of classification, while it has been particularly complex in the case of process workers as this involved the conversion of a system based on a job by job analysis into a new one based on the classification of workers into 5 grades only. This explains also why the introduction of the IU has been much more complex in the steel industry than in any other industrial sector.

15. The tendency for conflict and group claims to arise has always been a characteristic of the steel industry. This was the case in the years immediately after the Liberation, when the trade union movement was strengthened by the political events; plant representative structures were being reorganized and plant bargaining was taking place in several large factories in the North. Similarly, an upsurge of group and sectional conflicts arose when plant bargaining began again in the late '60s. For an analysis of sectional conflicts in the '40s see Pozzobon and Mari (1978) pp. 150-198. For the following period see Abbatecola (1975) for Dalmine; Carabelli (1975) for AFL Falck; Beccalli (1975) for Redaelli; and Vento (1981) for Cornigliano Italsider.

16. Mr Fantoli is General Personnel Manager at Italsider.

17. This, too, was quite clearly perceived by management in the public sector: "In fact, the pattern of the division of labour in the steel industry is not only a direct outcome of the layout of the installations, but it is also an instrument to direct and manage the labour force. The division of labour into job tasks and the consequent system of classification – JA and JE – were in fact, above all, a direct derivation from the hierarchical and organizational structure of the enterprise, a method for managing careers and for the control of productivity, and industrial relations system functional to the type of stratification of

skills prevailing in the labour market". (Fantoli,
1980, p. 201).

18. On the experimentation with work organization in the
     public sector steel industry see Della Rocca (1974);
     Micheli et al (1976); Del Lungo (1976); Uccelli and
     Amatori (1978); Butera (1977); Fantoli (1980).

19. Del Lungo (1976, pp. 245-251) made a survey of all the
     major changes that occurred in the Italian large
     enterprises in the public sector, up to 1976. Out of 24
     observed cases of innovations introduced in work
     organization, 22 were found in steel plants.

20. In the '70s, experimentation with new forms of work
     organization was carried out in several large
     enterprises, in many industrial sectors, but with few
     results both in terms of their diffusion and relevance,
     and in terms of their impact upon the division of
     labour. For the most part, experimentation and research
     tended to be limited to a few large enterprises and,
     within them, to a very few experimental cases.
     Moreover, they mainly consisted of a sort of job
     design, oriented toward the recomposition of job tasks,
     but without real substantial changes in workers'
     qualifications and skill. This seems to suggest that,
     in a large number of cases, the research done and the
     innovations introduced were more like an attempt to
     recapture workers' consent, than a significant and
     positive change in the division of labour. On the
     research and the experimentation carried out on work
     organization in Italy in the last decade see Del Lungo
     (1976); Segatori and Torresini (1979) pp. 85-106;
     Graziosi (1979) pp. 129-154; Butera (ed.) (1980);
     Della Rocca (1982) pp. 160-166.

21. The company agreement of 1978 decided to experiment,
     through collective bargaining, with new forms of work
     organization for the achievement of better efficiency,
     increased productivity and development of workers'
     qualifications. On the basis of the experiments carried
     out since 1978, a new company agreement was settled in
     1981, which decided on the extension (but not the
     generalization) of the "operative unit" to all its
     steel plants.

22. This was, originally, the idea underlying the workers'
     demands for a new classification system. See Lettieri
     (1970), (1971); Surrenti and Treu (1970); Regalia et al
     (1978); Veneto (1974).

23. For different evaluations of the 1981 Italsider
     agreement see Carlini (1981) and Italia (1981).

REFERENCES

Abbatecola, G. (1975). Dalmine. In "Lotte operaie e sindacto
    in Italia (1968-1972)." (A. Pizzorno, ed.). Il Mulino,
    Bologna.
Ancona, L., et al. (1957). "Iron and Steel Workers'
    Attitudes in the Face of Technological Change." Report
    on the research carried out by the Institute of
    Psychology of the Milan Catholic University, European
    Productivity Agency, Project 164 (mimeo).
Beccalli Salvati, B. (1972). The Rebirth of Italian Trade
    Unionism, 1943-54. In "The Rebirth of Italy 1943-50"
    (S.J. Woolf, ed.). Longman, London.
Beccalli, B. (1975). Redaelli. In "Lotte operaie e sindacto
    in Italia (1968-1972)" (A. Pizzorno, ed.). Il Mulino,
    Bologna.
Bonel, M. (1967). "L'industria siderurgica". Etas Kompas,
    Milano.
Botta, L. (1981) Gli anni '50 a Genova. Classe. XII (19).
Botta, R. (1978). Gerarchi professionali e competizione
    operaia all'ILVA di Novi Ligure: per un uso delle fonti
    orali. Movimento Operaio e Socialista, 4.
Broglia, B. and Galbo, E. (1961). Qualifiche e mansioni
    all'ILVA di Bagnoli. Economia e Sindacato. September.
Broglia, G. (1962). 'Le paghe di classe in Italia'. In
    "Lavoratori e sindacati di fronte alle transformazioni
    del processo produttivo" (F. Momigliano, ed.).
    Feltrinelli, Milano.
Butera, F. (1977). La ricerca intervento al laminatoio della
    Dalmine. In "La ricerca intervento
    sull'organizzazione". Cedis, Roma.
Butera, F. (1979). "Lavoro umano e prodotto tecnico".
    Einaudi, Torino.
Butera, F. (ed.) (1980). Le ricerche per la transformazione
    del lavoro industriale in Italia: 1969-1979. In
    Sociologia del Lavoro, nos 10-11.
Cai, F. (1976). L'esperienza italiana sulla job evaluation:
    Il caso Italsider. In "Ascesa e crisi del riformismo in
    fabbrica" (F. Cai et al, eds.). De Donato, Bari.
Cai, F. (et al) (1976). "Ascesa e crisi del riformismo in
    fabbrica". De Donato, Bari.
Carabelli, G. (1975). Falck Unione. In "Lotte operaie e
    sindacto in Italia (1968-1972)" (A. Pizzorno, ed.). Il
    Mulino, Bologna.
Carlini, F. (1981). Italsider. Cambia l'organizzazione del
    lavoro. Analisi di un accordo controverso. Il
    manifesto. 18th September.
Castronovo, V. (1978). L'industria siderurgica e il piano di

coordinamento dell'IRI, 1936-1939. In Ricerche Storiche
     (1978).
Chiaromonte, F. (et al) (1982). "La contrattazione aziendale
     dell'organizzazione del lavoro 1976-79". ESI, Roma.
Collettivo Tecnici Italsider (1979). Il caso Italsider.
     Sapere, No. 816.
Contini, G. (1980). 'Fonti orali e fonti scritte: un
     confronto', Classe, No. 18.
Coppola, A. (1971). Italsider: il padrone sconfitto due
     volte. Unita Operaia, 2, January.
Crespi, P. (1979). "Capitale operaia". Jaca Book, Milano.
Crouch, C. and Pizzorno, A. (eds.) (1978), "The Resurge of
     Class Conflicts in Western Europe since 1968" Vol. 1.
     Macmillan, London.
Dal ferro all'acciaio. La Breda Siderurgica (1967). Autori
     Editori Associati, Torino.
D'Andrea, R. (1976). "Scienza operaia e organizzazione del
     lavoro". Marsilio Editore, Padova.
Della Rocca, G. (ed.) (1974). Due documenti sulla ricerca
     sociale in fabbrica. Prospettiva Sindacale, No. 14.
Della Rocca, G. (1982). "Sindacato e organizzazione del
     lavoro". Franco Angeli, Milano.
Del Lungo, S. (1976). Esperienze organizzative in alcune
     aziende metalmeccaniche a partecipazione statale.
     Quaderni di Sociologia, Nos. 2-3.
De Rosa, L. (1978). La siderurgia italiana dalla
     Ricostruzione al V Centro Siderurgico. In Ricerche
     Storiche, (1978).
Elbaum, B. (1983). The making and shaping of job and pay
     structures in the iron and steel industry. In
     "Employment Practices in Large Firms" (P. Osterman,
     ed.). MIT Press.
Elbaum, B., Lazonick, W., Wilkinson, F. and Zeitlin, J.
     (1979). The labour process, market structure and
     marxist theory. Cambridge Journal of Economics, 3 (3),
     September.
Fantoli, A. (1980). L'approccio dell'Italsider ai temi
     dell'organizzazione del lavoro. Sociologia del lavoro,
     Nos. 10-11.
Friedman, A. (1977). "Industry and Labour". Macmillan,
     London.
Giugni, G. (1964)." L'evoluzione della contrattazione
     collettiva nell'industria siderurgica e mineraria".
     Giuffre, Milano.
Graziosi, A. (1979). "La restrutturazione nelle grandi
     fabbrichi 1973-1976". Feltrinelli, Milano.
Italia, G. (1981). L'organizzazione ritorno dell'accordo
     Italsider. Il manifesto, 29th July.

Kahn, L.M. (1976). Internal labor markets: San Francisco
    shoremen. Industrial Relations, 15 (3), October.
Lettieri, A. (1970). Factory and education. In "The Division
    of Labour" (A. Gorz, ed.). The Harvester Press.
Lettieri, A. (1971). Inquadramento unico e strategia delle
    qualifiche. Quaderni di Rassegna Sindacale, No. 35.
Lorenz, E.H. (1983). "The Labour Process and Industrial
    Relations in the British and French Shipbuilding
    Industries, from 1880 to 1970: two patterns of
    development". Unpublished Ph.D. thesis, Cambridge.
Manzini, G. (1976). "Una vita operaia". Einaudi, Milano.
Micheli, S., Mighetto, F., Montobio, P., Parodi, E. and
    Rovery, S. (1976). Esperienza di ricerca intervento
    sulla organizzazione del lavoro di una grande aziende.
    Quaderni di Sociologia, Nos. 2-3.
Ministero dell'Industria, Commercio e Artigianato (1979).
    "Programma finalizzato, Industria Siderurgica".
    Instituto Poligrafico e Zecca dello Stato, Roma.
Mondo Economico (1981). Il crack dell'altoforno. No. 11.
Neufeld, M.F. (1954). "Labour Unions and National Politics
    in Italian Industrial Plants". Cornell International
    Industrial and Labour Relations Reports, New York.
Parenti, G. (1958). Livello di meccanizzazione e modi di
    remunerazione. Universita degli Sudi di Firenze,
    Instituto di Statistica, Firenze, October (mimeo).
Pesce, A. (1970). L'autunno '70 si chiama Italsider. Mondo
    Nuovo, 29th November.
Pizzorno, A. (ed.) (1975). "Lotte operaie e sindacato in
    Italia (1968-1972)". Il Mulino, Bolognoa.
Pizzorno, A., Reyneri, E., Regini, M. and Regalia, I.
    (1978). "Lotte operaie e sindacato: il ciclo 1968-72 in
    Italia". Il Mulino, Bologna.
Pozzobon, M. and Mari, R. (1978). Le AFL Falck (1945-48). In
    "La ricostruzione nella grande industria" (L. Ganapini,
    M. Pozzobon, R. Mari et al). De Donato, Bari.
Quaderni di Rassegna Sindacale (1982). Organizzazione del
    lavoro e contrattazione collettiva. Special Issue, No.
    94.
Regalia, I., Regini, M. and Reyneri, E. (1978). Labour
    conflicts and industrial relations. In "The Resurge of
    Class Conflicts in Western Europe since 1968" (C.
    Crouch and A. Pizzorno, eds.). Macmillan, London.
Rubery, J. (1978). Structured labour markets, worker
    organisation and low pay. Cambridge Journal of
    Economics, 2, March.
Scortecci, A. (1961). Rapporto sul progresso tecnologico
    nell'industria siderurgica italiana. In "Il progresso
    technologico ne la societa italiana: Effetti economici

del progresso technologico sulla economia industriale italiana. 1938-1958". Giuffre, Milano.

Segatori, R. and Torresini, D. (1979). "La professionalita difficile". CEDIS Editrice, Roma.

Sette, M. (1973). Intervento di M. Sette al Convegno dell'Instituto Gramsci. Scienza e organizzazione del lavoro. Torino 8th-10th June. In "Sindacati e lotte operaie 1943-73" (V. Foa, ed.). Loescher, Torino.

Stone, K. (1975). The origins of job structures in the steel industry. In "Labour Market Segmentation" (R.C. Edwards, M. Reich and D.M. Gordon, eds.). Heath, Lexington, Mass.

Surrenti, G. and Treu, T. (1971). Esperienze in tema di inquadramento. Dibattito Sindacale, Nos. 3-4.

Torneo, C. (1970). Basta con le paghe di classe. Unita Operaia, I, (1).

Uccelli, S.E. and Amatori, F. (1978). "La fabbrica ristrutturata". Franco Angeli, Milano.

Vallini, E. (1957). "Operai del Nord". Laterza, Bari.

Veneto, G. (1974). "Contrattazione e prassi nei rapporti di lavoro". Il Mulino, Bologna.

Vento, S. (1981). Portuali, siderurgici, marittimi: tradizione e nuovo protagonismo. Classe, XII (19).

Villa, P. (1985). "The Structuring of Labour Markets: a Comparative Analysis of the Steel and Construction Industries in Italy". O.U.P., (forthcoming).

Wilkinson, F. (1977). Collective bargaining in the steel industry in the 1920s. In "Essays in Labour History: 1918-1939" (A. Briggs and J. Saville, eds.). Croom Helm, London.